BREATHING SPACE

BREATHING SPACE

A Spiritual Journey in the South Bronx

HEIDI NEUMARK

BEACON PRESS, BOSTON

BEACON PRESS
25 Beacon Street
Boston, Massachusetts 02108-2892
www.beacon.org

Beacon Press books are published under the auspices of the
Unitarian Universalist Association of Congregations.

10 09 08   8 7 6 5 4 3

This book is printed on acid-free paper that meets the uncoated paper ANSI/NISO
specifications for permanence as revised in 1992.

Text design by Isaac Tobin
Composition by Wilsted & Taylor Publishing Services

Library of Congress Cataloging-in-Publication Data

Neumark, Heidi.
Breathing space : a spiritual journey in the South Bronx / Heidi Neumark.
p. cm.
Includes bibliographical references (p.).
ISBN 978-0-8070-7257-8 (pbk.)
1. Neumark, Heidi. 2. Lutheran Church—Clergy—Biography.
3. Women clergy—United States—Biography. 4. Trinity Lutheran
Church (Bronx, New York, N.Y.)—History. I. Title.
BX8080.N463A3 2003
284.1′092—dc21
2003006201

To Gregorio

Perdona mi amor
por tanto hablar,
es que quiero ayudar
al mundo cambiar.
!Qué loca!*

y a los queridos santos de
Transfiguración con muchísimo amor

And to the beloved people of
Transfiguration who have transfigured me

* "El Tiempo es Veloz," David Lebón

*Have mercy on your people, Lord, and give us
a breathing space in the midst of so many troubles.*

MISSAL OF PIUS V

CONTENTS

Construction

PREFACE

Break forth together into singing you ruins of Jerusalem.
Isaiah 52:9

The stone that the builders rejected has become the chief cornerstone.
Psalm 118:2

This book began in the spring ruins of Oklahoma City in 1995 and reached completion seven years later in the aftermath of the September 11 attack on the World Trade Center. At the time of the first bombing, I was experiencing some weariness after a decade of pastoral work in the South Bronx, and found myself in serious need of breathing space. Watching the televised grief of people in a distant city was like looking into a mirror and seeing what I hadn't wanted to see. I needed to grieve. I thought of the Bronx mother who raced to get a basin of water to scrub her murdered son's blood off the street before the cars and buses could desecrate what to her was holy. She went out alone and held off the cars until she was finished. I needed to stop the busy traffic that barrels through each day, stand vigil, pause, and remember. Grieving was a way for me to say that this blood mattered, the blood that had flooded my heart.

In the early eighties, I joined with people who'd been working long and hard before I was ever called here, dedicated agents of transfiguration amidst the rubble. At that point, the South Bronx had gained international infamy as the ground zero of urban blight. More often than not, I was the witness of deep faith and inspiration, heroism and indefatigable dignity, but other realities were taking their toll: AIDS, crack, heroin, methadone, cutbacks, kickbacks, corruption in virtually every corner of the borough's infrastructure, never enough time, never enough money, never a night without gunfire, or a week without funerals.

Just as our son Hans, then eleven, wanted us to turn off the news in the wake of September 11 and return to more cheerful activities, I wanted to turn my attention from the pain and focus on the uplifting moments. One of the reasons I avoided giving voice to my own grief was out of respect for the other grievers. There is an idolatry of lurid, inner city images—a colleague calls it urban pornography, slick one-dimensional takes that titillate but invite no true relationship. There is a certain fascination with objectified extremities of the urban scene, safe to gawk at on an airbrushed screen or page, but far too threatening to engage in any meaningful, life-changing way. I've never wanted to foster this and feed into the stereotypes that bring tourists with cameras looking for the rumble and the rubble.

I am drawn to a different vision—the walls rebuilt, the land reclaimed, the people who rise up like grass improbably breaking through slabs of stone. But the losses took their toll. To stand here is also to stand in the center of so much that is wounded and wrong in this nation and world, in a well of catastrophe that is, at the same time, a center from which springs amazing grace. I was busy like a politician putting the right spin on things, not just for others, but for myself—the "grace" spin, but I didn't need to do that. The denial of loss and difficult truths are not the attendants of grace. I have learned that grace cleaves to the depths, attends the losses and there slowly works her defiant transfiguration.

At the end of the summer before September 11, I cleaned out old toys and games with Hans. Together we sorted the wooden blocks, the Legos and K'Nex. At one point, when Hans wasn't looking and I was tired of sorting, I dumped a bunch of mixed-up pieces in the garbage. There seemed to be an ample supply of building materials that remained. I almost took the boxes to my mother's attic, thinking that sixth grade would bring other interests and entertainments. Now I thank God that the boxes never left home. This is one time when procrastination paid off.

Soon after watching the televised images of the Towers' collapse, Hans reached for the wooden blocks he'd been building with since before he could walk. As we sat mute and motionless before the news, Hans reenacted it. Block upon block went up in one tall tower and then another. After that, he found an old model airplane and knocked them down. "Just leave it there," Hans told us, and later, he put it all away. A few days after this reenactment, Hans got out the K'Nex and began a building program that lasted for months. The first thing he built was a replica of the Empire State building, strikingly accurate and almost as tall as he was. New creations were added daily. Some were taken apart and rebuilt, although the Empire State Building continued to tower over the rest. In the beginning, Hans gave us daily advisories with his building plans. We lived in a construction zone and had to negotiate an increasingly intricate display of structures to get from room to room.

There was something almost compulsive about Hans's need to build and in his daily efforts, which he had to fit between homework, meals, and other frustrating interruptions, I saw my own need and struggle to write. When more things seemed to be falling apart than coming together, I reached for words as Hans reached for the K'Nex. But it was easier for Hans to find the right K'Nex to fit his architectural designs. For the longest time, I was just lifting up pieces without knowing where to place them.

What shall I preach? All flesh is grass ... the grass withers, the flower fades.
Isaiah 40:6ff.

The prophet Isaiah, that ancient correspondent from the sixth century B.C.E. is a good companion in the wake of urban ruin. The mighty army of the Babylonian Empire had ripped though the inner city of Jerusalem, destroying homes, businesses, and the temple itself. The hallowed site of a people's history, tradition and pride became a place of disaster and corruption. When Isaiah looked around, he saw a traumatized community taken captive and deported to Babylon, the smoking ruins of the city still blurring their vision, and choking their souls.

Isaiah was one of them and their questions were his own: *What shall I preach? All flesh is grass ... the grass withers, the flower fades.* (Isaiah 40:6ff.) What was there to say? What difference could it make? And yet, the story cried out to be told. Deep sadness seems to swallow up language and simultaneously compel speech. Reflecting on the transiency of life after the fall of Jerusalem,

Isaiah bewailed his loss of words but then went on to write some of the most passionate and eloquent poetry in the Hebrew scriptures.

The sacred stones lie scattered at the head of every street, sighed Isaiah's prophetic contemporary in lamentation, Jeremiah ... *the precious children worth their weight in gold—how they are reckoned as earthen pots ... For these things I weep; my eyes flow with tears; my children are desolate.* (Lamentations 4:1-2, 2:16) The prophet could have been describing the devastation wrought on September 11 here in New York City. And the prophet could have been describing the inheritance of the children who played among skeletal remains of burnt-out buildings that covered 300 acres of vacant land in the South Bronx in the seventies and early eighties.

Break forth together into singing you ruins of Jerusalem ... says Isaiah. Singing? Isaiah tells us that the song will come. He too searched through wreckage and lifted up dismembered pieces, letter by letter, phrase by phrase, recovering an alphabet that scattered like acres of rubble and dissolved like tons of paper coating the city in silent, bone-white dust.

He had only the blackened remains of one ear showing, but the nurses told me they believed he could hear. I'd been visiting Felipe who worked at the World Trade Center keeping the vending machines stocked with candy and chips. That was his job. His vocation was playing the bass with his band, *Fuerza Brava de Honduras*. His wife, Elba, joined the *via dolorosa* of thousands, walking from hospital to hospital around the city, showing her picture of a proud immigrant, a father with his arms around the two young children he adored. She held out the picture to anyone who would look, hoping against hope that she would find him alive. And then, miraculously, she did. Alive, but barely. Alive, but covered with burns from the fiery explosion. His children wanted to see their father but Elba shook her head and she was right. While most of his body was hidden beneath layers of dressing, the part of his face that showed was swollen and charred, disfigured beyond recognition.

After visiting him in the hospital, I came home and lay in bed feeling sad and helpless. My husband, Gregorio, also an adoring father to a son and daughter, said, "Why don't you have his children record a tape for him—*eso le dará ánimo*—that will strengthen his soul." It gave me *ánimo* too—something to do when one is helpless. Ten-year-old Leonel knew immediately what he

wanted to say: "I miss you Daddy. I wish this never had to happen. I want you
to come home. I love you Daddy." But five-year-old Rosalina was mute. I was
holding a strange machine that had nothing to do with her father who was in
some strange place her mother disappeared to every morning in tears and
came home from at night in anxious exhaustion. Rosalina had nothing to say
to the gray box. Why should she? But I was desperate to capture her voice
for Felipe. "Do you like to sing?" I asked and a smile played across Rosalina's
face as she nodded. I turned on the recorder and she sang to her father:
a,b,c,d,e,f,g ... I played it for a week, holding the machine close to Felipe's ear
like a cell phone and saw no response. I also read Psalms and prayed prayers,
and yet I was sure that if anything would get through the fog of morphine and
pain, it would be the voices of his children.

   Toward the end of the second week, following grafts on his arms and chest
and after much of the dead skin on his face, head, and ear had been removed,
I played the tape again and I saw Felipe, eyes still shut, trying to speak. I
watched two words take shape on lips so fragile they bled from the effort:
Thank ... you. The words made no sound but filled the burn unit as a hymn of
gratitude breaking forth from the ruins. Connection is everything. Relationship to God and to each other is life itself.

This book is also a song of thanksgiving. Thanksgiving for the people whose
courageous witness has transfigured this community—and this pastor.
Thanksgiving for the gift of these stories that cry out to be told and retold because in the midst of death they rise to fill the air with life. The small stories
that make up this book are part of some larger ones—the story of a people refusing to submit to the ruins at their feet and reclaiming their land to build new
homes and a new future, the story of entering a church about to fold and rebuilding it with new people and a new wing. And finally, there is the story of
the urgent struggle to frame some breathing space in my own life. I offer it all
to honor those who have taught me how to sing in the ruins and in deep gratitude for the connections we share.

When Teresa of Avila, the sixteenth-century Spanish mystic and reformer,
was seeking a structure for her treatise on prayer, she turned to the realm of architecture. Her book, *The Interior Castle,* traces a spiritual journey described

as a progression through a series of mansions or rooms of a castle. When I first encountered this book in college, I aspired to follow Teresa's path, but to this day have never reached the innermost mansion of ecstatic rapture that seems as remote as some fairy-tale room of spun gold. Here in the South Bronx, I have traveled a different path. The only castle in the vicinity sells small, cheap hamburgers, and onion rings. Nevertheless, like Teresa, we have engaged in an architecture of the spirit which has included construction with brick and mortar along with heart and soul. Teresa herself oversaw more than one building renovation project in the founding of numerous convents. In structuring this story, I decided that I could do worse than follow Teresa's blueprint, however loosely. Perhaps she will be gracious enough to add this project to the many she has prodded to completion.

At the conclusion of *The Interior Castle*, Teresa begged God to "give light to the Lutherans." I assume she was being generous toward those reformers who, in her mind, must have been wreaking havoc in Christendom. Nevertheless, from her new vantage point beyond all earthly confines, I hope Teresa is still praying for the Lutherans. *Santa Teresa ¡mil gracias!*

Refer to the Notes on p. 277 for all citation sources and some additional explanation of passages in the text.

ONE

Preconstruction

CHAPTER ONE

CHURCH DOORS

If you come upon Transfiguration Lutheran Church on the corner of East 156th Street and Prospect Avenue in the South Bronx, the first thing you'll notice are the doors, spray-painted with a bright mural. It shows an open fire hydrant with water splashing down into a baptismal font. Water brims and spills from the bowl onto the grass below as new buildings rise up from the sidewalk. An arm reaches out from the altar, with bread to place on a plateful of food—turkey, greens, and rice for the hungry. Across the top of the doors, you will read a line from the prophet Isaiah: *My house shall be a house of prayer for all peoples.* The doors swing open into the history of this place and my arrival here.

La Casita

It was a long time before anyone thought of backhoes and concrete mixers. Keeping the old doors open—and undefiled—was challenge enough. The first construction tool I lifted was a paintbrush. It was May of 1984 and I didn't need to check the first item in my daily date book. It never varied: "repaint door." The members of the church had given the doors a fresh coat of red paint as a gesture of welcome for me, their new pastor. Someone had the foresight to leave the can in my office. I needed it. Each morning as I crossed the street, walking from the house to the church, I met fresh graffiti. The church doors had become a convenient canvas for neighborhood youth to vent anger and frustration, emotions that double locks and bolts sought to keep firmly outside the sanctuary. Yet it was not so easy to erase the crude, potent message in those ragtag lines. Each night, they were relaid like lines at a construction site, staking out their claim to identity and space.

The doors to Transfiguration Lutheran Church had not always been bolted. For years, they swung open as easily as the screen doors to the airy *casitas* that brighten the Bronx landscape to this day. In fact, the church had much in common with these *casitas*, "little houses" fashioned with scraps of wood or lumber their small group of builders pitched in to purchase. The architecture of the *casitas* mirrors that of their island antecedents on Puerto Rico. There, the *"casitas de madera,"* or "little wooden houses," were first built by the native Taino people and later adopted by their descendants. Here in the Bronx, they are usually found at the center of a community garden on a once-vacant lot. Nestled amidst sunflowers, roses, day lilies, and geraniums, the *casitas* are built to be a garden refuge, a paradise island plunked down in a sea of concrete. Their presence announces a joyful rebellion of *independencia*, although being built on city-owned land, they remain dependent on development decisions made elsewhere which can and do sweep them away. In the meantime, the *casitas* offer a place to relax, to eat and drink, talk and laugh, play cards or dominos, make music and dance—breathing space and fiesta amidst the rush and pressures of city life. They are a refuge to restore dignity and remember roots, room for celebration and sanctuary.

Transfiguration began as just such a space. The first members arrived in New York City from Puerto Rico in the 1920s. They came as active Lutherans due to the mission work of an American Swede named Gustaf Siegfried Swensen who gathered the first Lutheran community in Puerto Rico in 1898. Others from Germany continued his initial labor so that a small but vital Lutheran church took root on the island. Enough of these members then immigrated to create concern that there was no Spanish-language Lutheran congregation to welcome them in their new island home of Manhattan. The church in Puerto Rico arranged for leadership so that worship could begin in Harlem in 1924. By 1930, the church had its own full-time pastor, the Reverend Jaime Soler, who served for forty years. For a decade after his arrival, the growing flock of Transfiguration worshipped in borrowed and rented space. Eventually, when most of the members had moved to the South Bronx, they bought land, built and dedicated their own sanctuary and parsonage. It was 1941.

From those early years, the church's sanctuary was not only a place to meet God. It was also space to meet, sing, laugh, and eat with one another. Church was no place for private religious experience. Church was community. It was a place where the community's native language, food and music could flower without the pressure required to assimilate the rest of the week. It was a lovingly tended island on an island. This piece of Puerto Rico on Prospect Avenue in the South Bronx was solid and built to last. The graceful lines of the concrete walls with their pink stucco facade and bell tower reflected a Spanish influence. But like the *casitas,* Transfiguration was in danger of being swept away by development decisions made elsewhere.

Planned Shrinkage

The late 1950s brought an influx of new urban refugees as poor families from Manhattan were forced into the South Bronx by Robert Moses's "slum clearance project." Robert Moses was the New York state and city official whose vast array of public works projects transformed the urban landscape of New York. His idea was to push the poor out of parts of Manhattan in order to build middle-class housing there. In the words of then-Manhattan borough president Stanley Isaacs: "My God, they're hounding the people out like cattle. Tens of thousands, indeed, hundreds of thousands of people were thrown out of their homes by Moses with very little provision for relocation." Moses steered the poorest of the masses into the South Bronx.

Soon afterward, he oversaw the construction of the Cross Bronx Expressway, which ripped through the area, unsettling and displacing 60,000 more families, who had no say in the matter. Hundreds of solid, six-story apartment buildings were bulldozed away at the same time that more housing was needed for the forced refugees coming from Manhattan. The decimation Babylon's armies wrought on Jerusalem was reenacted by our own city planners.

The intense concentration of overcrowded housing and poverty that resulted led to increased crime, drug use and gang violence throughout the following decade. Landlords saw arson as a way to bolt responsibility for their investment in the community and to escape with a tidy profit. Welfare recipients were encouraged to join in by signs posted in welfare offices promising new public housing for burnt-out families. There were close to 70,000 documented fires in the South Bronx between 1970 and 1975.

In 1976, Roger Starr, New York City's administrator for Housing and Urban Department, announced a response to the devastation. It was a policy targeted for the South Bronx that he called "planned shrinkage," a purposeful cutting back of city services such as police, fire, and ambulance as well as the shutting down of hospitals and schools. He stated that the city could thereby "accelerate the drainage" of the most battered sections of the South Bronx. The money saved could be invested in more worthwhile neighborhoods. Almost half a million people moved away. The Bronx hit bottom.

Planned shrinkage quickly contributed to the unforeseen shrinkage of the church, which had completed an addition to double its space in 1967. This building project began years earlier as I learned from searching through an old box of files down in the boiler room. The cracked, yellowed clipping from a *New York Times* article dated October 7, 1959, almost disintegrated in my hands. It was headlined: *Pastor Says Leibowitz Slurs Puerto Ricans.* Pastor Jaime Soler is quoted as charging Kings County Judge Samuel Leibowitz as "unfairly maligning" the Puerto Rican youth of the South Bronx: "The Puerto Rican is in the spotlight today . . . because he is the newcomer to New York. But he is no more inherently delinquent than anyone else. Puerto Rican youths learn crime here, not in Puerto Rico. The problem is ours, not theirs." The *Times* reported that

> the Rev. Mr. Soler's all-Puerto Rican congregation, concerned with gangs in their own East Bronx area, have taken part of the problem into their own hands. They have raised $10,000 among them towards the construction of a new community center. "This is an example of how Puerto Ricans are contributing to better living, not to crime," the pastor said.

It took another eight years of fund-raising before the new wing was built and dedicated.

During those eight years, as neighborhood violence escalated, the church withdrew from its strong identification with the struggles of the street. Many of

Transfiguration's working-class members had the means to move out and did so. Few chose to commute back. Those who did and those who stayed felt increasing alienation from the neighborhood. Once a place to come home, relax and regroup, the air was now poisoned with smoke, gunshots, screams and sirens. A rapid succession of pastors came and left. More members moved. Others died. The doors that once swung open in hospitality were fitted with larger locks to keep danger on the outside, and the dwindling number of members retreated behind them.

Near the end of the 1970s, the parade of pastors came to an abrupt end and left the congregation untended for five years. A supply pastor would show up on Sunday morning and when the little flock arrived for worship, the doors were unlocked to admit them and then relocked. No one expected visitors. On other days, the doors didn't open at all. There were only about twenty people left, but they were a people in love. Like a lover clinging to his dying beloved, they cleaved to their church. The bishop would have to drag them away, which he almost did. For church officials in their Manhattan offices, Transfiguration had become an island of dry bones, a relic from another era. Nothing was developing here. The money saved could be invested in a more deserving church. It was about time to sweep this one away, part of an unplanned but seemingly unavoidable shrinkage in the number of mainline inner city churches.

Institutions and social services were not the only victims of planned shrinkage. Urban planning for the South Bronx began to cause the shrinkage of breathing space itself, closing up airways in children's throats and lungs. When you live in this community, breathing space is not a figurative expression referring to longed-for leisure amid a hectic lifestyle. Breathing space is a matter of life and death. In the South Bronx more children die of asthma than almost anywhere else in the nation. Children pack asthma pumps in their pockets the way other kids pack action figures. The ecology of urban poverty is one cause. Rodent droppings, cockroach remains, apartments with flaking paint, poor ventilation, and air pollution are all contributing factors. Inconsistent health care aggravates the epidemic.

But the worst contributor has been the growing industry in other people's garbage: sewage treatment, waste-recycling plants, and incinerators that burn hazardous hospital waste from around the city. The pollution is a result of environmental racism. While services for the South Bronx were cut back, services from the area are in high demand. As an editorial in *El Diario*, the Spanish-language daily, put it: "The Bronx Has Become the City's Toilet." Seventy percent of the city's sewage is processed right here. Until it was recently shut down, much of the city's medical waste was also incinerated in the same area. The Niafrigo plant converts sewage sludge to fertilizer pellets, 220 dry tons a day. At one point, they hired a full-time odor consultant. Any child on the street with a pump in his or her pocket could have been consulted for free. This plant, and others, stank and clogged the air with noxious bacteria, making breathing difficult for increasing numbers of residents.

One summer night, the stench woke me up. I thought it might be a gas leak and called the gas company. Two men arrived with their detector meters and went through the house. They were baffled. They could smell the odor but could not detect the source. They checked the stove and the dryer and even went out to their truck to bring in a new meter. Finally they left, assuring us that whatever it was, it was not a gas leak. The house would not explode. Nevertheless, "make sure to leave your windows open," they cautioned. Of course, the air coming through our wide-open windows did nothing to abate the stink!

At the time, we didn't know about the sewage, and the foul aroma disappeared as mysteriously as it had come. Perhaps the wind changed direction. We later found out that there were so many complaints about the smells from Niafrigo, that the company took action. They found chemicals to kill the odor. Now the same old sickening air sports a refined chemical mask. Would that the zeal to save our citizens from secondhand smoke in the workplace would extend to these streets and schools with open windows where ambulances are regularly called to cart gasping children away. Nearby Lincoln Hospital counts 15,000 visits, 2,500 admissions and 22 deaths a year—just from asthma.

After twenty-five years working at the hospital, Dr. Harold Osborn has noted a marked correspondence between the increase in asthma admissions and deaths and the growth of the garbage industry. The sewage plants are located in Hunts Point, a peninsula in the heart of the South Bronx with major transportation arteries that bear the traffic of more than one million trucks each year. The trucks carry food to and from the Hunts Point Market—40 percent of the meat and 80 percent of the produce distributed in the New York metropolitan area; and the trucks carry garbage. The area is packed with waste transfer facilities, iron and metal scrap yards testing high in lead particles, auto graveyards, fuel-oil transport stations, all-purpose dumps and, of course, the fumes that accompany the barrage of trucks barreling in and out from the Major Deegan and Cross Bronx Expressways. In addition, of the eight major bus depots for Manhattan, seven are in Harlem and the South Bronx.

Someone did tree research and discovered that locust trees can be planted in front of the few offices in the area because they are resistant to pollution. Unfortunately, a breed of resistant children has not yet been discovered. This does not appear to bother those who now see the same place as prime property to handle more and more of New York's waste, especially with the closing of New York City's largest dump, Staten Island's Fresh Kills landfill. Clearly, the asthma epidemic here is not an accident. It's an extension of planned shrinkage from the seventies. Would Transfiguration close its doors too? The church itself was gasping for breath. Was it even possible to keep the doors open? Plans were afoot for the closure, but grace pleaded one more chance.

Reformation

The congregation called me as their new pastor in February of 1984, and I began in May. I had been preparing for this day since the beginning of my seminary training. My fieldwork was all done in inner-city Philadelphia parishes, with my pastoral internship in Jersey City. Fifteen months in Argentina and Peru had given me usable Spanish and a powerful experience of church life among the poor in Latin America. When the members of Transfiguration voted to call me as their pastor, it was a dream come true, and I eagerly accepted. As I got ready to lead worship for the first time, I noted that under the altar, a box of rat poison was set alongside a box of Communion wafers. The baptismal font was pushed into a back corner and kept covered. I lifted the lid to discover a film of dust and the remains of a few dead cock-roaches. Paradise had become a desert, and I felt like I had stepped inside of Sarah's womb.

Why Sarah's womb? The biblical story that came to my mind as I sur-veyed my new parish was the story of Sarah. By the time she was in her nineties, Sarah, the long-suffering wife of Abraham, had long since resigned herself to the bitter fact of barrenness. When three visitors appeared at her tent door, where Abraham was resting from the desert sun, and announced her imminent pregnancy, Sarah was not impressed: "After I have become worn out with use and my husband is old, shall I have pleasure?" The Hebrew word here for "pleasure" has the same root (*ednah*) as Eden, the primeval par-adise. "Shall my barren life be changed to Paradise?" Sarah's question is rhetorical. She knew the answer. "Is anything too wonderful for the Lord?" the visitors asked; but Sarah only laughed.

When I arrived on the scene as the new pastor, I was spared the sound of bitter laughter, if there was any, but there was little pleasure and much dis-couragement. Most of the members felt worn out and worn down, despite their love for Transfiguration. They could easily identify with the dismal view from Abraham and Sarah's tent in the heat of the day. The Bronx had inter-national infamy as an urban desert, a landscape of withered hopes, barren of economic vitality, battered by violence, fear, and death. The church's mem-bership was steadily aging. Most were resigned to the fact that their child-bear-ing years as a congregation were over. At ninety, the statistical probability of pregnancy was nil for Sarah. The statistics in our surrounding community were no more promising: 60 percent of families on welfare, 80 percent of chil-dren living in poverty, 70 percent unemployment, only 3 percent of adults graduated from college, 80 percent of births to single mothers (and 20 percent of those teenagers), 20 percent of adults and teens testing positive for HIV, 28 percent of all deaths annually were due to drugs, AIDS, or violence.

But there were other truths about Sarah and her husband, other truths about Transfiguration. Abraham had been seeking some quiet relief from the heat when the visitors arrived. Nevertheless, he immediately jumped up, ran to greet them, bowed down and invited them in to wash, rest and eat. Sarah may have doubted these strangers' absurd intentions, but that didn't prevent her from baking bread with the best flour and serving up the fattest calf, and the creamiest milk. Maybe Sarah and Abraham expected little, but they gave in abundance. The hospitality I received upon my arrival at Transfiguration was no less extravagant. What could they expect from this inexperienced Anglo pastor? With plenty of reason to doubt my competence, my commitment, and my untested hopefulness, they took me into their tent, fed me, mothered me, taught me, prayed for me and with me, and drew me close to that holy of holies named trust. And they wanted to install an iron fence around the church to protect me. I said no.

I took time to begin getting to know the members and the neighborhood. I visited homes and walked the streets. I talked with community leaders, shopkeepers, and drunks on the corner. And I repainted the door. After a few months, I'd come to the bottom of a second can of paint and grown tired of my dispiriting morning chore. In walks around the neighborhood, I began asking teenagers and children I met if any of them would like to be part of an art class a friend had offered to help lead. It wasn't long before a group of enthusiastic young artists came through our doors. Together we read stories from the Bible, which they then illustrated right on the doors.

At one time, the members would have insisted that the proper place for such artwork was on a bulletin board somewhere inside, but no one could deny that this beat the graffiti. Week after week, the youth painted their hearts out on those doors. It was a joyous, messy process. In spite of all the newspapers taped down, some paint always splattered on the sidewalk, but no matter. It soon faded under the parade of feet that daily passed by, feet of people who stopped to look, to check out what was going on, to offer compliments and suggestions, and to inquire about the church. There has never been another stroke of graffiti on those doors.

Even when closed, the doors now shouted a new word of openness. Reformation on the doors has good precedent in our church. In the sixteenth century, Martin Luther set the Reformation in motion with his 95 theses posted on the church doors of Wittenberg. His theses called for significant rethinking about church life and reversals in attitudes about power and privilege. Our theses did too. Our doors proclaimed: this community has a vision, a voice and a future. These young people do not represent an uneducable underclass better off locked away in prison. Created in the image of God, they come bearing life.

Malabarriga

Against all odds, new life began to stir at Transfiguration. The changes brought on a healthy case of ecclesiastical morning sickness. It was only later that I became familiar with the signs. I knew I was pregnant with our second child, Hans, when I was putting on my robes for Sunday worship and a wave of nausea swept through me. In both pregnancies, I suffered a bad case of what the Puerto Rican mothers in the church call "*malabarriga*," which translates as "evil belly," and seems more to the point than the comparatively benign English equivalent. My sickness was never confined to the morning. It was bad enough during my first pregnancy with our daughter, Ana, but the second time round, I could barely eat or function. Getting up from the couch was a major achievement.

I was immensely grateful to be in a community that embraced motherhood, *malabarriga* and all. I know of other women clergy who have met with less acceptance. I remember one friend's description of her first interview with a church committee charged with assessing potential candidates. She and I were interviewed around the same time. The church she met with is noted for its intellectual openness and liberalism in issues of gender and sexuality. How lucky for her! Mutual friends were skeptical of what my reception would be in the South Bronx by a committee made up of working-class Puerto Rican men and women. I got expressions of sympathy over the machismo and sexism they assumed I would encounter. My friend's interview began with questions of theology but moved quickly on to other matters that weighed on their minds. She was already the mother of one child. How was she going to balance motherhood and being a pastor? What if her son became sick? Where would he go to school? What did her husband think? And most important of all, what if, God forbid, she were to become pregnant again? These were the questions of the well-educated, politically correct.

My supposedly unenlightened committee focused on theology, vision, pastoral style, and a mutual sharing of hopes and dreams. Of course, I didn't have any children yet. Perhaps it was only a matter of time. It was. But the question, when it came, was quite different: "Pastor, when are you and Gregorio going to start a family?" Instead of seeing pregnancy and childbirth as inconveniences and obstacles to job performance, they considered motherhood a natural and joyful part of life that they hoped I would share. As I said, this world view was most welcome when *malabarriga* set in. On the Sundays I had to leave the altar to dash into the church kitchen and throw up (no time to make it to the bathroom), wash my face and reappear at the altar, I knew how fortunate I was to be in a place where people accepted this as natural and brought me soothing herbal teas instead of shaking their heads in dismay or disgust.

After some tests, the doctor said the sickness was caused by a hormone level three times higher than normal. It was unusual enough to demand a sonogram, which ruled out triplets or twins. Apparently, it was just our lively son, Hans. The doctor happily assured me that my belly was not cursed at all. On the contrary, the prodigious hormone level was a healthy sign of strong new life taking hold. This *"malabarriga"* was a sign of blessing. It would just take my body time to adjust to the changes.

And so it was at Transfiguration. Two years before my own experience of *malabarriga,* we were adjusting to new children in the body of Christ. Children who had little to do after school were not satisfied with door-painting once a week. They began coming in from the elementary school across the street every afternoon, seeking a place to do homework, to hang out, eat a snack, and get a hug. From these simple beginnings, our after-school program began. It was the children who brought their parents and invitations to visit their homes. Within a short time, Sunday school classes began, and an English worship service was started in addition to the Spanish mass because the neighborhood was now a mix of both Hispanic and African-American families.

For the church, this meant an influx of rapid changes in race, class, age, language, and music. So many new hormones inundating Sarah's womb and charging around the body of Christ were giving Transfiguration a bad case of *malabarriga.* The typical signs were there: discomfort, upset, and fatigue.

There were complaints about the noisiness of the children, the irreverence of the teenagers, and the instability of the adults. If only I had had the wisdom then to know that these were indicators not of something gone wrong but of something going right. There was new life in the body of Christ, and the body needed time to adjust. If I had known, I would have been more secure, more patient with others and with myself, more gentle.

Instead, I cried. I worried in bed at night. I wasn't sure what to do and, as hard as it was, I realized that this was good. I knew that I didn't know.

Lessons for Jonah

*Like Jonah himself, I find myself traveling toward my destiny
in the belly of a paradox.*
Thomas Merton

Jonah was a know-it-all. When God points him in one direction, Jonah knows better, and sails off for another. When a storm threatens to break up the ship he's traveling on with a company of sailors, Jonah sleeps soundly without a worry—or a prayer for help. Jonah's arrogance lasts until the sailors toss him overboard in hopes of appeasing the storm. It works and Jonah appears to come to his senses too. *The Lord provided a large fish to swallow up Jonah; and Jonah was in the belly of the fish three days and three nights.* (Jonah 1:17) There he is, seasick in the smelly dark, bumping up against oversized innards, as Luther put it: "How often lung and liver must have pained him! How strange his abode must have been among the intestines and the huge ribs!" Talk about *malabarriga!* Even a know-it-all like Jonah has lost his reference points and he begins to pray. Then Jonah gets another chance … *the Lord spoke to the fish, and it spewed Jonah out upon the dry land.*

In 1998, more than a decade after arriving at Transfiguration, I visited Hamburg, Germany, for a conference on urban ministry. There I was struck again by the blessing of being without answers, "traveling in the belly of a paradox." One day, when I was out for a walk, I came upon the handsome statue of Archbishop Ansgar who is said to have brought Christianity to that city in the ninth century. Judging from the statue, Ansgar appears to have arrived in

Hamburg carrying a perfectly structured, ready-made church in his arms. I don't know what Ansgar himself would have thought about his statue, but for me it served as a reminder of an arrogant ecclesial model that assumes we carry a prefabricated, everything-included, unquestionably correct, model church around in our arms to plop down wherever we find ourselves. On the contrary, we have discovered the church at Transfiguration in relationships where we encounter the life of the Spirit already present and at work. The church is established as we are built together, "living stones," as St. Peter put it. There are no shortcuts. Claiming to come in knowing everything, possessing the complete package, would be particularly dangerous for a white pastor in the South Bronx. I keep the photo I took of Ansgar as a reminder of what I don't want to do or to be.

Like Jonah, I wasn't born with this understanding. One memorable lesson came from Miss Ellie. I met her when I took a year off from Brown University and lived on John's Island off the coast of South Carolina. At the time, I was torn between campus classes and the independent study I was doing in poetry therapy, which took me into a large group home for children removed from their families by the state. When I was in the classroom, I'd daydream about the kids. When I was with the kids, I felt guilty that I wasn't spending more time in the library.

If my parents were less than happy about my decision to leave Brown at the end of my sophomore year and take off for a year on an island they'd never heard of, they didn't let on. They helped me pack. Since I was taking half the Brown bookstore with me in case I ran out of reading material, my mother's packing expertise was essential: never put cartons of books in the car—you can squeeze more books in loose, one by one. Then they drove me down 95 South until we reached Charleston and took the bridge over to Johns Island.

My parents always gave me, their only child, space to be myself. My father grew up in Germany in the first quarter of the twentieth century. As soon as he'd earned a doctorate in chemical engineering, his father, worried about the future, put him on a boat for New York. It was 1938, and Hitler was threatening to invade Czechoslovakia. My father had a visceral aversion toward any kind of group-think, a trait shared by my mother. Although both of my parents were of a highly literalistic, scientific bent of mind (my mother also majored in chemistry), they recognized my affinity for fairy tales and poems, which neither of them enjoyed. When I was very young, they plied me with poetry, respecting and nurturing what was unique in me. They never made me feel that I should conform to some predetermined idea in their minds but freed me to discover and follow my own path, which then became part of their own life adventure.

We arrived on Johns Island and found the two-room cabin that was to become my home. While my dad went off to find something that would rid the place of the huge water bugs that were already at home (a fruitless errand, but being from the North, we didn't know), my mother set to work scrubbing the sink which was plastered with fish scales. I was cleaning too. The strange thing about it was that the more we cleaned, the more the place stank. Finally, my mother's chemistry background asserted itself and she identified the foul odor as hydrogen sulfide, the smell of rotten eggs. The water was laced with the compound and had to be boiled before drinking.

Before they headed home, we went to church. I remember my German Lutheran father sitting through a three-hour AME Zion church service. He sat through the eighty-three minute sermon without complaint, although after the accustomed twenty minutes, he was unable to resist regular glances at his watch, and one final, incredulous tally. Then my parents bought me a week's worth of groceries and began their long drive back.

I was on the island as part of a volunteer program sponsored by a group called Rural Mission. Looking back, I see that I didn't have much to contribute. I filled my time reading stories and singing songs with the children at a day-care center and visiting the elderly. Mostly, I learned from the people of Johns Island—from the sons and daughters of plantation slaves, who allowed me to listen in as they sat around, chewing snuff and telling stories. I also learned from the few lawyers and social workers who supported the islanders in their fight for land rights. Real estate developers, anxious to build resorts, were investigating old records and going up to Philadelphia, Chicago and New York to knock on the apartment doors of the islanders' distant relations, often poor, who were happy to sign away their portion of a property they'd never heard of for a quick $100 in cash.

But the most important lesson I learned on Johns Island was from Miss

Ellie who lived miles down a small dirt road in a one-room wooden home. I loved to visit her. We'd sit in old rocking chairs on the front porch, drinking tall glasses of sweet tea while she'd tell me stories punctuated with Gullah expressions that would leap from her river of thought like bright, silver fish: "Girl, I be so happy I could jump the sky!" Hummingbirds darted in and out of bright zinnias and magenta cockscombs where her old, gray cat slept in the sun.

All the while she talked her hands were busy knitting, quilting, darning, and embroidering. I loved to watch her deep brown, gnarled hands putting out delicate work for her granbabies like the tender leaves that would emerge each spring from the branches of the island's ancient Angel Oak. Many tourists would come to see the fourteen-hundred-year-old Angel Oak, but failed to notice the people who weathered so many storms and still put out so much life. I never could find out Miss Ellie's precise age, but it was somewhere between ninety and one hundred. Maybe she didn't know herself. She still chopped her own firewood, stacked in neat piles beside the house.

One thing Miss Ellie did know was her Bible—by memory. She would rock and tell her own version, stitched, patched and embroidered from years of hearing it read and preached. I liked her version of the crucifixion: "And the hammer rang out—Repent! Repent! Repent!" as she hammered her fist into the open palm of her other hand. Even the sleepy cat would open an eye.

Miss Ellie had a friend named Netta whom she'd known since they were small girls. In order to get to Netta's house, Miss Ellie had to walk for miles through fields of tall grass. This was the sweet grass that Sea Island women make famous baskets out of, but it was also home to numerous poisonous snakes: coral snakes, rattlesnakes, water moccasins, and copperheads.

Actually, Netta's home was not that far from Miss Ellie's place, but there was a stream that cut across the fields. You had to walk quite a distance to get to the place where it narrowed enough to pass. I admired Miss Ellie, who would set off to visit her friend full of bouncy enthusiasm, with no worry for the snakes or the long miles. I also felt sorry for her. Poor Miss Ellie, I thought, old and arthritic, having to walk all that way, pushing through the thick summer heat, not to mention the snakes.

I felt sorry, until I hit upon the perfect plan. I arranged with some men to help build a simple plank bridge across the stream near Miss Ellie's house. I scouted out the ideal place, not too wide, but too deep to cross. I bought and helped carry the planks there myself, like Ansgar who, by the way, presides over a Hamburg bridge. Our bridge was built in a day. I was so excited that I could hardly wait to see Miss Ellie's reaction. I went to her house, where she wanted to sit in her rocker and tell stories, but I was too impatient with my project. I practically dragged her off with me. "Look!" I shouted, "a shortcut for you to visit Netta!"

Miss Ellie's face did not register the grateful, happy look I expected. There was no smile, no jumping the sky. Instead, for a long time, she looked puzzled, then she shook her head and looked at me as though I were the one who needed pity; "Child, I don't need a shortcut." And she told about all the friends she kept up with on her way to visit Netta. A shortcut would cut her off from Mr. Jenkins with whom she always swapped gossip, from Miss Hunter who so looked forward to the quilt scraps she'd bring by, from the raisin wine she'd taste at one place, in exchange for her biscuits, and the chance to look in on the "old folks" who were sick.

"Child," she said again, "can't take shortcuts if you want friends in this world. Shortcuts don't mix with love." Her wisdom washed over my hot embarrassment like cool, spring water, and we went back for some sweet tea.

Some lessons, however, take a while to stick. The next one would come two years later when I graduated from Brown and went to seminary. Ironically, while one of Luther's chief foes was Tetzel, a monk of the Dominican order, it was a member of the same order who would put me on the path to a Lutheran seminary. At the end of my year on Johns Island, I had a summer before heading back to school and called a Trappist monastery where Thomas Merton once lived. Being a Merton fan, I was really excited about visiting there, but it turned out that women were not welcome. The monk on phone duty recommended that I try the Springbank Retreat Center in Kingstree, South Carolina. It was there I met John Egan. Since his death, I have often felt that he is watching over me. In many ways, I owe my vocation as a Lutheran pastor to this wise and compassionate Dominican priest. His hospitality allowed me to spend the summer at Springbank. I spent a good part of the time under great, old magnolia trees draped with Spanish moss, reading the Bible, Thomas

Merton, Thomas Aquinas (new to me but essential for any Dominican library), Teresa of Avila and Luther, trying to decide what God wanted of me and pestering the patient priest with questions, opinions and ideas.

When the summer was over, I returned to Brown with a renewed passion to dedicate my life to working for justice and to increasing agitation over the thoughts, planted by John, of going to seminary. I applied for and received a grant that paid for a trial year at the seminary of my choice, still unsure about my vocation. There is a huge difference between private conversation or personal writing on matters of faith and public witness and proclamation. The first was comfortable, the second was not. The pastor of the church where I grew up, Pastor Franklin Fry, calmed me by saying that even if I decided that the ordained ministry was not for me, a year of seminary study would not be wasted. Then I had to choose a seminary. I thought I'd be open to working in any context except for one—the city. If I wouldn't work there, why study there?

I was a nature girl. True, I'd grown up in the suburbs of New Jersey, but it was a suburb with lots of woods. In fact, when I was born in 1954, the area hadn't been built up and our house was surrounded by woods where I spent many contented hours playing. I played by myself, but never felt alone in the woods. I was absorbed by the fascinating presence of so many living things—mayapples, skunk cabbage, birches and oaks, squirrels, chipmunks, moss and lichens, mushrooms, ants and the rare mole.

During college, I liked retreats in the country. Springbank had been in the heart of the rural South, forever associated in my mind with the voice of God. Cities seemed too noisy, too chaotic. I wanted nature. I wanted intimacy with creation. The desire clung to me stubbornly, like the green cockleburs stuck on my socks and jeans whenever I came home from playing in the woods.

But Pastor Fry was even more tenacious in convincing me that if I cared about justice, I ought to at least try a year of seminary in urban Philadelphia. The tree-lined streets of its Germantown location and its gardenlike campus with broad green lawns, flowering bushes and trees seemed creation-friendly anyway. But then, being in Philadelphia, I decided to seek out an area where some of the people on Johns Island had relatives, the Southwark high-rise housing projects that surrounded Emanuel Lutheran Church.

During the first two years of seminary, fieldwork is required. You leave the seminary campus to spend several hours a week at a congregation, performing assigned duties such as teaching Sunday school, helping to lead worship or visiting the sick. I requested and received my placement at Emanuel. It wasn't long before I discovered something. No place on planet Earth has more nature to offer than what people call the inner city—human nature. Human nature in close urban quarters makes for plenty of intimacy with creation. Once again, I was absorbed by the fascinating presence of so much life, and I was hooked—by the city and by the vocation.

I was also studying Hebrew and reading Jeremiah. The words of this prophet who ended up where he never expected to be, stung my heart like a cocklebur that has never let go: *If I say, "I will not mention him, or speak anymore in his name," then within me there is something like a burning fire shut up in my bones; I am weary with holding it in, and I cannot.* (Jeremiah 20:9) I knew that I had to go public.

At the time, John Cochran was Emanuel's pastor. He had an infinite store of patience and compassion when called upon by the Southwark congregation and community, but less with fellow clergy and seminarians. John worked daily until late at night or early in the morning hours. He was single and, from what I could tell, his mother took care of the cooking, washing, and household chores. His interns didn't have the benefit of a live-in mom, but I think he basically expected them to keep the same schedule. As a part-time seminary student, I didn't have to live up to such expectations. On the other hand, I was eager to prove myself.

After an orientation that included setting up and completing interviews with a range of community leaders, visiting neighboring institutions and walking for miles around the city, drawing and labeling my own maps to better learn the area (very good but highly unusual activities in most fieldwork placements), I was given my first big assignment: to create a Sunday school flier and place it under every door in the four twenty-one-story projects. Sister Jean, who basically ran the church's daily operations, told me to wait for her or for Pastor Cochran to accompany me, since it was my first foray into the projects, where I was both unknown and unknowing. I waited. And I waited. But, after all, I was on a schedule. I had seminary classes to attend. There were only certain hours for fieldwork, and I was wasting them waiting around for some-one to hold my hand while I delivered leaflets. I came to the conclusion that this was ridiculous. Besides, I was wearing my new black shirt with its white clerical collar, so there would be no doubt about my public business in the buildings.

It was a hot and humid day at the end of August. On the sidewalks outside, the temperature was in the high nineties and climbing. Inside the buildings, it was easily three digits. Every fan and air-conditioning unit must have been on. I took the elevator straight up to the twenty-first floor and stepped out with my stack of fliers. The doors closed. That's when the electricity went off. There were no windows in the hallway. I couldn't see my own hands, much less, floors, walls, or doorways. There were no working exit lights. I felt my way to-ward a wall, to a door and knocked. No answer—I tried the next door, and the next. Anyone with any sense was outside where you could breathe a little. I put my fliers under the first three doors and decided I needed to find the stairs. It took a while.

By this time, I was sweating so much that my new black shirt was plastered to my body. I pulled out the white collar tab and opened a few buttons. So much for pastoral identity. I found a door that pushed open and carefully felt my way to the stairs. I was gingerly taking the steps toward the landing—the first of twenty-one—when I stepped on an empty bottle, slipped and went down. I landed in the landing which doubled as a garbage catch-all. I wasn't hurt, just shaken, sore and as smelly as the used diaper I had to peel off my back. Still unable to see a thing, I decided to leave the fliers where they lay rather than feeling around in the trash to collect them. There I was, like Jonah, in the odoriferous belly of darkness. My mission had changed. I just wanted to see daylight again.

After several floors, I heard voices and decided to see if anyone had a flash-light. A door opened and wonderful, shadowy light flooded the hallway. "Vicky Heidi, is that you?" (For reasons that are uncertain to me and even less clear to others, Lutheran seminary interns are often called vicars.) Children, who are masters at making sense of nonsense, often used the more familiar-sounding names of Victor and Vicky. One girl couldn't get over the amazing coincidence that all the interns had the same first name. I was a fieldwork student and not an intern, but this distinction was lost on Roger and Jerome. There was no flashlight, but they took my sweaty hands in their own, sticky from candy, and led me all the way down the stairs until we hit the light. I was Jonah spit out from the sunless bowels of the whale onto dry land. Stubborn Jonah who ignored divine directions, who eschewed the outstretched hands and heartfelt wisdom of his fellow sailors, who clasped salvation to his chest like a clammy shirt, eventually became Jonah set straight by the grace of God. I thanked the boys who cheerfully told me they'd see me in Sunday school and headed back toward the church office to face Sister Jean, borrow a clean shirt, and find a bathroom. That time, the lesson stuck.

My urban education was just beginning. The church was located in an African-American neighborhood, and the membership and ministry reflected that community. Not too far away was a large Italian community and, strangely enough, in its midst was one lone street of African-American families: Beulah Street. *Beulah,* which literally means "married" in Hebrew, is a biblical name used by a people wedded to their land: *No longer will they call you Azubah* [forsaken], *or name your land Shememah* [desolate]. *But you will be called Hephzibah* [my delight is in her] *and your land Beulah* [married]. (Isaiah 62:4) Many Black churches have taken the name Beulah, which bears powerful meaning for a people torn from the beloved earth that was home.

Pastor Cochran's next assignment for me was to go to Beulah Street and see if the youth there would be interested in forming a club. The church had begun a series of youth clubs as an alternative to gangs. There was only one problem. I had no experience. I had received no training for this sort of thing in seminary. I was shy. I once missed a party in college to which I had been invited because I was afraid to knock on the door, worried I wouldn't find anyone I knew inside. No one on Beulah Street had invited me to their doors. What would I say? What would I do? What if no one wanted to talk to me? And the bottom line—what if I failed? Did I mention that I didn't know anybody on Beulah Street? The prospect of that particular street seemed less than delightful to me.

I remember discussing my concerns about the Beulah Street assignment with Pastor Cochran. As I indicated, he was not big on commiserating with insecure seminary students. "How can you fail? Whatever you do won't be so bad as doing nothing." While I didn't agree with that, he had made his point. He had said what I needed to hear, and it wasn't long before the Beulah Street Bunch (the name they chose) became a regular fixture on the Philadelphia Seminary basketball court, on practice runs along the Schuylkill River, and around the altar. And Beulah became a delight to me.

The delight in Jonah's story is more ambiguous. After the whale vomits him out, Jonah finally heads off for the city he had first avoided. Things go remarkably well as the whole city turns to God. Any other prophet would be overjoyed, but not Jonah. He cannot accept that things have turned out so contrary to his expectations. At the very least, if he had to go to this rotten city, it was only to call down God's judgment and wrath. If the city was going to undergo such a transformation, Jonah decides that he would be better off dead:

> Oh Lord, is this not what I said when I was in my own country? That is why I fled to Tarshish in the beginning . . . And now, O Lord, please take my life from me, for it is better for me to die than to live. (Jonah 4:2–3)

We don't know if Jonah ever emerges into the light, but tragically many churches have not. There were once thirty-one Lutheran churches in Newark, New Jersey. There is now one. Basically, some in the church decided that death was preferable to change and openness to the city and people around them. I thank God that that did not happen at Transfiguration.

Five Weeks

Like Beulah's bunch and the gracious children who led me out of the rank belly of the project building, there were members of Transfiguration who took my hand and led me through the period of *malabarriga*. There was Manny, who would sense when a particularly stressful situation was approaching: "Now Pastor, please don't cry," he'd say. "Crying is fine, but in this instance it would really be better if you didn't cry. It gives the wrong impression." The wrong impression? What would that be? That I was unsure and insecure?

Ready to fall apart at a moment's notice? That wasn't an impression, some days that was the truth. When he left my office, the tears would flow, but then, on the strength of his kindness, I'd pull myself together to face whatever it was.

Ernestina, an active member of the church since the 1930s, would tell me, "Oh *Pastora,* I'm sorry I can't do as much as I used to. I'm too old now, but every day I'm praying for you. Don't worry. Don't give up. God has sent you here. Everything will be all right." On shaky days, I'm sure her prayers were, and are, the ground beneath my feet. Then there was Esperanza, a retired school teacher. She brought the same firm and soothing presence to the congregation—and to me—that she'd demonstrated over years of calming children and giving order to their days. She corrected my Spanish preaching grammar and helped me with difficult idioms. It took me time to loosen from the less demonstrative style of my upbringing into the free and frequent embraces and kisses that are the cultural norm of this community. Esperanza not only translated for me, she interpreted for those who found my style of greeting cold and uncaring. She represented an oasis of tranquility until the evening I visited her apartment during a boxing match. Her husband let me in the door. There was a strange woman on the couch, fired-up and screaming at the TV set. It was Esperanza. I knew then that I had a fiery bush as well as an oasis on my side. There were others, too, passionate and patient in teaching me their ways.

With this help, despite the insecurities and anxieties roiling around my gut, I was determined to ride out the early days of morning sickness because I really did believe that nothing was too wonderful for God and that a new day was coming forth. Didn't a rainbow of vibrant color on the church doors greet me each morning and on the smiling faces of children each afternoon? Weren't there now punch and cookies in addition to *café con leche* during coffee hour, in deference to the new children? Wasn't there monthly bilingual worship, where everyone tried valiantly to sing each other's songs and embrace with wordless understanding at the kiss of peace?

Then it was time for my vacation. Since we were going to visit my husband's family in Argentina, I requested our church's elected leadership body, the council, to take my allotted four weeks at once. "No problem," the council told me, "in fact, take five!" "This is great," I thought, "they really like me. They're going to give me five weeks instead of four!" So off we went to the land that had brought us together.

I had been inspired to go to Argentina after a chance meeting with Juan Cobrda, a native of Czechoslovakia, who served as a Lutheran bishop in Argentina for ten years. He came to the United States in exile from the dictatorship that he had criticized, and soon afterward, he visited and spoke at my seminary. Listening to his story of imprisonment and torture left me deeply shaken and simultaneously awed. I was amazed that a man who had descended into hell with his adopted nation and his church was able to get up in the morning and face the world with a genuine smile, with obvious faith, hope and love. How could this be? I wanted to know more. When he finished speaking, I approached him and we talked. He encouraged me to visit Argentina for myself and learn from the people there. I applied for a scholarship to study in Argentina for my final year of seminary, and Bishop Cobrda wrote me a letter of recommendation. Sometimes a conversation can change your life. Little did I imagine that my brief exchange with the bishop would lead me into the arms of my life's companion.

I first met my future husband, Gregorio, in a squatters' area that I moved to from the seminary dorm in Buenos Aires. I made contact with the squatters through Aldolfo Perez Esquivel, the Nobel Peace Prize winner in 1981 for his human-rights work in Argentina and throughout Latin America. I was volunteering with his organization, *Servicio Paz y Justicia* (SERPAJ), translating and answering letters he received in English. One of SERPAJ's projects was with a group that took over vacant land on the outskirts of Buenos Aires.

A priest in the area, Padre Raúl, had been inspired by the landmark 1968 conference of Latin American Roman Catholic bishops in Medellín, which had called for a church reformation from the grass roots. Instead of a passive flock dominated by a hierarchy with close ties to political dictatorships ("all the leading families produce three sons—a general, a judge and a bishop," went the Argentine saying), the church would re-form from the ground up, among the masses of poor, with small groups of lay people reading the Bible together and relating it to their context. Rather than promoting dependence and unthinking obedience to church and state, Padre Raúl and others like him encouraged the people to assume strong leadership roles in their church and community. The squatters I came to know organized in groups called base communities which met for biblical reflection, song and prayer one night a week and developing strategies on how to get electricity, water and land rights, the next.

My interest in these base communities was one of my reasons for taking the year to study in Latin America, and through Esquivel's group, I visited several times. Some of the women leaders I met invited me to move in with them for a deeper experience of their life and work. Gregorio had recently moved there with his family from the northern Argentine province of *el Chaco* where he had grown up picking cotton and cutting sugar cane while I was playing on our suburban New Jersey lawn and in the woods out back.

Like my father, Gregorio doesn't like talking much about his past. In both cases, the sociopolitical context of their homeland brought heartbreak and reticence to discuss it. I think they would have understood this in each other, but my father had died a year before I met Gregorio. From time to time, Gregorio is willing to relate the good memories: hunting rabbits, birds and armadillos, picking cotton as a child, side by side with the adults, more working and playing with eleven brothers and sisters, frying bread and stuffing sausages, singing sambas and playing the guitar with friends and family around a fire while meat was grilling.

But these memories are often mixed in with pain he occasionally alludes to but declines to dwell on: having too much cotton to pick when his hands were already bleeding, going to bed hungry, not being able to go to school, one sister dead at twenty and another in her thirties for lack of medical care, national prejudice against the tawny skin of his indigenous heritage and watching people "disappeared" in the Dirty War which brought terror to Argentina from 1976 until 1983. A military junta seized control of the government and waged a campaign against the left-wing that caused far more instability and ruin than those it sought to eliminate. Dissidents and innocent civilians alike were arrested and then vanished without a trace. Thirty thousand people were among the *los desaparecidos,* the "disappeared." The economy was in a shambles too and Gregorio watched helplessly as many of the men around him sank into drink and depression.

Finally, like thousands of other families, Gregorio, his mother and some brothers came to the capital city seeking better opportunities when the rural economy was offering nothing beyond the yearly cotton harvest. His father had died several years earlier. Like so many others, Gregorio's family could not find affordable housing in Buenos Aires and settled on vacant land outside the city, constructing a simple home from scraps of metal and lumber. The floor was dirt, and there was no running water, but Gregorio's house had something others didn't. It had a door, painted pink. At this door, my own heart's reformation began.

Gregorio and I landed in the same base community where he played the guitar and led the music. I remember looking forward to the moment for saying the Lord's Prayer, when all the worshipers would join hands. Somehow we frequently managed to be reverent side by side, *mano en mano*. The kiss of peace was nice, too. But it was evangelism that really brought us together. The community members were divided up into teams to visit other squatters and see if they wanted to organize their own group. Gregorio and I were assigned to be a team. We weren't particularly successful at the evangelism, but we did become a team.

Before the squatters' arrival, the land had been empty because it was low, often flooded and muddy. There were some slaughterhouses nearby, and workers dumped animal hides right outside along with whatever else they didn't use. Lack of affordable housing in Buenos Aires (literally "good air") pushed the poor to this land where the *aire* was definitely not *bueno*. A foul odor pervaded the area, especially when the ground was damp. The absence of plumbing throughout the settlement didn't help. When I moved there, I began commuting by bus to and from the seminary. After falling in love with Gregorio, I'd ride the bus and, as soon as it would near the area, I'd catch the slaughterhouse stench. I was usually sleepy with closed eyes, but my dozing senses were no match for the invasive odor. I'd wake up and know we were near—and begin to feel glad. Before long, the disgusting smell became a heady perfume. Whenever I caught the scent, I was happy thinking of joys behind the pink door. It became the most marvelous smell. Gregorio is not fond of this story, but I think it's a great example of how love transfigures perception.

This first vacation I was taking after coming to Transfiguration was to be our first visit back to Argentina since getting married, so it was great to have the five weeks generously allotted to me by the church. The time was important because we were going to build a concrete house for Gregorio's mother, Anastasia, who still lived in the shack with the pink door. My mother was going also—to meet Anatasia and to help with the construction. Three years earlier, when I called her to say that I'd fallen in love with Gregorio and wanted him to come visit, she helped us get the visa, becoming his sponsor. She did it because she believed it best for the two of us to realize on our own that we were not meant for one another. Since that's not how it worked out, she's embraced him without reserve. She too had married a man who grew up in another country, and although they had a similar educational background, there were twenty years of difference in age between them. So she had some experience of love leaping distances.

My mother rented a car so we could drive around and order all the building supplies—concrete mix, bricks, windows, sheets of zinc for the roof and a new door. The car became another unexpected adventure for my mom, who had grown up with a mother who did everything possible to shield her and her sister from life's unpleasantness. If a disabled person was walking toward them, my grandmother would quickly take them across the street so her daughters wouldn't note any deformity. Naturally the girls took every unplanned street crossing as a cue to pay particular attention to everything and everyone around them. My mother vowed never to do the same with me, and she succeeded.

There were no other cars in the squatters' area, so the presence of ours attracted attention. One day when my mother and I walked a few blocks to buy bread, a neighbor ran after us, "Hurry! They have a gun pointed at your husband!" Three policemen had surrounded Gregorio, and one was pushing the barrel of a gun hard into his chest. They wanted to know where the car came from, where was his ID, where were the keys to open the trunk. My mother had helpfully put all of our identification, as well as the car's papers and keys, into her purse for safe keeping. The police thought Gregorio's story about a North American mother-in-law who'd rented the car to be a big joke. ("If that's true, she must be a *curandera* . . . a witch.")

When my mother produced the documents and the keys and opened the empty trunk, they laughed and went on their way. Luckily, she and I hadn't gone farther. Many police trained under Argentina's military dictatorship during the Dirty War retained the same mentality of unrestrained brutality when the government changed. Shooting some guy in a squatters' area who probably stole the car or had guns hidden in the trunk was doing the *patria* a favor. It took several days for Gregorio's heart to calm down. Little did he know that the same thing could easily happen in the Bronx.

After that, the house went up without incident. With lots of help from family, neighbors and friends, it was completely finished at the end of the five weeks. Building a house was a great vacation from church work. I could see immediate results every day. Things were different in the parish. We were returning to the Bronx on a Saturday, and the very next day was our annual congregational meeting. While I was away, I prepared my sermon. I didn't know that some other preparations were going on, too. A key leader had decided that things had gone too far in a new direction, and he drafted a motion to, essentially, divide the church. The congregation, which for sixty years had been a homogeneous Hispanic group, would not integrate the new English-speaking members who were African-American. Instead, they could form a separate congregation with their own council and would be allowed to rent space in the church, which would remain basically as it had been.

On Saturday my plane landed, and Sunday morning I stood up to preach, aglow in blissful ignorance . . . "What a marvelous thing God is doing here!" I told the congregation, "What a powerful witness to Christ you are. What a sign of the Holy Spirit! Why if you were just acting with your human instincts, you would be seeking division, but look at the unity represented here in this church. People of different races, classes, languages, and musical tastes, united in the Spirit!" On and on and on I went, praising them, giving thanks for them and pointing out the positive, wonderful things God was doing through them. The motion to split never came up. And the leader behind it later moved away to a distant state.

If I had been wiser to the ways of the world, if I had realized what was really going on, I would have been depressed and frustrated. I don't know what I would have done, but surely I would not have stood before the church radiating joy and thanksgiving in the power of God working through imperfect human beings. And yet, that's what really was going on. It was a turning point. There was never any further question about the doors staying open to everyone. Nor did it mean the immediate end to *malabarriga*. But we'd turned a corner, and the worst had passed.

CHAPTER TWO

NEIGHBORHOOD DOORS

"The door of entry into this castle is prayer and meditation," wrote St. Teresa on her way to ecstasy. *Ecstasy* comes from the Greek *"ek stasis"* and implies moving out of stasis, out of a set position. Of course, the word is used for spiritual transport, but it strikes me that the church ought to see its daily role as following a path of ecstasy, leaving behind all that is stagnant and staid and stepping out into the unknown, allowing ourselves to be displaced as we enter into relationship with others in their space. Ecstasy, then, is not just interior communion with God but communion with our neighbor. The passion implied is not just the passion of erotic power but the exciting power of relationships, one by one, creating a new community, a new city, a new world.

Long before we could knock down the physical walls of our church to make room for a larger building, we had to step out and rebuild relationships from which the church had retreated behind its closed doors. Since I was new to the neighborhood, it was important that I too step out and seek out new relationships and understandings, especially as a white pastor coming from a history fraught with racial and class divisions. As Miss Ellie had taught me, there are no shortcuts, just a wide range of patiently built relationships made one by one, day by day. And so I began by spending many hours praying on my feet, visiting neighbors.

Visitation

Debra lived on the fifth floor and the elevator never worked. This was a problem for her two young sons who suffered from asthma and easily became short of breath. One of them also had a heart condition. Debra, a single parent, first came to the church seeking activities for her boys and help with her landlord. In addition to the stairs, the apartment had broken window locks and water dripping through the kitchen ceiling. Visits to the apartment led to visits in housing court. The visits also forged a relationship that has spanned almost twenty years. Debra is now a trusted friend and colleague. She is the director of our youth ministries and the secretary of our church council. I often turn to her for advice and counsel. Over the years, she has been a source of guidance and support for hundreds of neighborhood youth, but it all begin with the initial visits, up and down the stairs, many times.

Sometimes, another visitor beat me to the door. I took the stairs two at a time and pushed open the unlocked door, but it was too late. Julio's neck had snapped instantly when he stepped off the chair, hanging himself from the light fixture in the living room ceiling. I'd spent the morning listening to him talk, an unemployed Salvadoran immigrant telling a story of frustration and shame at being unable to find a job while his wife worked as the domestic servant for a wealthy family in Brooklyn. They required her to live in, leaving her just one day a week at home with Julio and their children. It was the only way they could pay the rent. Mostly Julio spoke of his quickly assimilating teenage children who, he felt, despised him.

They came running to my house several hours later to say that their father was on a chair trying to hang himself. I dialed 911 and raced to the apartment. I didn't know where the teenagers had gone, so I stayed with his body, which hung from a rope hooked to the ceiling, and waited for the useless ambulance. Should I have called the ambulance that morning when we talked? Did I fail to take his despair seriously enough? A futile question that sat immobile on my heart like a big, heavy stone.

When the police finished their interrogation, Gregorio drove me to Brooklyn to tell Julio's wife. Making the trip was the job of the police, but they asked us to do it, which seemed better anyway. Hours later, back home, it was time to finish my sermon for the following morning. I was speechless. The stone had risen from my heart to my throat.

What to preach wasn't the only question. What about purifying the place of a hanging? We have a worship book for "occasional services," but it has nothing for occasions like this. The family was afraid to go back into the apartment and something had to be done. We brought water from the baptismal

font and used sections from Psalm 51: *Purge me with hyssop and I shall be clean
. . . create in me a clean heart, O God, and put a new and right spirit within me.*
We did it that way and then we changed "me" to "this place." We voiced our
rejection of evil as we do at the beginning of the baptismal rite and said the
Apostles' Creed, our confession of faith, and prayed a baptismal prayer: "Jesus
from your wounded side flowed streams of cleansing water; the world was
washed of all its sin, all life made new again. Fill this room and those gathered
here with your newness of life and light."

There was terrible irony in the fact that Julio hung himself from the windowless room's one source of light. After sprinkling the area and ourselves
with water in blessing, we lit candles: *The light shines in the darkness, and the
darkness has not overcome it.* We held hands in a circle under the light fixture
and prayed for Julio, for ourselves, and for the many immigrants who seek a
better life. The landlord came, too, fearing a curse on the building. After that,
the family stayed for a while, but moved out as soon as they could.

Julio lived on the same block of Union Avenue behind the church as Ruby. I
met Ruby for the first time when she came to our food pantry. Later I decided
to visit her. Once again, I found an elevator that didn't work, so I walked up the
six flights of shaky stairs. There were signs that it was once an elegant address.
Fluted concrete columns planted on either side of the building's front door still
sprouted sculpted flowers. If you looked hard beneath the chipped, scuffed
and stained floor of the foyer, you could see the marble mosaics polished to
glistening. Once, solid stairs had led the way to a landing of dreams. Now the
center of each marble step is caved in from the weight of so many trips up and
down, up and down.

At the sixth floor, I knocked on Ruby's door. I could hear her movements
inside, and then there was tense silence as a shadow passed over the peephole.
I knew she was considering whether or not to open that door, her door. Then
locks clicked open as Ruby made her decision and invited me inside, all the
while apologizing for the condition of her apartment. She hadn't been expecting visitors.

It was dark in the windowless living room, since her electricity had been
cut off, but it was not so dark that Ruby and I couldn't see the accumulated
garbage; old cartons of Chinese takeout on top of the silent TV, paper plates

crusted with dried macaroni and cheese made from the box picked up at the food pantry, soda-streaked glasses, Styrofoam boxes heaped with old chicken bones, cigarette butts, and balled up napkins. A small kitten busied herself by pouncing on roaches while a rat, easily twice her size, scuttled along one wall and disappeared in back of the couch. I had not yet met the little boy who sat on the floor in his underwear using his fingers to pick soggy pieces of pastel cereal out of the milk in his bowl.

I knew I would never, ever have had the courage to open that door. Ruby did. It was bold courage, not sloth that stood up and welcomed me. She pushed aside a pile of clothes on her sofa to make room for me to sit, and after another moment of decision, Ruby opened one more door. Out spilled the story of her depression, her battle with crack, her ex-husband's abuse, her mother's rejection, and worries over her daughter, Thea. Thea had recently returned from a relative where she'd been staying because of an older brother's abuse. Just turned twelve, Thea hated going to school because, with the electricity turned off, there was no way to iron her clothes even if there were enough quarters to wash them. The night before my visit, Ruby woke up to Thea's screams as rats chewed on the bottom of her mattress. And finally, Ruby came to the most difficult subject—her recent HIV positive test results.

But this was still a landing of dreams . . . "You know what I want?" said Ruby, "I want my children to have a photo album of happy memories of their life with me to look at after I die . . . I want to start making some happy memories." Then Ruby, ever courageous, took my hands and pulled me through the final door, way past the locks, the mess, the rats and the rags, into her pure cry for mercy. Ruby's strong, trembling hands pulled me into her prayer—rare and radiant in the dingy shadows of the room—Lord, have mercy . . . mercy . . . mercy!

The foundations of the wall of the city are adorned with every jewel. (Revelation 21:19a) One of them is named Ruby. She taught me about prayer that burns through all the crap. I never saw Ruby again. A few weeks later, the apartment was empty, boarded up.

I went to see Marisol, twenty years old and beautiful like her name—sea and sun—*mar y sol*. I remember her hair—long, black, thick and shiny. Irrepressible strands spring from their braid, swinging with a lilt down Longwood Avenue. Her eyes hold the warmth of the Salvadoran sun, and her belly holds a baby, afloat in its own private sea. She left beaches behind for the cold deserts and colder terror of dangerous crossings, traveling north, to build a future safe from war. Marisol left her mother's hands behind, the hands that plaited her hair each morning as she leaned back into her lap. She left to make a living. She left to live and landed in the Bronx.

That's how I want to remember her. Each month, Marisol would go to the clinic for her check-up. It took most of the day as she sat awaiting her turn. Friends said she was wasting time. "No," said Marisol, "I want to make sure my baby is healthy." Finally her name was called and a nurse took blood. A doctor appeared for the examination. Marisol had a bad cough, but no mind. She heard the words she'd waited to hear: "Everything is fine. Come back next month." Faithfully, Marisol returned each month. The baby was growing. Blood was taken. The cough was worsening. A doctor appeared. Different doctors appeared. Same words: "Everything is fine. Come back next month."

After seven months, the cough was so bad that an X ray was taken. Everything was not fine. Marisol's lungs were wasted by tuberculosis. One month later, warm salt waters streamed down her legs. She longed for the strength of her mother's hands. She longed to lean back into her lap. As tides of pain crashed through her body, Marisol heaved her son onto a sterile shore. Within an hour, she was dead. Dead in the promised land, in the Bronx. Her eyes held the warmth of the Salvadoran sun. Now someone else holds her baby.

Marisol's girlfriends stood weeping around the coffin, stroking the pink satin, fingering the pillow's lacy edge. "Doesn't she look beautiful?" they said. No she didn't. She looked dead.

Some visits required a certain kind of street diplomacy. Dealers dominated many buildings. I remember going to visit the family of some children who came on their own to Sunday school. When I approached the building on Southern Boulevard, I saw a long line of people stretching around the block. Long lines were a fact of life—at the bank, the post office, the drugstore, at food pantries and soup kitchens, welfare offices and clinics. This time, it was a line for crack. I had to ask permission to enter and visit from the dealer who controlled the front door. On my way out, a woman in the line stopped me, "You a Reverend?" she asked. "Yes." "Where's the cheese?" Where's the cheese?! She thought it was a cheese line. Cheese was a popular government surplus commodity that generated long lines like the one she was waiting in. I told her she was in the wrong line.

Dealing with the dealers to get into buildings became routine. In the eighties, drugs were sold openly here, and crack rapidly became the drug of choice, moving like wildfire through the streets. I can't imagine that the spread of anthrax or an epidemic of smallpox could wreck more lives. The sidewalks were dotted with empty crack vials sporting jellybean-colored tops—pink, yellow, lavender, red, green, and robin's egg blue—very appealing for unattended toddlers to pop into their mouths. It is no exaggeration to say that on the five-minute walk from my house to the church, I would step over hundreds.

In the summer, I'd daily check the crevices in the rubber bottoms of my sandals to pick out any of the tops that had become stuck there so as not to track them home when my own children were of the age to put such things into their mouths. One summer, a dealer set a ratty armchair on the sidewalk in front of our house to do business in comfort until I asked him to move. There was a constant chorus of dealers calling out the latest brand names for their wares: Flamingo, Kiss, Spider Woman, Fatal Beauty, DOA, Undertaker. Bad Boy was a popular moniker for heroin, and the teenagers selling it stood on our corner chanting, "Bad Boy, Bad Boy, Bad Boy," to anyone who walked by. This was upsetting to Hans when he was three and assumed they were referring to him. His eyes filled with tears, "But mommy, I'm not a bad boy!"

That same summer, there were eight shooting incidents in which someone was killed within a block of our home. We heard gunshots every night. For the most part, the children slept through it. Their bedrooms don't directly face the street as does ours.

Because of visitation to their homes and because of our open doors after school, neighborhood children kept coming to the church. Many came without parents. Some walked. Some we picked up. When I went to pick up Shanna for Sunday school one week, she was crying and had blood on her dress. "It's my Uncle Joe!" she said. I knew that her family was "going through changes" because of Uncle Joe and his drug addiction. Shanna had particular reason to feel bitter toward her uncle. For years, she had dreamed of owning a bicycle, and that Christmas a donation from another church made her dream come true. Shanna rode her shiny, new, blue bike everywhere, bragged on it, polished it, and treasured it.

Within a month, her uncle had sold the bike to buy drugs—ample reason to embitter a nine-year-old. Now, on this morning, there was one reason more. Uncle Joe had come home wearing a T-shirt that read; "Say No to Drugs." Shanna commented, "Why don't you read your own shirt?" He hit her, causing a nosebleed. The white collar and yellow lace of her Sunday dress were a mess. Nothing else was clean, and everyone else was still asleep. We went to church where her teacher washed out the bloodstain.

When it came time in the service for individual prayer petitions, Shanna's voice sounded bright and clear as a trumpet: "I pray for my uncle Joe. He needs your help, Lord. Please, Jesus, help my uncle." What a privilege to drink from the same chalice as Shanna.

The demographics of this neighborhood favor the young, but there are still elderly members to visit. While I needed to immerse myself in the neighborhood, it didn't mean forgetting about the folks who'd held the church together for so many years. When I arrived, Alma was one of the few members who still lived in the area. In her nineties, she loved to walk. She invented daily errands to get out on the streets. She often went to visit friends unlikely to be home. Whenever we announced the need for chaperones on a youth outing, Alma raised her hand. Then she was confined to bed with a missing leg, amputated because of diabetes. When she came out of surgery, I found her in the hallway, still groggy from anesthesia. As soon as she saw me, she smiled: "How are your children, Pastor?" "How is your husband?" This is typical. I know of many pastors who feel that ministry is a one-way street; they give, but they don't get, at least not from their parishioners. My experience here is utterly different. I am given far more than I can give, and those doing the giving are often perceived by most as the neediest of all, folks looking for hand-outs. On balance, I find many more hands here are stretched out to give than to take.

I went to visit Alma again when she came home from the hospital. Before we prayed, it was important for her to lift the bed covers, unwrap the long strips of gauze and bare the stump where her leg used to be, so that in praying, I might see her wound, her loss. At the end of the visit, she touched the metal railing of her bed, smiled widely, and said, "this is my cradle now."

The next time I saw Alma, she didn't know where she was. In her mind, she was still in the old Bronx neighborhood, but in fact she had been moved to a nursing home in Brooklyn. She sat in her wheelchair, parked in the hallway, and I found a loose chair for myself. Soon we mercifully left the confusing corridor with its odor of urine-soaked diapers and entered the limpid geography of the psalter. Once there, Alma knew every turn and detail of the landscape. The hills rose with familiar grace. She moved unimpeded across this holy land and her mind leapt up in glorious lucidity.

Most of the 150 Psalms seem etched into her DNA—not just memorized but woven through the very strands of Alma's being. *Alzaré mis ojos a los montes. ¿De dónde vendrá mi socorro? Mi socorro viene de Jehová que hizo los cielos y la tierra.* (*I lift up my eyes to the hills—from where will my help come? My help comes from the Lord who made heaven and earth.* Psalm 121:1-2) Together we roamed the hills, free of wheelchairs, prostheses and canes, leaning on the everlasting arms.

I visited Mirta who was hospitalized after an asthma attack. It was hard for her to be in the same hospital where her mother, Cordelia, had recently died of AIDS, after years of drug abuse. Near the end, Cordelia wondered if it was too late to receive her First Communion. Of course not. "But I haven't done the class," she worried. No matter. What matters is the hunger. She wanted to confess and receive absolution, then Communion. *This is the body of Christ, given for you. This is the blood of Christ, shed for you.* Cordelia lay in the white sheets, smiling. "*Gracias,*" she said, "*gracias.*" It was the last word I heard her speak.

I think Mirta's grieving contributed to her hospital admission. I sat with her as she lay in bed, wheezing and struggling for air, and reflected on the powerful kinship between this illness that constricts the passage of breath and the struggle for silence and prayer in my own life. So often, I wheeze and am brought low by the stress, all the environmental irritants that swirl invisibly through my life evading awareness. Like Mirta, I've found myself weakened and debilitated, again and again. Perhaps I simply need to accept this and get on. "Prayer is a battle all the way to the last breath," said one of the Desert Fathers, Abba Agathon.

Physical breath, metaphysical breath—I think they belong together. In the Genesis creation story, God breathes over the waters, and chaos swirls into shape. God breathes the *ruah,* or holy wind of life, into human beings, which propels them to their feet. In Hebrew, *ruah* is feminine, what the poet Gerard Manley Hopkins called, "world-mothering air." What this story communicates to me is that life is holy, all of it.

Ezekiel saw the same thing when he pictured his community as a field of dry bones:

Suddenly there was a noise, a rattling, and the bones came together, bone to its bone. I looked, and there were sinews on them, and flesh had come upon them, and skin had covered them; but there was no breath in them. (Ezekiel 37:7–8a)

At first, the bones link up in their individual skeletal frameworks. But as bodies disconnected from one another, without community, they still can't move. They're all fitted out with sinews and skin, going nowhere. *"Come from the four winds, O breath,"* cries the prophet, *"and the breath came into them, and they lived, and stood on their feet, a vast multitude."* Like Ezekiel's bones, we might rattle through the motions, but without *ruah*-spirit-breath, nothing gets up or or moves forward. Space becomes claustrophobic, literally a closed-in place where fear sucks out the air. Many people shut in their project apartments feel like this—isolated with no exit. The welfare system does it, too, knocks the wind out.

It's the same place Jesus' disciples found themselves in after his death, like the locked church where I first met Transfiguration's members huddled together:

The doors of the house where the disciples had met were locked for fear ... Jesus came and stood among them and said ... "Peace be with you. As the Father has sent me, so I send you." When he had said this, he breathed on them. (John 20:19, 21–22)

It was breath that set them free to open breathing space for others.

* * *

Mirta can do little to change the conditions in the small apartment she shares with her grandmother, aunt, and two brothers. The doctor wrote a letter urging the aunt to limit her smoking to outside the building. When I asked Mirta about it, she threw up her hands. Her aunt tried for a few days, but smoking in the hallway was not like sitting on the couch with a cup of coffee. Soon she went right back to chain-smoking in the living room. I, on the other hand, have options. I can do things that I don't do. I am, as Auden put it, "craving the sensation but ignoring the cause."

The doctors prescribed a new pump for Mirta. They thought it would work better than the bulky machine she'd been dragging around in case of an attack. What should I take for emergencies with this asthma of the spirit? I hope Pius V doesn't mind recurring use of his prayer by a Lutheran: "Have mercy on your people, Lord, and give us a breathing space in the midst of so many troubles."

I finally came to my senses and began to take regular detours from neighborhood visits to visit with my spiritual director, Ellie. Sister Ellie, not Miss Ellie, but like the latter she's loving, patient, and wise. I told her how not having a set time to pray every day used to be an obstacle. I wanted to take time early in the morning, but that's when Hans, as a toddler, would come into bed with us for a cuddle. Then it would be time to get both children ready for school—making breakfast, packing lunches, gathering homework, library books, gym clothes, instruments. Shouldn't we have done this the night before? Of course, and that knowledge only makes morning chores more stressful.

Hans has his own wisdom. He often notices things in passing that I miss in the rush to get from here to there. Sometimes in the midst of the morning frenzy, he'd grab my hand and lead me to a window to see the sunrise or show me a cloudlike morning moon. When he was quite small, he'd pause for instant theology with a mouthful of toothpaste: "Mommy, if God and Jesus are the same, how did God live before Jesus was born on Christmas? How can they be the same?" I'm not up for theological conundrums so early in the morning, but I was supposed to answer this question, which created one of the greatest schisms in Christendom, and look for matching socks at the same time. Maybe this was rubbing off. I found myself so longing for moments of reflection, meditation, and silence that I'd snatch them as I could, here and there. Sometimes, I felt guilty, as though I were having an affair—sneaking away from my pastoral responsibilities to pray—as though it were some elicit pleasure. I also told Ellie that I was sure this wouldn't last, and she said that I should simply savor the present grace. I did and it didn't!

We discussed nursing, one of my favorite things as a new mother. The memory is still strong in my body. Sometimes, when I hold a baby, my breasts will stir with the feeling of letting down milk. I often had a glass of water nearby when I nursed because I became so thirsty. I took extra vitamins, too. The milk draws strength wherever it can, if need be, directly from the mother's bones, leaving her increasingly weak. My walks around the neighborhood left me thirsty. I am often thirsty.

What I long for is simple, like the city tap water we drink. I used to fantasize about prayer—Perrier-prayer, champagne prayer. I was a voyeur in the upper echelons of prayer. It was a compulsion: John of the Cross, Teresa of Avila, Bernard of Clairvaux, *The Cloud of Unknowing*, Dame Julian of Norwich, Meister Eckhart, Thomas Merton, the Desert Fathers and Mothers. The books cover eight yards of shelving and centuries of lived grace. That's not counting the Native American, Hindu, Sufi, Buddhist and Zen traditions; another two yards' worth of Peeping Tom piety. That used to be my relaxation reading. I can't imagine how I had the energy or will. I gave it up and became addicted to reading mystery novels, struggling to stop. Now that's over, except for some moments of relapse, especially in airports.

Teresa of Avila didn't have her first mystical experience until she was forty. That was comforting when I first read her at twenty, but not now. Fortunately, that's not the point anymore. I'm grateful for the thirst, the desire, the longing. I've stopped considering prayer as a matter of discipline that I must make myself do or, alternatively, an undeserved vacation from duty. I'm just thirsty for some silence, and I've learned that praying on my feet is not enough.

Mother's Day at Zarephath

The idea for the party came from Lucy, the woman who was working with our domestic-violence program. A couple of years earlier, she happened to be walking by the church during a youth-choir practice. She liked the music and stood in the back of the church listening. Burnice, the mother of one of the children in the choir, spotted Lucy and invited her to come inside and sit down, but she declined. Burnice stayed outside and talked with her. She told her about different church activities and invited her to our newly formed women's group.

Lucy didn't trust churches and didn't like God. A priest had told her to stay with her husband through thick and thin. It was pretty thin. When she was eight months pregnant, her husband threw her down a flight of stairs because he was angry that she wouldn't give back the money he gave her for food. He wanted a fix. According to the church, this was her cross to bear. So was her mother's abandonment of her as a child and leaving her to grow up in a series of foster families and group homes where she was sexually molested and beaten. After her baby was born, Lucy left her husband, and she left the church that refused to baptize a fatherless child.

But this was different. Here was Burnice, a church leader, herself a survivor of abuse, who'd walked in Lucy's shoes and wasn't judging her. Lucy began to attend the women's group and women's Bible studies. She volunteered to help in the food pantry once a week. It was two years before she attended her first Sunday morning worship and eventually joined the church. She received training and worked in the AIDS-outreach and domestic-violence programs (both examples of programs begun in response to needs identified by the new people coming into the church). We began with the after-school and added a pantry, a food cooperative called SHARE, Narcotics Anonymous meetings, and ESL classes. In time we joined with other churches to get funding for some of these and other programs. Our goal was to identify and train local leadership, people like Lucy, to run them. Lucy is a good listener. She inspires the trust of other women and helps them locate the inner courage and outer resources they need. Sometimes, when the outer resources aren't available, she invites battered women to sleep on her couch.

She came up with the idea of a Mother's Day party because she knew that day was a hard time for many women, those abandoned like herself or mothers who'd lost their children to the system because of their own drug addiction, immigrant mothers whose children lived with relatives in other countries until they could make enough money to send for them, women being abused along with their children. A number of us were giving out the invitations. Irma was on my list.

Three years earlier, she had left four young daughters in Ecuador, to come here, hoping to prepare the way for a better life in this country. It was not going well. She tried to learn to be a manicurist like her sister. Her training began by scraping dead skin off unwashed feet that she had to hold up to her face to see properly. She was compelled to do this from eight in the morning until eight at night—without pay! Like so many before her, Irma held on to the promise of a real job once the training period was over. Irma would arrive home by nine or later with aching arms and a headache from eyestrain. Usually she was unable to stomach any dinner.

For the sake of her daughters Irma persisted until she was told that the business wouldn't be hiring anyone in the foreseeable future. She left, and they doubtlessly found someone else to labor in delusion. She showed me pictures. Her daughters stared out of the worn photos, barefoot, in their best lacy dresses. Irma spent her days dreaming of the girls, fingering the photos like rosary beads and caring for her sister's son and her brother-in-law's epileptic daughter. She was thinking about moving back to Ecuador, uncertain if the husband who had sent her here would still be waiting. She said she'd like to come to the party.

Lucy asked to speak to me in private. She had been planning to make a big pot of *arroz con pollo* (rice and chicken) for the party, but now she was worried that she could not. The women working at the church in AIDS prevention under a city grant couldn't be paid for at least twenty days because the city had not passed its budget and the agency through which our funding was channeled was in big debt. Twenty days is an eternity when you live from check to check and are already owed back pay. I was angry but could do nothing. Lucy didn't know how she and her kids would eat, never mind cook for others. Burnice alone was owed $2,400, a fortune. What lessons did this teach people working part-time, trying to develop a resume and eventually get off of welfare altogether? Welfare checks come on time, paychecks don't.

The blow was more than economic. Burnice and Lucy had been proud of the change and growth that allowed them to serve others at the pantry rather than having to get food there for themselves. Now they would need the food again. Lucy felt shame at withdrawing her offer of party fare. Burnice couldn't buy a wedding gift for a friend's upcoming wedding. She couldn't buy the new dress she'd been eyeing for the big event. These simple pay-check perks were out. She apologized that she couldn't put much of an offering in the plate. Seeing my distress over the entire situation, she tried to comfort me.

The economic distress of our neighborhood pervades the church as well. Manny, our treasurer, is often the bearer of grim tidings from the bank account. When I was called to Transfiguration, it was not only due to the willingness of our church members to invest in an uncertain future. It was also because our local bishop and national church offices contributed to the ministry. But before long, those monies and our church offerings could not keep up with growing needs. Fund-raising is time-consuming. I often feel that if I spend more time raising money, I can't really serve as a pastor. But if I don't raise money, how can we remain here as a church? How much longer is it possible to go on like the widow of Zarephath? I don't know, but I cling to her example.

As we struggle, I have been increasingly drawn to the biblical story of this nameless widow. She appears in what commentators refer to as the Elijah cycle, a series of stories vaunting the prophet's miraculous powers. I think the cycle holds a different truth, a different power. In one installment of the series, God tells Elijah that a time of drought is at hand, a consequence of the nation's perverse behavior under King Ahab. First, Elijah lives by the Cherith brook, where he survives by eating bread and meat delivered by ravens and drinking the water, but after a while the brook dries up. At that point, God sends Elijah to a small village, Zarephath. He's told that a widow there will feed him. Elijah finds the widow gathering firewood.

By all rights, this widow should be in worse shape than Elijah. She is one of those most affected by the drought. In a time of national need, her needs would be considered last, especially under the arrogant regime of King Ahab, who lost no sleep because a large part of his population was threatened with starvation. Instead, he took his chief servant on a frantic hunt throughout the countryside for grass and water to keep his horses alive. Ahab was no animal lover: his horses represented military power. Concerned only to secure his own position, the king had no thought for the likes of the widow and her child. In fact when Elijah shows up and requests a drink, she was gathering sticks to cook a last supper for herself and her son. The woman wants to be hospitable, but when he asks her for bread to go with the water, it's too much. She tells him that she's gathering wood to bake the handful of meal and bit of oil that's left for herself and her son, who will eat it and then await death. The Cherith brook that streamed through this woman's heart has run dry. Then she hears another word:

> Do not be afraid, go and do as you have said, but first make me a little cake ... for thus says the Lord, the God of Israel, the jar of meal will not be emptied and the jug of oil will not fail until the day that the Lord sends rain upon the earth. She went and did as Elijah said, so that she as well as he and her household ate for many days. The jar of meal was not emptied, neither did the jug of oil fail. (1 Kings 17:13–16)

Here is a woman about to die with her child, a mother unable to feed her little boy; nevertheless, she loves her neighbor as herself. Sure, Elijah predicts the miracle, but she is the one who sets the miracle in motion by her trust and risky generosity. So why is this story part of the "Elijah cycle"—as though the widow is just there as a backdrop to show off the powers of Elijah? Perhaps it is because he is the same male prophet who later triumphs in the spectacular showdown with his opponents, the prophets of Baal. In that story, when Baal failed to ignite his prophets' sacrifice, and before Elijah called down fire on a mound of lumber, he had his servants soak the wood with jars of water. The wood was good and drenched before God made it catch fire.

In contrast to the prophet's mega-miracle, all the poor widow does is set fire to a few sticks in order to cook a little cake; however, I can't help but think that her wood was good and soaked too. This widow is the mother of a little boy who came into the world gleaming with her blood, a little boy she nursed, rocked, bathed, soothed, fussed over and taught to walk. I cannot imagine that this mother was preparing her child's last supper with dry eyes. Surely the sticks she gathered were wet, not from jars filled by servants, but with rivers of her own tears. Surely, that wood was immersed in the waters of her grief when hope caught fire and she heated the bread and shared supper with Elijah.

This story never appears in our church's assigned cycle of Sunday readings. Instead, we get the next installment in which Elijah raises another widow's son from the dead. In that story, the woman is portrayed as dependent on Elijah's miraculous power, a guilt-ridden sinner who sees her son's illness as God's punishment. By omission, why does the lectionary seem more comfortable with the second story?

I am ordained in a predominantly white, middle-class church, and I believe we need to be careful that the poor do not become a backdrop for our miraculous charity, that quotas and programs and conferences on women, children, and poverty do not become a forum to show off our goodness and compassion on the fringe of the problem while the church goes about its other business as usual, dry-eyed and silent at the cruel heat of poverty drying up the whole Cherith brook. Pastors, priests, and official prophets (mostly white) are often cast in the role of a miracle-working Elijah for the poor widows and children (mostly not white). It's not only paternalistic and racist, it's impossible. Most of us can't keep up the mega-miracles for long.

There is no point in romanticizing poverty. It stinks and it kills. There is, however, a point in recognizing the power of those who, despite it, fight for life and bear witness to a death-defying hope. We could say that Elijah, the male prophet, does this and therefore that he deserves the spotlight he gets in the lectionary text. After all, he raises someone from the dead. Yes, but the widow raises a child—without a husband, without a safety net, without welfare or workfare. She does it in a time of idolatrous national arrogance, famine, and drought. Raising the dead required a single act of trust and prayer from Elijah. Raising a child requires countless acts of trust and constant prayer, especially for a single mother faced with famine.

The official commentators call it the "Elijah cycle," but looking closer, I see it was the open hand of that widow in Zarephath that kept the cycle spinning. It's still spinning. I see it every day. The hands of those who continue to open out to others in spite of so many closed doors, in spite of drought and famine—these are the hands that nurture life and witness grace.

One of the best examples is Burnice. When I met her, she was a single mother like the widow, facing life beside a dried-up brook. She dropped out of school as a teenager when her first baby came along. A series of men battered her heart and broke her bones, much as her alcoholic father had done. She sought relief in beer and crack and ended up selling her body to get it. The brook was bone dry. She moved to the Bronx to escape an abusive husband in Brooklyn, but still couldn't get away from drugs. Her bones had healed, but not her heart.

One day, after dropping her children off at school, Burnice came by my office with a friend. Ben, a church member who volunteered at their children's school, told them that we gave out Christmas gifts. They wanted to make sure that their families were on our list. I wrote down the names and ages of their children and invited the women to come to church on Christmas morning. I told them we'd begin with a breakfast, have church, and then give out the presents. They thanked me and left.

Burnice's plan was to pick up presents for her children, sell them and buy enough drugs for an overdose. She told me later that this was her solution to being sick and tired of being sick and tired. On Christmas morning, she came to get the gifts and met our intern at the time, Janell. I was busy with the happy bedlam of handing out hundreds of presents, but Janell saw something in Burnice's face that made her stop and invite conversation, listening, and prayer. When I noticed them, they were sitting in a wordless, tearful embrace. Burnice later said that Janell's tears had opened her heart.

Burnice came back for our women's Bible study. She asked if she could detox by sleeping in the church, and we agreed. She slept on the rug by the altar and made it through that first week clean. By Easter, she was baptized. Hope had caught fire in her heart. Burnice began to open her hands to other women, reaching out to addicts as they hit bottom. Through the church, she signed up for training and a part-time job as an HIV/AIDS outreach worker. She led workshops and talked with people on the streets. She listened, counseled, and helped others get into detox and rehab programs. I worked with her so that she could lead the Bible studies she once sat in silently.

While Burnice helped others, her own struggles persisted. The first man after the husband she left was much older and tried to take control of her sobriety. He was determined to make sure she stayed sober no matter what. He would show up at church demanding to know where she was and what she was doing, explaining that "you can't trust an addict." One day, he broke her ribs. She called the church, and I called the police. By the time I reached her apartment, he'd disappeared for good.

The next one was young and charming, gentler on her body, but not on her heart. There were other women in his life, and he made sure Burnice knew it, telling her their names, showing her their pictures and assuring her that she was his main squeeze. They were just side dishes. Hoping to hold him closer, she became pregnant. Twice.

After the second baby was born, the apartment they shared became infested with rats. The baby, Darrin, had just come home from the hospital. The building was city-owned, and the rent office wanted proof of the rats. Burnice asked if I could come over with the church's Polaroid camera. I worried that the rats might be camera shy. They practically posed. My desk still holds a file of Polaroid shots I took of those brazen rats. We used the pictures as evidence to try and persuade city officials to grant Burnice a transfer to another building. All they would do was send an exterminator. It was not enough. The conditions outside the building were too inviting for future rodents. So Burnice took Darrin and her two other children and moved to a shelter, preferring homelessness to the danger posed by the rats.

Eventually, after months of searching, prayer, and stress in the shelter, she moved into a new apartment on the block where I too live. We joked that the only good thing about the rats is that they helped get rid of the Rat. He had never contributed toward the rent and didn't want to start paying to stay with the rodents, so he moved out and in with another woman. I hoped that Burnice would stay clear of men for a while, but she wasn't at that point.

Burnice met her second husband through her outreach job. He was doing similar work, and his life seemed to be moving in the same positive direction. Before long, her new husband began picking up the crack she thought they'd left behind. He blamed her for his drug use, in fact for everything. After a year, she found that he'd infected her with the HIV virus.

There are ups and there are downs, but Burnice has not closed her hands. She hasn't let go of her children. Nor has she let go of her dreams. She began working on a GED in preparation for a full-time job. In my eyes, this was a mega-miracle. She was elected and served as the president of our congregation. "From crackhead to council president," she likes to say, "Transfiguration has made a transformation in me." Yes, but the reverse is also true. Burnice and the many others who have come into the church from the surrounding community have transformed Transfiguration into the place it is today.

On Sundays Burnice stands before the altar holding out bread to share with all who come to receive it from her hands. As Elijah received the bread of life from a widow who defied the certainty of death, so people come to take the bread of life from Burnice, a woman who also defies doomsday statistics, a woman who defied King Ahab by her travels to Albany and Washington to address legislators on welfare reform, who offers counsel and comfort, leadership, and challenge even when her heart is near collapse, a woman who holds on and keeps the cycle spinning: *The jar of meal was not emptied, neither did the jug of oil fail.*

I had one more woman to visit before Mother's Day—Carmen, who requested that I stop by her home. I stepped out through the church doors and found myself walking toward a big commotion that had erupted across the street because one boy ripped off another's gold chain. Suddenly, an angry crowd appeared where a moment before there was only reggae on the radio and easy conversation between a few neighbors. More came running—the ripple effect of rage. Shouts, curses and threats drowned out the dance music. Someone ran upstairs to get a gun. The police arrived before the gun, but when they'd gone, nothing had changed. It was not about losing a few inches of gold, but about a lifetime of loss, link by link, suddenly remembered. The chain was returned. The loss remained.

I got to know Carmen when she was active in a community of squatters who were rehabilitating a building left vacant by the city for twenty years. It was used only by drug dealers and prostitutes. Carmen and her husband, Luis, came to New York from Santo Domingo and joined with other Caribbean and Central American immigrants to create their own housing. They spent their spare time and money fixing up the building where they began to live even before the water and electricity were hooked up. When the renovation was nearing completion, the city decided to take the building and have a developer re-renovate it under a $2 million contract. The building would then be used to house the homeless, thus rendering homeless the people who were fixing the building at no cost to the city.

One morning near Christmas, I was having coffee with Carmen, who was six months pregnant, when the police arrived. They advanced with a mighty show of force—guns drawn and dogs straining at their leashes. Looking out the window, I could hardly believe the sight of a large, antiterrorist vehicle and several hundred police charging this humble building on Crotona Park where fewer than twenty persons were present, all women and small children. The rest were in school or at work. The media had also been called in. Evidently, there was a point to be made: people should not take their housing needs into their own hands. I thought of the bulldozers that showed up to knock down the squatters' community in Argentina. Gregorio and I had joined the thousands who stood in their path. There, the squatters prevailed and gained legal rights to the property, but not in New York City.

Gesturing with the butt of his gun, a cop indicated my exit route and escorted me down the stairs, while Carmen was roughly dragged from the apartment in which she and her husband had invested all their savings, all their weekends and so much pride. These investments were of no account. Emptied of people, the building was further defiled. Carefully installed windows were smashed, doors were knocked down, phone lines were cut and staircases, recently reinforced with so much hope, were wrecked so that no one might ever climb up again.

Most of the families were never able to recover their belongings. Some furniture was thrown out of the windows, chairs and tables splintering as they hit the sidewalk. I followed as Carmen was taken by van to an overcrowded shelter where her husband would not be allowed to stay with her. The next day her water broke, and she went into premature labor. When I first visited the hospital where her son was born weighing less than two pounds, I could not even pray for his life. I stood and watched his valiant struggle to breathe, his vital organs unprepared for life outside the womb. Carmen held my hand as we baptized him with a few drops of sterile water mixed with tears. I didn't believe he would live, but he did.

Stevenson, named by his father for a Mexican boxer, fought all through that Christmas season inside his prickly manger of needles and tubes and wires, and he emerged a victor. This brave child's survival transformed Luis from a gambling philanderer into a doting father and faithful husband. Stevenson gave impetus to his parents' own struggle in the face of realities for which they were not prepared.

When Stevenson reached his second birthday, Luis was shot during a robbery while driving his taxi. Witnesses testify that he was still alive when brought into the Lincoln Hospital emergency room, a place that was often the butt of macabre jokes: "How is the Lincoln ER like a Roach Motel?" "You check in, but you don't check out." Luis was tagged as dead and left unattended in a hallway to bleed to death.

Stevenson would go to the window every afternoon around four o'clock looking for his father to come home. That was the hour when Luis normally arrived to care for his son so that Carmen could go to her job at a candy factory. After his death, Carmen continued at the factory and added a second job in our AIDS-prevention outreach program during the day.

On one occasion, I visited her because she was worried over her upcoming hysterectomy. She'd had unusually heavy bleeding and for months had pains in her uterus. The doctor at the clinic told her that it was "*el cambio de vida,*" the change of life. He didn't speak Spanish, but had learned this special phrase, pronounced slowly and loudly as though Carmen were deaf: "EL CAM-BI-O DE VI-DA." "Just relax!" he told Carmen. Relaxation was not a big part of Carmen's life since her husband's murder. After working for six hours, four days a week in outreach, her six-day-a-week factory job began at four o'clock in the afternoon and ended at midnight. Then off to the babysitter's to pick up her sleep-heavy son.

Like Carmen, most of the women at the factory were recent immigrants working for below the minimum wage. They traded Caribbean fields for this factory floor, each woman rooted in position in a row like a plant. Their harvest piles up in the shadows, under a ceiling that blocks the sky, the sun and the rain. Instead of corn or beans, this harvest is candy, Pampers, perfumes and soaps sheathed in plastic, packed in boxes. In time, the women themselves are ploughed under like dry stalks to make room for a new crop. That way the boss doesn't have to pay benefits. Meanwhile, in their rows, the women work and talk. To them, Carmen described the symptoms that worried her. "It sounds like a fibroid tumor to me," said one coworker never educated beyond the fourth grade. "You should have a sonogram."

Carmen returned to the clinic. "Maybe I have a tumor," she suggested to the doctor. He poked and prodded and put her off. "Nothing there ... just relax!" The women packed and listened and told her she definitely needed a sonogram. Carmen returned to the clinic. Each trip meant lost time, lost wages. "I know I have a tumor," she said. "I can feel it!" This was a lie, but Carmen was determined to get the sonogram. Once again, the doctor poked and prodded, repeating that he felt nothing. "It moves around," she said. At last, he gave in and ordered the sonogram. "Well," said the doctor, "you have a large fibroid tumor." Her experience did not leave her feeling particularly confident about the upcoming operation. We drank strong coffee and prayed strong prayers.

Most of the women we visited came to the Mother's Day party. It was not what one might expect for Mother's Day. Rosa, who cooked the pernil and coconut bread, got up and spoke of her mother in Guatemala who tried to abort her twice and continued to reject and hurt her throughout childhood. She asked for prayers that one day they might reconcile. Caridad, a Honduran immigrant, was there. Her mother had stood by as her stepfather raped her as a child and later forced her to live with a much older man in exchange for money. He was the first of many. She lifted her shirt to show us some scars. This is common. People often show off their scars like badges—"Look what I have survived! I'll still here!" Of course, Lucy was there, still bearing the wound of maternal abandonment, and there were Burnice, Carmen and Sharon, too, present through her drawings, and not a single happy mother-daughter story among them.

And yet, these women knew how to party! After the stories came music and laughter, eating and drinking, hugging and, at the end, praying. Rosa wore a suit covered with a fiesta of roses and sunflowers. Isaiah might have had her in mind as she led her sisters in the *punta*, a sexy dance common in Honduras and Guatemala, followed by others leading *salsa* and *merengue:*

> The wilderness and the dry land shall be glad,
> the desert shall rejoice and blossom . . .
> the glory of Lebanon shall be given to it,
> the majesty of Carmel and Sharon. (Isaiah 35:1–2)

These women blossomed in the desert and bloomed in the furnace with beauty to take one's breath away—the glory of Lebanon, the majesty of Carmen and Sharon, Honduras, Guatemala, La Republica Dominicana, Puerto Rico, Ecuador, the Bronx. "The jade burned on the mountain retains its natural color. The lotus blooming in the furnace does not lose its freshness." (eleventh-century Vietnamese Zen monk)

Back home, Ana wanted me to sing her to sleep. She picked a hymn with more verses than any lullaby we know, "For All the Saints." Its appeal was neither melodic nor thematic. What mattered is that the hymn has eight verses. From the start, Ana knew how to manage me. If pleas for one more story didn't work, she begged for "just one more prayer." If she knew that extra lullabies were not likely, she'd pick a lengthy hymn. When I got to the last verse's "unwearied praises," gunshots began. Thankfully, Ana had fallen asleep.

After getting up at five to go over my Mother's Day sermon, then celebrating two masses, attending two receptions and a raffle, driving with Gregorio, Ana, and Hans to New Jersey to have dinner with my mother and then driving home, getting stuck for two hours in a post-celebration traffic jam, I was tired when we finally got back at 11 P.M. Gregorio had already undressed when he remembered that we were out of toothpaste. Since we'd been out of it for two days, I decided I'd better go find an open bodega.

The first bodega was already closing for the night, but the second—I pushed open the door and stepped into a party. Though forced to work on Mother's Day, the family had turned duty into delight, drudgery into fiesta. *Merengue* pulsed through rows of macaroni, rice, and kitty litter. The rhythms of a Caribbean Paradise Lost swept the floors and air clean of debris. Giddy children laughed and swung, dancing through the narrow aisles while their elders stood swaying or sat on overturned crates drinking rum from paper cups. People kept coming in, drawn to this defiant bodega that insisted on transcending its lowly station in life. By the time I'd paid for the toothpaste, I felt like dancing back up the street, past the trio of drug dealers who wished me a happy Mother's Day.

It's like this: you go for toothpaste and find yourself swept into the arms of a cosmic dance. You step outside the doors and there it is—real ecstasy, and not in a pill.

Rizpah's Table

Rizpah, a grieving mother, is one of many biblical sisters all too rarely invited into our congregations. It is a shame because these ancient women often spark contemporary recognition and connection, especially with those who feel like outsiders. Once, when we studied Rahab, often perceived as a prostitute, a woman new to the Bible study group turned out to be a prostitute herself. She was so excited to see Rahab in Matthew's list of Jesus' forebears. "Maybe there's hope for me," she ventured. Of course! Another woman commented, "I never knew the Bible was about us!" It's not only prostitutes who feel that way. A woman who attended proper middle-class churches all her life, listening to countless sermons and participating in women's groups and Bible studies month after month and year after year, visited Transfiguration one Sunday. I preached on Tabitha, a widow who sewed clothing for other widows, offering the destitute women both clothing and the hope that they were not powerless or alone. After the service, the visitor told me that it was the first time in her life she'd heard anything from the Bible specifically about women. She was eighty-four years old.

Since many in our women's group had recently lost loved ones, we'd chosen the theme of biblical women facing death. Before we could even introduce Rizpah, Lucy had to get up and leave because the part about death was simply too much for her to sit through. She'd been dealing with one violent death after another. A friend had just been found stabbed twenty-three times, but the worst was the death of her baby goddaughter, who drowned in the bathtub. Lucy's *co-madre** Josie, the baby's mother, was facing murder charges and Lucy accompanied her day after day to court for the trial. The day of our study, autopsy photos were presented as part of the evidence. Making it even more difficult was that fact that Lucy was not convinced of Josie's innocence.

*The term *co-madre* expresses the relationship between a child's parents and godparents. The mother of the child and the godmother would be each other's *co-madre*. There is no comparable word in English.

Lucy would return from a day of deeply conflicted feelings at the court-house to face an evening of fighting at home between her older teenage son and grown daughters. She felt helpless to bring harmony to either sphere. Her blood pressure and diabetes were getting worse. Other health problems led her to fear a diagnosis of uterine cancer. It was unclear whether tension was spreading through her body like a cancer or whether cancer was growing like a heavy mass of pain in her womb.

When I visited, I saw that someone had gone into the elevators in five of the John Adams high-rise project buildings and sprayed "Fuck you and fuck your family" in every one. In Deuteronomy (11:20), the people are instructed to write the commandment of love on the doorposts and gates of every dwelling place. Living a loving life is hard enough even when such good counsel marks the portals of our comings and goings. In these buildings, one goes and comes surrounded by the violent assaults and stench of Babylon, a biblical city of notorious corruption. The pool of urine in the elevator left no dry space to stand, so I walked up to her ninth-floor apartment and thought of her homecomings, having to decide whether to stand in the urine or walk, with swollen legs, up the stairs. Lucy spoke to me about feeling helpless. She said that when she wakes up in the morning and thinks about getting up, she can barely open her eyes. It is as though the muscles in her eyelids won't work, won't lift the weight of darkness off to open up and face another day. She also said that she felt ashamed of being so weak.

Weak? I think of Job when he writes of deep darkness pressing down on his eyelids already swollen shut with tears (Job 16:16). It is the same deep darkness the prophet Jeremiah speaks of as *a land of drought and deep darkness, a wilderness of deserts and pits* (Jeremiah 2:6). It is *the valley of the shadow of death* in Psalm 23. Psalm 107 mentions it too as a miserable, imprisoning force clamped down like bands of iron. (verses 10,14). With all this pressure, I told Lucy that the very act of opening her eyes is, in itself, a mighty feat. I think of the many women rising early to get to some gym and work out. This woman is bench-pressing enormous weights before she even gets up—with her eyelids.

The day that Lucy left our Bible study, we had turned to the story of Rizpah found in 2 Samuel, chapter 21. Rizpah had two sons, both hanged in a revenge killing. She spread sackcloth on a rock and stood watch over the bodies of her murdered sons for five months, fighting off wild animals and the indifference to her grief of those in power. Unfortunately, this was not a conversation that required any leap of imagination for those who remained at the table. We also considered the daughter of Jephthah in Judges 11. Hers is a disturbing story in which Jephthah makes a vow that if he wins a battle, on his return he will make a burnt offering of the first person who crosses his path. After his victory, by chance out comes his only child "with timbrels and with dancing." A vow is a vow. The daughter and her friends head for the mountains for two months of mourning, after which she returns for the sacrifice—which is carried out.

The women admired and approved of the girlfriends who spent two months wandering the mountains in solidarity with their sister, to talk and pray and grieve their upcoming loss. We spoke of wandering and walking, how physical motion can help to relieve deep stress and how often we do the opposite, lying in bed or glued to the TV, feeling paralyzed. *Solvitur ambulando.* "It is solved by walking," said the early monks. The women were also unanimous in saying that they would never, ever come back from the mountains as victims willing to meet death at Jephthah's hands, but in truth most deaths are out of our hands.

Burnice pointed out that at her father's funeral the week before, the women stuck together—talking, cooking and hugging, while the men went out and got drunk. The others nodded and hummed with recognition. I told them about the mother who stopped traffic to wash her son's blood off the street. The Bible study itself is a time to stop the traffic rushing through our days and honor what is sacred to our hearts. It may not be two months, but it is two hours that the girlfriends take off, two hours that say "Our grief is not just something to get over. Our grief is holy ground."

I needed this time as much as anyone in the group. Time for my own feelings had seemed like a luxury for a busy pastor attending to others, but I have also needed to pause and take the basin overflowing with tears and pour it over everything before going on. Like Rizpah, if we don't do this, who will? After the World Trade Center collapsed in dust, taking so many with it, a cloud of death descended over our city. The very air wrapped us all in sackcloth. Many of those who worked close to the scene have suffered serious respiratory trouble, but virtually everyone in the city was affected. Who could breathe freely while thinking about all those who disappeared into thin air, while, in the words of the late Reverend Will Herzfeld, we literally "inhaled our fellow citizens"? On the other hand, back in the late seventies and eighties the air in the South Bronx was smoking with death, and the ground was stained with bloodshed, but it felt like more people were shaking their heads than wiping their eyes. It helped to believe that the ground was consecrated by God's own grieving. It became the desert of my contemplation.

In the eighties and early nineties, it seemed that whenever I sat down to pray, I was interrupted by gunshots. It has been said that prayer is easy when bullets are flying, but I never found it so. It's one thing to be gathered into silence on a retreat, but what was I supposed to do back home? I had a terribly distracted time at prayer and not for any of the usual reasons. I've always found the counsel of spiritual elders—to incorporate mental distractions into one's prayer rather than to fight against them—to be sensible advice. At times it even works. But I found it increasingly difficult to incorporate the POP POP POP POP POP POP POP POP POP of bullets and automatic weapons. Scarcely a night went unviolated—bullets stealing lives, stealing childhoods and stealing, too, the calm and the bright of the night.

I realize that my meager prayer life is of negligible weight when placed in the balance along with all that is lost through such violence. I would forgo all prayer if that would bring back Tomas, Alex, Pedro, J.J., Derrick, Ruben, Ricky, Paul, Carlos, Pipo, Tommy, Jessica, Rose, or any one of those whose names are written in our hearts and spray-painted on our neighborhood's walls in so many colorful, graffiti memorials. On the other hand, without prayer we cannot stand against these powers that are greater than metal and flesh and blood. The work of teaching and preaching, celebrating and organizing and just loving one another into something better would collapse like the rotten building across the street from the parsonage, taking with it anyone foolish enough to be playing around inside.

Is contemplative prayer even possible here? I want to believe that it is possible everywhere or nowhere. But how does one reach the calm beyond the night rocked by squadrons of violence, sirens, screams and shouts? The agitation was borne not just of an overstimulated thought process and an undisciplined spirit. It was physical, shocking the rhythm of pulse and breath. Each bullet shot adrenalin into the pit of my stomach and burned its way up into my ears. Surely this was a primitive flight reaction, but there was no flight possible.

I am suspicious of a silence without bullets as long as bullets fly. I am skeptical of contemplation that requires rarefied, privileged circumstances. It doesn't feel real or right to me. I refuse to accept a spirituality that functions as a silencer, dulling or blocking the sound of these shots in the dark. Such a device seems more accomplice than alternative. And yet—the bullets rend silence as surely as flesh, leaving a wound that perhaps only the balm of paradise can close.

Why does silence matter? I went on a retreat, and the moment that the leader gave us permission to be silent, I walked to the woods and dissolved in tears of gratitude for the quiet, which has so often been unattainable. If it is not gunshots, it is boom boxes and the Mr. Softee ice-cream truck. I overestimated myself. I can't survive without some silence. I need it like I need air to clear out my mind and restore my heart. Perhaps silence is simply the space to hear the echo of a deeper voice or a place apart to grieve or a way to deny bullets the last word—or all of these. Breathing Space.

I have seen layers of skin and flesh blown away to reveal the pale, raw edge of cracked bone and the body's inner sheen—sights never meant to be exposed. In those moments at an emergency room or in the street, I have been able to pray: in fact, to do little else. But the *pop-pop-pop-pop-pop* in the night left the layers of my prayer life blown away to expose what? Some pale, raw edge of the spirit? A slow, hemorrhaging cry that saturates the night? It seemed so distant from the evening prayer I enjoyed in seminary that rises as incense through starry, bullet-free space, but amid the gunshots, it was all I could manage. Perhaps the other was never more than the fantasy of breviaries.

Being a mother, thinking of the mothers, made it worse. And being a mother made it better. Even after the hardest nights, there would come a lull near morning when everything slept, or at least collapsed in quiet exhaustion, all violence temporarily spent. When Hans was a toddler, he would climb into bed with us at dawn and rest his hand on my neck, softly breathing on my face, into my ear, warming the early notes of sparrows and starlings that stirred in the trees and on the telephone wires, as we woke to live another day.

* * *

On the way to school one morning, Ana wanted to listen to Hot 97, a local hip-hop station. I agreed, unless the lyrics were about killing people, in which case I would turn it off. When we got to school twenty minutes later, Ana asked, "Mommy, how come you like murder in mystery books but not murder in music?"

How could I explain this to my daughter? I didn't want to. I didn't want to tell her that I don't want to hear music that brings to mind the very scenes I want to forget, but the images float unbidden to the surface, like the faces of the babies who were victims of a different kind of murder. They died choking on formula left propped in their mouths by overworked nurses on an under-staffed ward of Lincoln Hospital. For a year, our church sent volunteers who went to hold, feed, and play with the growing number of boarder babies await-ing foster care placement. I did it myself, but we couldn't be there around the clock.

Since then, South Bronx Churches, the ecumenical community-organiz-ing group we helped to found, has successfully advocated for an investigation into corruption at the hospital. It brought some positive change. We marched to the hospital and rallied outside: "Lincoln needs major surgery!" We made calls and wrote letters. We acted and got action. The State Department of Health investigated, uncovered wrongful deaths and made administrative changes. But the babies still visit my dreams. The babies still choke and drown in the night.

The images are too many to remember; too vivid to forget. I remember Miguel's skull bashed in by a baseball bat. He was the brother of a church member. They called me to the hospital where he lay surrounded by family and useless machines. His sister rested her hand on the side of his head that was left, and I lay mine on top of hers. Tears splashed down as we prayed, and hospital staff stood around waiting impatiently to wheel the body away.

I can't forget the sound of the pounding feet of a man running desperately from armed pursuers before jumping up on the side of an oil delivery truck. It was the only escape that presented itself. Almost immediately, he lost his grip and was sucked under the huge wheels that crushed his skull and brains on the street right in front of the church and the school that faces us. A large group of people, mostly homeless, were standing in line to eat at the soup kitchen next door. They gathered around his body before the police arrived, beckoning me to join their circle. Together we prayed, a spontaneous congregation joined around a grim icon of human frailty. Fifteen minutes later, I was hosting a meeting with some clergy at the church. The purpose of the meeting was to plan a special joint liturgy, but I could only wonder how the street would be cleaned before the children walked across it on their way home from school. I had to excuse myself.

I remember the Bronx Valentine's Day massacre, February 14, 1993. One of the little girls in our after-school program went home to find her twelve-year-old brother had been shot dead. Christian had gone into his building and met two men in the elevator who asked him to point out the apartment where someone they knew lived. He did the favor, got pushed inside and lined up on the floor with five others. One by one, they were shot in the head. The *Daily News* titled their front-page coverage of the carnage "Prisoners of Prospect Ave." Since our church is also on Prospect Avenue, a few blocks away, I wrote a letter to the editor to say that we are most definitely not the prisoners of Prospect Avenue. We are the promise of Prospect Avenue. But Valentine's Day will never be the same for me. Perhaps it never was. Valentine himself was beheaded by the Roman emperor Claudius, a Valentine's Day image I believe Hallmark has never promoted.

I remember the many moments that should have been acts of simple tenderness—a mother gently fixing the collar of her son's shirt to make it more comfortable—except that the son was lying in his coffin, beaten to death by six other youths at a local swimming pool, each wielding a bat. Richard was too slow when the gang approached, and he fell while trying to run away. "I'm his mother," she sobbed. "I'm his mother," and she grabbed my arm for support with one hand while the other sought solace with the collar and smoothed hair that no one would comb again. Death after death, after death, after death. There are just not enough tears.

I told Ana the truth: It's too real for me. I don't want to hear lyrics that promote violence, which still doesn't explain why I like the mystery novels. But the books seem like so much fantasy. The rappers are often for real. Our strength around the table is real, too, as we are joined by our elder sisters, women like Rizpah and Jephthah's daughter, who've walked this road before us.

Rizpah means "glowing coal." A Hasidic tale tells of the disciple who asked his rabbi the meaning of community one evening when they were all sitting around a fireplace. The rabbi sat in silence while the fire died down to a pile of glowing coals. Then he got up and took one coal out from the pile and set it apart on the stone hearth. Its fire and warmth soon died out. With Rizpah and Rahab, Jephthah's daughter and Zarephath's widow, our community spans millenniums. The table where we spread our sackcloth, meet, study, laugh, cry, pray, talk and drink coffee is our hearth. There we bear the unbearable together.

Longwood Avenue

The Mother's Day bodega is on one corner of Longwood Avenue, one of five such stores in a stretch of just three blocks near the church and parsonage. These bodegas all dispense the same mix of household necessities and attract enough local customers to stay in business. So do the liquor store, the hair salon, the laundromat, the long-distance phone-call store and the Chinese takeout, which doubles as a hangout for drug dealers when life on the corner gets too cold (in the winter) or too hot (when police are around). The rest of the businesses come and go: video stores, "99 cent" stores, jewelry stores, clinics. None of them lasts.

Mi Jesus Fruits and Vegetables is a welcome recent addition. For years, there were virtually no fresh fruits and vegetables available other than bananas, plantains, lemons, garlic and an occasional avocado. I yearned for easy access to carrots, broccoli, green peppers, cucumbers and lettuce. Also low-fat milk and yogurt. While the rest of the city cut back on fat, only whole milk was sold here. Now one of the five bodegas carries low-fat milk on occasion (but never yogurt), and Mi Jesus Fruits and Vegetables takes care of the rest, with a bonus. Nestled somewhere in between the lettuces and eggplants is a radio with the volume turned up high to broadcast Pentecostal-style salvation day and night. When the preacher really gets going with a powerful Spanish vibrato, even the oranges tremble in their crates. But not Chango the Indian presiding over the Botanica next door, a longstanding business on Longwood that is a spiritual supply center for the Santaría faith, a widespread syncretistic religion with Afro-Carribean roots. The Botanica sells plaster saints, wooden statues, beads, powders, potions, herbs, urns and other items that remain a mystery to me. They also sell bootleg videos and designer jean knock-offs.

If Pentecostals or the Botanica are not your thing, a vendor spreads holy paintings on the sidewalk. Jesus and his disciples sit around at the Last Supper as though it were a carnival with giddy red lights darting all over them. Then there's the Pieta: showers of sparkling lights fall from Mary's eyes in lieu of tears as she cradles her dead son, dotted with blinking blood. Batteries not included.

The Longwood mini-shopping district is typical for the area in that there are no banks or bank machines, but you can visit Pay-O-Matic Check Cashing and Financial Services for a fee. There are no mailboxes. Red, white, and blue flags hang year-round from the windows and wires, rippling with Puerto Rican or Dominican pride. Used sneakers swing from streetlights and telephone wires. Despite the housing construction and renovation of recent years, there remain some boarded-up, abandoned buildings that become a dumping area for uncollected garbage and a nesting place for rats, whose flattened carcasses often evade the street sweepers.

Around the corner from Longwood on Southern Boulevard is a "Restaurant Sports Bar" with a green awning that proclaims it as "the finest restaurant in New York." The place has no windows, and I have never seen anyone waiting to get inside. Zagat hasn't discovered it yet, but they should discover Longwood's El Nuevo Gran Cafe. Inside there is a large mural that surrounds diners with scenes of the Puerto Rican countryside, while a jukebox plays the latest Latin hits. Like virtually every other Spanish restaurant in the area, El Nuevo Gran Cafe used to be owned and run by Puerto Ricans but has changed hands to Dominicans. That is when it became "Nuevo." The newer immigrants took over these businesses when the children of the first owners grew up and moved on to other fields.

The food is consistently fine: fried plantains dipped in garlic sauce, salt cod fritters, chunks of chicken in yellow rice with olives and cilantro, sweet bananas stuffed with spicy ground beef, pork shoulder marinated in garlic. The shellfish soup on Sundays is delicious, too, if you don't mind the whole shrimp with their beady, black eyes staring up at you from the surface. Personally, I don't like eye contact with my soup. After the meal, there's espresso with flan, coconut custard or a slice of guava jelly-roll cake.

On one visit, with a new seminary intern and his parents, the older man asked: "So where's the steak and potatoes?" I was about to point out the *bistec encebollado con papas fritas* (onion-smothered steak with french fries) when the father raised his challenge a few decibels: "All I want is some normal food— steak and baked potatoes! What's wrong with this place?" The waitress didn't completely understand his words, but she sure caught the attitude. I understood more than I wanted to about the father's relationship with his son, who had graduated from Harvard and chose an internship in the South Bronx.

Longwood has its Angel, too, the guardian of the street. When he's not hospitalized for ailments related to alcoholism, he's out sweeping the streets and emptying garbage for the store owners. He feeds pigeons discarded rice, and sometimes seagulls join them in the winter when pickings nearer the water are getting slim. Angel makes no distinction between those who pass up and down his domain. Mothers and children from the shelter around the corner or the social workers who come to service them, drug dealers or people on their way to legal jobs, African-American, Hispanic, young, old, drunk, sober—it matters not to Angel. He is the self-appointed greeter and always has a warm word for everyone, qualities that many church ushers could do well to emulate.

Last Christmas, Angel set up a tree on the sidewalk. From the distance, you could read its hand-lettered, cardboard sign: "Feliz Navidad, Merry Christmas" and see shiny decorations catching the light and the wind. Up close, I noticed that the ornaments consisted of empty beer bottles, soda cans, crumpled bags from chips, silver foil from candy—in other words, garbage. But from the distance, the tree was bright and pretty. Up close, it made me laugh. Who could not like it?

The neighborhood boasts stranger decor. There is a space between two buildings, behind a wire fence, where hundreds of identical beer bottles have been set up, side by side, in a snaking pattern like an elaborate swath of dominoes ready to be toppled. More sinister is a large, leafless tree from which hang several hundred stuffed animals. They have ropes pulled tight around their necks, causing their heads to hang lolling to the side. Once soft and fuzzy ducks, dogs, kittens and teddy bears are now grotesque, gray and matted with filth. It looks like a lynching of stuffed animals, of childhood itself.

Less sinister, but equally bizarre is the large billboard nearby that features Smokey the Bear, reminding all neighborhood residents of their special responsibility: "Only You can Prevent Forest Fires!" says Smokey. Is that so? My friend and colleague Lee Stuart pointed out that these signs were all over the South Bronx. Lee, who loves introducing urban youth to the Appalachian Trail and the woods around her Pennsylvania cabin retreat wondered, "How many folks here have even set foot in a forest?" Why were these signs all over the area? The company needed somewhere to deposit them, oblivious of their insult to a community that has probably suffered the worst urban destruction by fire since downtown Chicago went up in flames. As if there were not enough blame and work to deal with here in the Bronx, we're supposed to save the forests, too.

In the summer Longwood becomes a strip of beach. People unfold lawn chairs and stretch out in front of the stores, sprawled on colorful towels, washed in waves of *salsa* and *merengue*, unless you're near Mi Jesus Fruits and Vegetables where you get salvation. Vendors stop by with carts dispensing paper cups of lemon and coconut ice. Trucks park on the curb and set out tall stalks of sugar cane, piles of watermelons, mangoes and coconuts punctured for inserting straws to extract the sweet milk. In spite of these offerings, the children scramble for ice-cream money when they hear the siren jingle of the Mr. Softee truck. The domino players seek awnings for shade and drink Mabí, a popular drink made from bark left to ferment in sugar water, or cold beer while they move their pieces around the card table in games that never seem to end.

Vivero Live Poultry, otherwise known as Rick's Chicks, is not far and stocks a large inventory. I've often wondered what percentage of the chickens are sold to cook with rice or simmer in soup and what percentage are served up for Santería sacrifices. The latter get their throats slit and their blood poured over selected saints' statues. This is called feeding the warriors. One of our church members used to visit a Santería priest but left the religion because of the chicken sacrifices, which she herself had to perform over the priest's apartment sink. The ritual began to make her sick. She was told that she should be grateful to the chicken that was giving its life for her. In the end, she didn't want to entrust her life to a chicken. Still, there must be many people thankful for Rick's Chicks. Even the buxom chicks on the large sign above the store look quite happy as they sport tight dresses and high heels ready for a night out at some poultry-friendly Latin dance club.

The rest of the block is a series of car-part stores assured of continuing business. One of our interns found that a tire was missing from her car. She went to a nearby tire shop to replace it, and there it was—her tire. It had had a distinguishing yellow paint mark on it. They gave it back, free of charge.

Past Rick's Chicks and the car parts, you come to the mural of White Boy. Spray-painted murals to dead youth dot the area, but this one is different. The others simply commemorate the dead, this one packs a potent message: *"Solo de los cobardes se espera la traición, ven traidores, les espero ..."* ("Only from cowards do you await betrayal. Come on traitors, I'm waiting for you ...") White Boy was shot and killed in a drug dispute. His pale face looms over the street with lifelike scars. One hand points across to the spot where he was shot, toward the traitors he awaits. The other hand hoists a large machine gun. He wears a jacket made from the U.S. flag. A golden, jeweled San Lazaro medal hangs around his neck. The message: White Boy is risen and ready for revenge.

The message has profound appeal. To White Boy's right is a lovingly tended shrine with a holy water font, candles that are never allowed to go out and an elaborate flower arrangement that is kept fresh. I remember the celebration of what would have been his twentieth-birthday. I happened to be walking by and came across a paper plate with one hot dog in a bun and some potato chips, a cup of soda and yellow birthday cake with white-and-blue icing. This was all set out on the sidewalk in front of the mural, and as it was in July, everything was crawling with ants and buzzing with flies.

During the first year after White Boy's death, each holiday would bring a new addition to the shrine. A Puerto Rican flag appeared for the Puerto Rican Day parade. Then there was a plate of Father's Day cake on the ground and a card extolling him as a wonderful father who continued to watch over his beautiful daughter—with machine gun. There was a stuffed teddy bear in a little blue bag that said, "Number 1 Dad."

I have often been drawn to this particular memorial as an icon of the dominant street culture that elevates revenge and violence to a place of honor and adoration. Youth who never set foot in church stand at night in silent meditation before this perverse shine next to the C-Town supermarket. I find myself horrified and strangely moved at the same time. There is so much misplaced longing here. Every time I pass it, I've felt revolted, angered and alienated. It has reminded me of all that brings death—locally, nationally and globally. But sometimes I've felt something different—the strange stirring of communion with those who worship there. I've felt a tenderness and a hunger in the pieces of cake and the teddy bear under the shadow of the gun.

I made a poster-sized print of the mural, which I use in teaching First Communion class. White Boy and the meals set before him always command the kids' attention, so we usually begin by having the children draw pictures of their favorite meals. Aleidy drew her cousin's birthday in the Dominican Republic. She said it was her favorite because the whole family was together, "with no fighting." This memory is important to her now that the family is split between Santo Domingo and the Bronx. Her sister Leidy chose her own birthday and focused on the specialness of that day. When she showed the class her picture, she pointed out the decorations—red, blue and yellow balloons hanging between twisted crepe-paper streamers and a cake big enough for a wedding: instead of a bride and groom on top, there was a large number "7." She hunted through a big pile of crayons until she found the correct shade of lavender for her birthday dress. A third sister, Gladileidy, drew another birthday in Santo Domingo and told of the fun they'd had laughing when the lights kept going on and off during the party because of an electrical problem.

Eric simply drew a big pile of pancakes, topped with butter and dripping with brown syrup. Thin, black lines of steam rose up from the plate. Eric told us that pancakes were his favorite food, and it made him happy when his grandmother prepared them for his breakfast. The grandmother is caring for him until his brother graduates from college and can take over the job that their mother, dead of AIDS, cannot do. Lisa showed herself seated in solitary splendor at a table set with a bowl, a cup and a big vase of flowers. Her hair was braided, and she was wearing her favorite pink pants and shirt. She had a spoon in her mouth. She told us that she was eating her breakfast cereal, which was a good way to start the day. "Breakfast is the most important meal of the day," she informed the class. "It gives you energy, and it tastes good!"

The children make teaching easy and never fail to hit on many First Communion themes, as this class did: community, reconciliation, compassion, a special setting to honor the special meal, energy, goodness and joy—all are a part of this "most important meal of the day."

Eventually we come to White Boy and the sidewalk meals left in his honor. We discuss how when White Boy was betrayed, he picked up a gun seeking revenge and perpetuating the cycle of death. But Jesus made a different choice. "On the night in which he was betrayed, he took bread, gave thanks, broke it and gave to his disciples saying 'Take and eat, this is my body given for you.'" We talk about the difference between these meals, these choices, and these uses of power.

Guns and First Communion class have come together time and again. Alex was a ten-year-old fan of pizza, baseball, and the class. He and his five sisters came to church every day for our after-school program. On Wednesdays, they stayed for the class. Alex was always on the edge of his chair, keyed up with questions. Easter Sunday was to be the day of First Communion and Alex had a starring role in the Easter play. Alex would be the voice of God.

One Wednesday afternoon, Nerixabel, one of Alex's sisters, came rushing into the church with the news: "Alex can't come to class today. He's been shot." It was about a year after Christian was murdered on Valentine's Day and I immediately thought the worst. Around the corner from the church, in the hallway of his apartment building, Alex was shot in the leg by a sixteen-year-old neighbor. His leg bones were shattered. No one knew if he would ever walk normally again—or play baseball.

Why was Alex shot? Because the teenager who did it wanted to belong to the gang Power Rules. The initiation rite for Power Rules was to shoot someone—anyone—in the leg. Then you're in. You belong to the magic circle of power. Alex was the child sacrifice.

When I visited Alex in the hospital, his leg full of pins, suspended in the air, the first words out of his mouth were, "Pastor, now I can't be in the play." Well, why couldn't he? On the next visit, I brought along a tape recorder to record the voice of God. Wounded, but not silenced, Alex's voice rang out on Easter morning. Power rules indeed.

After four months in the hospital, with months of therapy still ahead, Alex, his sisters, and their mother all moved back to Puerto Rico. Their father had just been released from prison and had purchased a gun to take revenge. He came strutting into the hospital room and tried to convince me that God would surely smile down on his plans to avenge his son. God's hands were just itching to pull that trigger. Alex's mother didn't want to be around for any more sacrifices, and so they left. This is why White Boy is a repeat attendee at our classes.

Feast of the Transfiguration

The context of the neighborhood has transformed our teaching. Prepackaged lesson plans that come with a prepackaged church don't work. It is another example of how the neighborhood serves to transfigure the church. Many churches celebrate the annual feast of the Transfiguration, in memory of the transfiguration of Jesus on a mountaintop, but for us it takes on special meaning. In the story, Jesus takes three of his disciples up a mountain ... *and he was transfigured before them, and his face shone like the sun, and his clothes became dazzling white.* Jesus gives his disciples this "mountaintop" experience to strengthen them for struggles that would lie ahead. I don't know why the original members of the church chose this name, but they certainly chose well.

One year in the week before the feast day, we celebrated the graduation of those who had completed a series of workshops on domestic violence. Somehow, we began comparing stories about visits to the prison on Rikers Island. Joe told a funny story about the problem he had from a metal pin in his hip. It kept setting off the metal detector, and the guards wouldn't believe him. He had to endure a very thorough, unfunny strip search. Another man had the same problem with a bullet that couldn't be removed. I was reminded of my experience of having to stand still with my mouth open while they poked inside with a flashlight looking for drugs or razors. Then off came my sandals while they searched between my toes. This happened because I had arrived with a family and didn't get the special clergy treatment.

The regular treatment makes you feel violated and dirty. You go for a visit and get treated like a criminal. For many, it is a weekly ritual. There is a special bus stop in the main shopping district of the South Bronx to take people directly to Rikers. Other buses leave every Friday for the upstate prisons. Operation Prison Gap, which runs one such service, began in 1973 with a single van. Today it regularly charters thirty to forty vans and buses for the regular weekend outings. I had to change our First Communion class schedule from Saturday because too many of the children had prison visits with fathers or brothers over the weekend. One sign of the growing gap between the rich and the poor in New York City is the meaning that "going upstate" has for children. Here in the South Bronx, it always means a trip to prison, but in other parts of the city children use the phrase to talk about a trip to their country house.

After rice and beans, macaroni salad, and chicken, I invited everyone to come for Transfiguration Sunday and handed out a flier. "Where is this taking place?" asked one man, even though the flier had the church address clearly printed on it. I told him that it was here. He had wondered where it was since the flier said, "A mountaintop experience in the heart of the city." "I don't think of this as the city . . . the city is Manhattan," he explained. So what would he call the South Bronx? Lenny answered for him, "This is the leftovers."

"Lord, how good it is that we are here," said Peter on the mountaintop where Jesus was transfigured. I hoped we could all feel that, at least for a while, on that Sunday. I hoped Lenny would feel it. The Gospel of John tells the story of a blind man whose affliction became an occasion for the disciples to speculate: Who sinned, him or his parents? They speculate and pass on by until Jesus stops them. The same thing goes on in relation to the poor and the inner city today. People become objects for speculation: Who is to blame? Is it this generation or their parents? It is always someone disconnected from the one who is speculating. Radio talk shows, TV, books and magazines speculate, speculate and pass on by. Like the blind man, a host of people are defined by what is wrong and what others think about it. No wonder many folks feel like leftovers.

O Christ God, you were transfigured on the Mountain, and your disciples saw as much of your glory as they could hold. . . .
(From Byzantine Daily Worship)

One day when I walked down the block, I heard a street preacher on the corner shouting: "Power and glory! Power and glory!" As I got closer, I saw that the preacher was a pusher creatively advertising a mix of crack and heroin—

power and glory. Your disciples saw as much of your glory as they could hold. The rest of us could hold a little more glory than we see now.

On Transfiguration Sunday, I woke up to dazzling snow, shining everywhere. It is always a special day for me, the anniversary of my ordination. I was supposed to be ordained the day before, but couldn't because of a big snowstorm. I lay in bed and cried as friend after friend called to say it would be impossible for them to come because of the snow. Finally Bishop Herluf Jensen called to say that he couldn't come either, so that was that! The ordination had to be put off until the next day, Sunday—the feast of the Transfiguration.

It's hard to believe now, but at the time, that coincidence meant almost nothing to me. The readings for the ordination had nothing to do with the feast. The gospel I'd picked was Mary's song, the Magnificat: "*My soul magnifies the Lord, and my spirit rejoices in God my Savior ... he has brought down the powerful from their thrones, and lifted up the lowly ...*" (Luke 1:47,52). I guess the real powers knew all along that in just over a year, I would be called as the pastor of Transfiguration Lutheran Church. To make sure I didn't miss the connection, I would preach my first sermon here and be called by the congregation—on Transfiguration Sunday. Seeing all the shining snow that morning reminded me and made me feel very happy and grateful.

When I got to church, I realized we had forgotten to make sure someone was going to bring flowers. We still had some stalky poinsettias left over from Christmas, but I felt a little upset that there wouldn't be any special flowers for Transfiguration Sunday. This was a minor point—the poinsettias didn't look half bad, and probably no one besides me would even care about it. I was just about to go and do some visits, when Ben came in with two huge flower arrangements, exquisite with yellow orchids, daisies, white carnations and small, pale, purple flowers.

Ben had worked at a florist for Valentine's Day and the next day. They didn't need him any more, but he begged them to let him work one more day without pay—and be paid in flowers. He worked all day on Friday, twelve long hours, in order to earn these flowers for the church. How could anyone not love being allowed to be a pastor in this place?

Augustine wrote of the experience of being an alleluia from head to foot. That's how I felt—a song from head to toe. I walked in boots through heavy snow but felt like I was gliding through the air. *Magnificat, magnificat, magnificat anima mea dominum!* I used to sing the Latin refrain from Mary's song to Hans in the rocking chair. It calmed me down in the midst of his colic and startled subway riders one day when he sang out the Latin words loud and clear from his stroller: *Magnificat, magnificat, magnificat anima mea dominum!*

As part of the sermon for Transfiguration Sunday, Rick, Evy, and Lucy gave testimonies. Rick spoke of his addiction to drugs, his anger and guilt before God, and finally of coming to our men's Bible study hoping for something better in his life. He spoke of volunteering and working at the church, but feeling unworthy to come and worship. He described the paralyzing shame that prevented him from moving toward the altar. It turns out that our new-members' retreat at which we read a sermon of Luther's on Holy Communion as medicine had made the difference, and he's been communing ever since. Now Rick leads the men's study.

Evy told the story of how she used to come as far as the church door on Sunday mornings for the sole purpose of collecting money for Avon. For months she did this, refusing to enter despite weekly invitations, just waiting at the door for the Avon money, perusing the latest lipsticks, perfumes and eye creams in her catalog. One Sunday, she got tired of standing and decided to come inside and sit at the back of the church. What harm could it do? "Well," she said, "the sermon hit me on the head!" Now instead of coming to sell cosmetics, she teaches Sunday school and prays at the altar with those who seek healing.

Lucy spoke of her years in the valley of the shadow of domestic-violence when she felt forsaken by God. She said that now she knows God as the very one who bore her safely to this place where she calls others to new life through the domestic violence workshops that she runs.

Each one stood up and spoke with courage, honesty, and eloquence. Three stories of transfigured people in a transfigured church. Everyone was shouting with Peter; *"Lord, it is good that we are here!"* *("¡Señor, que bien que estemos aquí!")*

But the Transfiguration story does not end with shouts on the mountaintop. Instead, Jesus leads his disciples down, where all is not brightness and light. Immediately, they are approached by a father seeking help for his epileptic son who flails about and falls into fires. Jesus casts out a demon, healing the boy, when the disciples cannot.

We came down too. The following week would be our annual congregational meeting, when we would join the reluctant disciples who had to come down from the mountain to face a desperate father and a sick child, as well as their own faithless impotence and distress: *"Why could we not cast it out?" He said to them, "Because of your little faith."* For Transfiguration Sunday the church is always packed. It's another story when we come face to face with the nitty-gritty of our budget, council elections, deficits, and demons that still drive suffering children into danger, while the disciples stand around worrying how to pay the bills and who is the greatest.

We closed our meeting with the Transfiguration prayer, "Give us the vision to see beyond the turmoil of our world and to behold Jesus in all his glory." I want to capture every show of glory so that long after the pale yellow orchids of Transfiguration Sunday have faded and disappeared, these words will flower in testimony to Ben's humble goodness and God's mercy. Will a few flowers change the face of the South Bronx? The obvious answer is no. The true answer is yes. It depends on the nature of the flowers.

People in the Windows

One by one, people added bright felt flowers to the banner standing before hundreds of participants in a South Bronx Churches assembly. We were there to celebrate past accomplishments and pledge ourselves to the future. Flowers appeared in homage to homes constructed, apartments renovated, and the Bronx Leadership Academy High School—a joint project between SBC and the Board of Education. The bouquet represented investments of $122 million in the rebuilding of the South Bronx.

When the neighborhood came through the church doors bringing vitality and renewal, in came pain, frustration, instability, and anger as well. Symptoms of social conditions that the church once sought to avoid were now embedded in its very life. As Pastor Soler said back in 1959, "the problem is ours, not theirs." The work of transfiguration was more than we could undertake alone. We had programs of social ministry, such as after-school tutoring, but large-scale social change was beyond our power.

The year I arrived was also the year that a fellow Lutheran pastor, John Heinemeir, began talking with local clergy about community organizing. He initiated conversations with dozens of clergy—listening and probing to evoke our motivations, passions, frustrations, and willingness to take a risk on a new venture of hope. We crossed the usual dividing lines of ethnicity and religion to build a broad-based organization including Latino, African-American and white lay and clergy leaders. There were Lutherans, Roman Catholics, Baptists, Episcopalians, Presbyterians, Methodists, Disciples of Christ and, eventually, Muslims who joined in the conversation. From the outset, building relationships with one another has been the heart of our work. We found more to be gained by thinking and working together on the basis of shared values and common interests than by fulfilling the city's expectation that we would pour our energies into the maintenance of separate and weaker fiefdoms.

I read a provocative article by Martha Ellen Stortz on "Friendship in the City." She quotes Hannah Arendt in *The Human Condition* (1958) writing about the instability I feel so intensely at times and try to restrain by writing. Arendt, however, points out the instability of language, while lifting up the city itself as " 'a kind of organized remembrance' against amnesia. The city ensures that 'the most futile of human activities, action and speech, and the least tangible and most ephemeral of man-made products, the deeds and stories which are their outcome, would become imperishable' " But what city is this? Not the one Robert Moses and Roger Starr sought to engineer. Instead of "organized remembrance," they tried to make the South Bronx a place of intentionally disorganized amnesia. According to Moses, the area was "unrepairable ... beyond rebuilding, tinkering and restoring. The people living there must be moved and it must be leveled to the ground." Not a shred of civic friendship in evidence. No wonder the current expression for disrespect among our youth has become "dissing," as in "he dissed me." Disrespect, disruption, displacement, dismemberment, disconnection, disorganization, disease ... a community dissed.

When we first moved into the parsonage on Kelly Street, many of the neighboring buildings were abandoned and sported metal decals affixed over the upper-story window spaces. These were painted in a trompe l'oeil effect to resemble windows with curtains, shutters or venetian blinds. Some depicted plants with flowers that never faded. One showed a black cat that sat motionless for years. Nobody on Kelly Street was fooled by this subterfuge slapped upon hundreds of buildings at taxpayers' expense to the tune of $100,000 in 1983 by the NYC Department of Housing Preservation and Development. The scene at street level was graffiti-covered, with cinder blocks and gaping holes where windows belonged. There it didn't matter because the artistic exercise patronized by our city on higher floors was not for our benefit. It was for those who would drive by on the Cross Bronx Expressway—that they might look out and see pleasant, populated blocks replete with lace curtains and plants that never wilted. Someone commented that perhaps the people of the South Bronx should paste pictures of steak on their refrigerators, too. Then Mayor Ed Koch gave this explanation: "In a neighborhood, as in life, a clean bandage is much, much better than a raw or festering wound." But a bandage protects the wound from further infection so that healing may occur. These sham bandages protected the illusions of those who drove on by. As long as they didn't make a wrong turn and descend from their elevated highway, to the "festering wound" below. There are five boroughs that make up New York City—Manhattan, Queens, Staten Island, Brooklyn, and the Bronx, but the *New York Times* real estate section lists upscale Riverdale separately from the rest of the Bronx. It gets the same typeface as the five city boroughs, as though it were a sixth. The label "Riverdale" is pulled over these properties to disguise their true nature, their connection to the undesirable borough.

Maybe those in the passing cars could forget and disassociate themselves from this inner city and the destruction that made their ride possible, but amnesia has not worked here. There remains a pervasive ache for the city that is home:

> If I forget you, O Jerusalem, let my right hand wither!
> Let my tongue cling to the roof of my mouth, if I do not
>   remember you,
> if I do not set Jerusalem above my highest joy ... (Psalm 137:5–6)

The memory-dream of that home is woven through our humanity. For some, it is so painful that chemical amnesia is used in an effort to block it, but for many others the pain yields anger alchemized to action. Community organizing is the recovery of sanity in the midst of Babel. It is dissing turned on its head—dissing dissed. It is remembering, reconnecting, renewing, restoring, reforming, repairing, respecting, resurrecting, relationship. It is civic friendship built on relational power, one-on-one meetings and real, face-to-face encounters that belie the welfare system's perverse use of the term for pro-forma meetings between "workers and clients." In Spanish the word for power is *poder*, which is also a verb meaning "to be able." Organizing creates power to act in ways we cannot on our own.

We contracted with the Industrial Areas Foundation, an organizing network founded by Saul Alinsky to hire our first professional organizer. Alinsky, the son of Russian Jewish immigrants who grew up in Chicago's Jewish ghetto during the Depression, was a pioneer of community organizing who believed that the democratic system could produce real social justice if people were taught the nature of power. In particular, he worked to teach poor and working-class people how to become politically savvy in order to shape the decisions that would affect their communities. Both the civil rights and farm workers movements were influenced by Alinksy's trailblazing work. He mentored Cesar Chavez, who in turn worked closely for fifteen years with a passionate young organizer named Jim Drake, who later joined the IAF. We hired Jim, through the IAF, as the first professional organizer of South Bronx Churches.

One of our initial actions was to hold a series of house meetings at which church leaders could invite other members, friends, and neighbors to voice their anger, dreams, hopes, and concerns for the community. Jim emphasized that we needed to encourage folks to be concrete. "Be concrete! Be concrete!" he kept repeating. The words were ringing in my head when I spotted a concrete block fallen from an abandoned building across the street from our house—the perfect centerpiece for our house meeting. I could place it on the coffee table. I went to retrieve it, but it was too heavy. I could barely lift it. A drug dealer noticed my struggle. He came over and offered to carry it for me. Why not? He brought it to my door and I thanked him.

We were concrete: drugs sold openly as children headed home for school: we listed the locations; job-training programs that offered no jobs: we named the generously funded programs; blocks of empty, burnt-out buildings: we highlighted the blocks on a map; schools without books for each child, schools with dangerous building violations, lunchrooms without chairs, bathrooms without doors: we named the schools, the babies who died, the people left for dead in the emergency room of Lincoln hospital. Certain themes were repeated in meeting after meeting, and those were highlighted in our Sign Up and Take Charge Campaign which garnered more than 100,000 signatures in ninety days for an agenda seeking decent, affordable housing, better education, health care, jobs and drug-free zones.

According to Arendt, it is the concrete city that gives ongoing life to "the most futile of human activities; action and speech." In my experience, the opposite is true. Our deeds and stories are what make a city live. Our action and speech laid the foundation for rebuilding the concrete city. I remember our first organizing assembly in 1987 at St. Jerome's Roman Catholic Church, when an elderly woman who'd lived through the building and burning of the South Bronx stood up and shouted, "I want to see real people in those windows!" "*Without vision the people perish*" (Proverbs 29:18). People here weren't about to lie down and perish. Now, in most cases, real people are in the windows, and the decals are gone.

CHAPTER THREE

PARSONAGE DOORS

Babies and Breasts

It's not clean. I wish it were clean, but it's not. Sometimes I envy the Catholic priests with their housekeepers. On the other hand, for me celibacy holds no appeal. It's not that the cleaning is my job alone, but between all of us, we just never get it completely done. The only time the house got really clean was when my nesting instinct kicked in before each of my babies was born. Actually, even with the nesting advantage, I was more interested in decorating than cleaning. With Ana bulging against my paint shirt, I got up on a ladder and stenciled around the dining room walls up by the ceiling. Now, years later, the rest of the walls need a whitewash, but I can't bear to disturb the stencil. While Hans was somersaulting against my ribs, I painted an ark and a rainbow on the wall near his waiting crib. Each month in kindergarten, the children of his class had to draw a self-portrait and each month Hans drew himself under a rainbow. The teacher commented to me about this, noting that some of the others were beginning to follow his example. She thought it was a lovely thing, but wondered why he did it. So did I until it struck me. I told her that he'd slept under a rainbow every night since his birth. In a way, it is the story of his conception.

My mother, Gregorio, Ana, and I were in Argentina visiting Gregorio's family. It was the first time that Ana met Gregorio's mother, her Argentinean *abuela*. At the end of our visit, my mother stayed in Buenos Aires with Ana so that Gregorio and I could go to Iguazu on the border of Brazil and see the waterfalls. We walked through tropical forests among brightly colored birds, butterflies, and many waterfalls and talked about having a second child. I worried about how we would manage, how I would manage. Gregorio, one of twelve siblings, was ready to make the leap before I was, the same as when we were considering marriage. Then we came upon the main waterfall and found ourselves in mist, ringed by multiple rainbows. I took it as a sign that, in the end, everything would be all right. Eight months later, I painted Hans's wall.

After the initial morning sickness with Hans, I felt well and had plenty of energy. As the day of his birth approached, I had a parishioner near death. Brigido was a longtime member of the church, and I really wanted to preside at the funeral, but the hours of death and birth were out of my hands. As it turned out, Brigido died first. I did the funeral with my white alb ballooning out, but went home before the burial, not wanting to go into labor at the distant cemetery. I remember walking into the house and saying, "OK, now I can have the baby." Within an hour, the contractions began. Soon, we brought Hans home to his room and his rainbow.

Both children co-operated in the timing of their births, a false indicator of things to come. I was even foolish enough to plan my first pregnancy to fit neatly into the most convenient slot of the liturgical year. Once Gregorio and I came to the mutual conclusion that we wanted to have a child, we were giddy with excitement. We toasted our decision with a celebratory bottle of champagne. All that remained was to pick the date. This was not something that occurred to Gregorio. Any date was fine with him, but I had a church calendar to consider. It wouldn't do to have a baby during Advent, the period before Christmas. Much too busy. Christmas was out, too, and right behind Christmas come Lent and Easter, also busy. Fifty days after Easter was Pentecost. Then there was the summer program—all day, every day—with upward of one hundred children enrolled.

Nevertheless, after much thought, I came to the conclusion that the best time to give birth was at the beginning of the summer. Our intern could oversee the summer program. I would trade oversight of a hundred kids for one baby. It never occurred to me that conception on such a precise schedule might be a problem. It wasn't. Ana was born on the first of July. I didn't, however, try this with Hans three years later. By that time, all thoughts of fitting children into liturgical calendars were long gone. Ana made sure of that.

* * *

There are many advantages to living a few blocks from the church. One of them was that when the children were nursing, I could easily go home during the day to visit, nurse and put the baby back to sleep. Having them at church never worked. I'd heard of working mothers who brought their babies to the office, so I tried it, too. I imagined Ana or Hans lying in a bassinet or playing happily in a playpen while I worked. One day in each case was all we could stand. Each child would be fine at home, but once inside the church, they wanted my undivided attention. I don't know how they realized the change in venue at two and three months, but they did. The same thing happened when I tried carrying them around on visits. I couldn't pay attention to anyone but the one in the carrier on my stomach. Gregorio was in cooking school during some of the time that the children were small, which often allowed him to be home when I wasn't. Between him and me, my mother, who came once a week, and Paulette, who babysat the children until Hans went to nursery school, we managed.

Sort of. Ana was four months old and an avid nurser. During the day, I went home to visit and nurse. If I had to be away for a longer periods, I expressed the milk. One Sunday, we were having a bilingual service. It was a particularly long morning. By the time we got to Communion, my breasts were so swollen with milk that they felt like two rocks. I lifted the chalice of wine and Ana began to cry. The flood gates burst open. I'm sure I must have been wearing a nursing pad under my bra, but it didn't matter. The milk poured through the pad, through the bra, through the shirt and out onto the front of my robes. The colorful stole I wore over my soaked white robe made it less noticeable, until the colors ran.

This story will probably provide someone with one more argument against the ordination of women. To me, it's a reminder that religion is not and should not be a disembodied affair. In fact, that's one of the oldest Christian heresies, Docetism, which held that Jesus didn't really have a body, just the illusion of one. Leaking milk is an undeniable sign of real flesh under, as well as on, the surface. Perhaps that's why menstruating and nursing women were barred from getting anywhere near an altar for so many centuries. Even in our own time, the body has been interpreted as an obstacle to priestly service:

"Since God is spirit, it seems appropriate that everyone who consecrates and devotes himself to this spirit should also in a certain sense free himself from his body . . . when someone has an office (the priesthood), is it not then proper that he must live as much as possible like a pure spirit?" I'll admit it is difficult to look or feel like a pure spirit when you're eight months' pregnant, but if that is hard to integrate into worship, then I don't think we are worshiping the Word made flesh. Flesh is not always convenient, prim and trim, neatly wrapped and rubric ready. Certainly, our Creator knows that. Does the ideal pastor wake up and say, "Well, this morning, I think I'll leave my body in bed and take my pure spirit over to the church"?

Church history is full of women who have been forced to cover up the offensive signs of bodily presence. Eugenia in the third century and St. Hildegund in the twelfth both disguised themselves as men and eventually became abbots of the monasteries they joined. Eugenia's true identity went undiscovered until she was accused of rape and revealed her gender in self-defense. St. Hildegund was known as Abbot Joseph until her death. There is compelling evidence of a female Pope Joan in the ninth century, who bound her breasts and put on monk's robes to enter a Benedictine monastery, from which she was elected to rule as pope for two years. Like Hildegund, she lived as a man until her death. Until 1601, a statue of Pope Joan stood side by side with busts of other popes in the Cathedral of Siena until, by order of Clement VIII, it became Pope Zacharias.

These women bound their own breasts and wore loose robes to conceal the contours of their gender, but others found themselves reconfigured against their will. While a few early frescoes depicting women as priests and even as a bishop have survived, some have been painted over to make them appear anatomically correct, i.e., male. This is not a history I choose to emulate as a pastor in a congregation where no one I know, male or female, feels like a pure spirit. It's not a history I choose to pass on to my daughter as she struggles with complex feelings about her own body in the throes of adolescence.

Two-Headed Monster

Of course, nursing is not the main reason it is good to live in the neighborhood. The nursing days are long over. I know that my understanding of this place and people and my acceptance by them as an outsider are immeasurably helped by living here. For me, it was a clear decision. I just didn't see how there could be any integrity in serving a church in the South Bronx while commuting in from someplace else. How could I preach that it was good for the church to be here, if I was not willing to be here? It was more complex for Gregorio. He grew up living in poverty, in a maligned community. He would have liked the chance to live in a different environment. But at the time, he didn't object because he shared my anger against the prejudices that create "undesirable" neighborhoods and my longing for a transfigured city. For me, as a person coming from relative privilege, living here has been a gift, opening my eyes and molding my heart. But for Gregorio, it has been something of a sacrifice. Only time will tell how it's been for our children, who are now teenagers. It's impossible to say how different choices would have evolved. In the end, this is home.

Being several blocks away from the church is just about right. It's close, but not too close. There is more privacy than in churches where the parsonage is next door. I've found that people both appreciate the closeness and respect the distance. The latter is important for our family, because my work is already a greater presence in our lives than most other jobs would be.

When she was three years old, Ana locked herself in a closet, clutching a bag of her outgrown clothes. She had heard me say that I was going to take them to church. She hadn't minded giving them away until she knew where they were going. I guess she felt she'd already shared enough of herself with the church by having to share her mother.

It came to a head one Sunday when she was two. Gregorio had to leave the church unexpectedly, and he carefully left Ana in the care of a couple she had always liked, Minerva and Manny, who magically produced pennies from her ears. Ana was laughing about the pennies until she realized that Gregorio had left. He told her he was leaving, but she didn't realize he'd meant for the rest of the morning. Suddenly, Ana was bereft and inconsolable. When I found her, she cemented herself against me, and that was that. I led the service with Ana in my arms. By the time of the sermon, she had relaxed enough to stand beside me holding my hand. Then it was time for Communion. Some churches commune infants, and I think it's a fine idea, but we don't do it. We have First Communion class beginning at around age seven. Younger children receive a blessing. While I said the Communion prayers, Ana let go of my hand and clutched my robes, unseen behind the altar. My spoken prayers over the bread and wine were silently mixed with prayers that Ana would not make noise, would not cry—that we would just get through this service.

People came forward to receive Communion. In our English worship, the congregation receives Communion from deacons standing in front of the altar, but in the Spanish mass, people kneel. Usually, Ana was in Gregorio's arms during English worship, and I gave her the blessing with a kiss besides. She would smile, her hands clutched around her father's neck. But this day was different. This was the Spanish service, and Ana was at eye level with the kneeling communicants watching her mother place food into every open hand except her own. She pulled on my robe and held out her hand. I kissed her and blessed her. She began in a relatively quiet voice, "Mommy share." I knew I couldn't ignore her. I leaned down and whispered that we'd soon go home to have lunch. I didn't have the time or the means to explain to a two-year-old why she couldn't have Communion. It was the final betrayal. Within moments, her quiet demand became an insistent whimper that crescendoed until she was screaming at the top of her lungs, "MOMMY SHARE! MOMMY SHARE!"

The congregation kept their heads reverently bowed except for a few people who tried to comfort Ana, but she was having none of it. What did I do? I suppose that I could make something up, but the truth is that I don't remember. Perhaps it was the day of Ana's First Communion—no white dress, no posing for the camera, just a sob-wracked body and a wafer soaked in tears. Perhaps not. All I remember is that somehow it was over, and I went home feeling like a two-headed monster: Mommy-Pastor, a horror to one and all.

Perhaps I should mention that the leaking-breasts incident and the Communion tantrum were one-time occurrences. My robes are otherwise pressed and milk-free. The loudest sound to be heard during Communion is usually singing. At thirteen, Ana began teaching Sunday school and occasionally, when she can be persuaded, brightens worship with her outstanding trumpet and cornet music. Hans often appeared to be paying no attention whatsoever, which was belied by the beautiful drawings he created of the sanctuary during the service and the insightful comments he would make about the sermon several days, or weeks, later. But other children and babies are welcomed in various states of attentiveness and volume. This pastor would be the last one to complain.

I cited these dramatic incidents as examples that the goings-on in the parsonage and in the parish are not so easily fit into neat compartments. Although this is rarely so obvious to the world, it is no less real. A visiting student from Germany once commented that the women theology students he knew had many worries about how they would balance family and church, adding "but that doesn't seem to be a problem for you." "Seem" was the key word there. Of course, it's a problem for me.

On the other hand, I never see the answer being to devise new and more efficient ways to compartmentalize our lives. Perhaps this is just self-defense. I once bought an organizational tool from "Time Minders" called *Time Power*. I came across it recently under a pile of old magazines, still unopened in its original box several years after I had ordered it. I hadn't had time for it! After that, just looking at the big, blue, reproachful box with the bright gold letters shouting TIME POWER!!! made my stomach flip flop. I couldn't get rid of it fast enough. Something in me resists the push to divide up life. That's what made me feel monstrous, that I was evolving into a creature with a different head for every role I play, a multi-headed beast.

Even my day off, every Monday, can be a challenge, even with a Time Minders plan in place. One time, I was going to spend the day evenly divided between (1) prayer and writing (2 hours) (2) entering names and addresses into the computer (2 hours) and (3) cleaning the house (2 hours). Then I was going to pick up Ana and Hans at school, spend the afternoon with them, and then make a nice dinner to have with Gregorio. This seemed like a good, balanced plan.

School was canceled because of a teachers' conference I'd neglected to note on my calendar. So much for planning ahead. We made French toast for breakfast, picked up two girls to play with Ana, which left Hans feeling miserable and whiny, made chocolate chip cookies, and took the girls home. By then it was time to think about dinner.

This was actually a fine day, and I should be able to leave it at that, but the names and addresses remained on a hundred scraps of paper spilling out of folders and bags. Prayer was interrupted by hungry children. The only cleaning happened when Hans played in my room and I picked clothes up from the floor of our closet. This didn't last long. Hans then helped me move piles of books from bedroom floor to study floor. I presented the task as an opportunity to build bigger muscles. He made two trips and informed me that his muscles were big enough. We left the books and played marbles. Another day off with no writing to show for it.

I'd forgotten another lesson learned from my children. Like John the Baptist, Ana began to assert herself from the womb. When John's mother, Elizabeth, was six months pregnant, her cousin Mary, pregnant with Jesus, came to visit. According to St. Luke, the moment that Mary greeted Elizabeth, John began kicking up a storm. Elizabeth took heed of this movement from her son, the beginning of his prophetic career. I should have paid attention to Ana. Maybe it was a bad day, "bad" because things weren't going the way I wanted, because I couldn't see the results I anticipated. Suddenly, there was Ana, with a kick to the gut, a poke against the ribs. The first time this happened, I was stopped in my tracks, and I knew that, while on one level things seemed to be falling apart, on another level new life was taking shape: tear ducts, fingernails, heart valves, brain cells were all forming and growing—invisible miracles that had nothing to do with my own futile busyness. It happened again with Hans, and fortunately the Spirit has other ways of stirring within us, but the first-time sensation of Ana's tiny kicking foot has never been surpassed.

That evening, Gregorio came home with a bunch of yellow freesias and played with the children. He told me to take some time for myself. I cleared a bookshelf in the bedroom and removed ninety-four mystery novels, all read in the last couple of years. Actually, I'd read even more mysteries, counting the ones borrowed from the library by my mother. Why did I choose to read these books? They offered distraction when I was tired and convinced me that I was incapable of attending to anything more demanding than books that engaged the busy surface of my mind. Someone told me of an article they had read about the propensity of women clergy in urban areas to read mystery novels loaded with murder. Perhaps when the violence occurs between the covers of a book, it feels more manageable. I see that I'm not so different from my parishioners who sit glued to Jerry Springer every morning. In fact, reading these books did not relax me, but merely offered a temporary mental diversion until I could get to sleep. I sold them to one of the sidewalk book dealers on Broadway. Now they could put someone else to sleep, or keep them awake, as the case may be.

So often love and energy feel divided, but even more often they are multiplied. For years, Hans had a recurrent bedtime question after I'd tell him that I loved him:

"Mommy, are you sure that you love me?"

"Of course, Hans, you know I love you. I love you with all my heart."

"With all your heart?"

"Yes, with all my heart."

"How many hearts do you have Mommy?"

"Just one."

"But how can you love me with *all* your heart if you love Ana, too?"

The answer was always the same: "Because love is a miracle. Because I can. Because I do."

Lepers in the Bed

There is a cathedral in Marburg, Germany, dedicated to St. Elizabeth of Hungary, who spent her final years there serving the poor. Elizabeth lived at the beginning of the thirteenth century. Born Hungarian, she was taken from her family at the age of four to be raised with her future husband, Ludwig, in the Wartburg castle where three hundred years later Luther translated the Bible. When Elizabeth turned fourteen and Ludwig was twenty-one, they married and had three children. Ludwig was a wealthy landowner and Elizabeth gave large sums of money away to the poor. Many neighbors criticized her unrestrained generosity, but Ludwig supported her. In addition to alms giving, Elizabeth founded two hospitals where she often nursed patients herself. She provided for orphans and prompted Ludwig to find employment for those in need of work. All of this was fine with Ludwig, up to a point.

Scenes from Elizabeth's life are painted around the church. In one image, a leper is seen lying in Elizabeth's bed, much to the shock and displeasure of her husband as he enters the room. A leper in the bed was going too far for

Ludwig. I have learned to keep our marriage bed relatively leper-free. In my early years at Transfiguration, I would often bring the suffering of the neighborhood into bed with me, with us. It was wrong, and Gregorio was no happier about it than Elizabeth's husband was at being displaced by the leper. A bedtime conversation about who was shot is not much of an aphrodisiac. At the time, I didn't know where else to turn. Gregorio was loving and patient, but it was a strain. Now I have a spiritual director. I talk to friends. I write. Our bed is for us.

But sometimes the rest comes slowly and after Gregorio has gone to sleep, other visitors sneak under the covers. I knew Ray for only a few months. After stopping by the church for information on our Narcotics Anonymous meetings, he'd also become a regular member of our Saturday morning men's group. Every Saturday for a couple of hours, he and a dozen other men, most of them homeless, would meet over coffee and donuts for Bible study, prayer, and no-holds-barred man talk. Martin Luther called it, "the mutual conversation and consolation of the brothers." For Ray, it was church.

One Saturday, the men were talking about prayer. Carl, recently homeless, told of walking the streets at night, sometimes experiencing pangs of fear and vulnerability and then simply praying aloud. He confided that a few times he'd been overheard and dissed as crazy. Ray spoke right up: "Man, I know what you mean!" He told of being locked up in a Veterans' hospital and really needing to talk with someone when nobody was around. Ray badly wanted to pray but said that he had so much going around in his head that he couldn't concentrate. "Then," said Ray, "I saw the chair. It was in the corner and I thought, well, Jesus is a king . . . a king sits on a throne. . . ." So Ray placed the chair before him and imagined Jesus sitting there.

As Ray told it, what followed was the best prayer time he'd ever known. Ray poured out his heart and soul to the king seated before him. "And I knew Jesus was listening," said Ray, "to every word." Jesus wasn't the only one listening. A nurse walked by and peered into the little glass window of the door. She saw Ray talking to a chair. A doctor was called. Ray's agitated protests only made things worse. A shot was administered. "I woke up with one mad headache," said Ray. He died two days after his most recent admission to the same hospital. While there, trying to recover from depression, someone dealt him a fatal blow to the head. Supposedly, no one knows the details of what happened.

I came home from his funeral, keyed up and tired with a sore throat and a headache. Gregorio was already asleep. I needed help to settle down and concentrate in prayer. Why couldn't I learn from Ray and take the ordinary furniture of my life as a locus for holy presence? A common head cold is sufficient to wreck my will and my focus. I remember five years of being tired, the time from Ana's birth until Hans, born three years later, stopped nursing and started sleeping through the night. I remember months on end, never sleeping more than two or three hours at a stretch—the times I tried to pray and fell asleep, the times I didn't even try. But there were other moments too, at 3 or 4 A.M., in the rocking chair, emptied of every strength by the sucking and sobbing of our colicky son. It was then, when all efforts at prayer became impossible, ludicrous, that I found myself rocked by mercy that swayed the night.

I remembered nights in seminary, praying compline before a candle lit icon ... how easy it was to focus. It's different after a funeral, lying worn out in the darkness, beside my sleeping husband. Through slits in the venetian blinds, a streetlight illuminated our rocking chair—thanks to Ray, icon enough.

Oma

Gregorio gives me encouragement and comfort, but this ministry is not his calling. His job cooking and selling gourmet foods is not his calling, either. He works to be useful and to help support our family, but his work is not a passion. It's work. Our family is his passion, and sometimes he feels it threatened by my vocation. Once when he was driving alone with Hans in the car seat, a drug dealer threw some bottles at the car. When I came home, Gregorio told me what happened and went on to say that if anything similar occurred in the future, he would take the children to my mother's house and stay with her. I could do what I wanted. "My husband is ready to leave me," I thought, "and he's going to move in with my mother!" I found the thought both terrible and comforting. A member of the church spoke with the bottle-throwers, and nothing similar ever happened again, but I know that Gregorio worries about safety more than I do.

My family has never had to move in with my mother, though she has spent countless days here with us. She makes the one-hour trip from Summit, New Jersey, almost every week. She buys toilet paper when we run out and cooks balanced meals. She helps drive the children to school and pick them up. When I have to go away on out-of-town preaching engagements and other work, she comes and stays. Up to this point, I don't know how we would have managed our work and family life together without her support. Having a grandmother, or Oma, as we call her, is entirely different from having a babysitter, and I know that the benefits are not ours alone. These are her only grandchildren, and I am her only child. Since my father's death when I was in seminary, our closeness is a boon to us all.

My mother can certainly not complain of encroaching boredom in the final quarter of her life. A few years after we moved to the Bronx, she called me at the church office to say that she had made sandwiches at the parsonage for lunch and wanted me to come home and eat. I walked back from church only to find the street completely blocked. Police and ambulances were everywhere. There were men in jackets labeled BOMB SQUAD. They assured me that everyone had been evacuated more than an hour ago, but I insisted that I had just spoken to my mother in the house. It turned out that they had rung the doorbell, but we'd forgotten to replace the battery. They assumed no one was home. My mother and her dog, Emma, were escorted out. After another hour, it was determined there was no bomb, but a house two doors down from ours turned out to have a big cache of drugs and a roomful of grenades. This is far afield from my mother's sheltered upbringing. It is her reward for raising a daughter to follow her own mind and heart. I can never be grateful enough.

My mother also gave me my earliest lessons about grace and race. The race lesson came first. I was five, and we were coloring together. The sixty-four colors of my new Crayola box had exotic names: orchid, magenta, sienna, cerulean and burnt umber. I especially liked burnt umber. It was much more evocative than plain old brown. Just hearing the names made me feel that I had my hands on rare ingredients of artistic inspiration. I would hold up a crayon and ask my mother to read me the label before I would test the color on paper. Then we came to one particular crayon. "What's this one?" I asked. My mother picked it up. "There's a mistake here," she said. A mistake on the crayon! This was interesting. "It says 'flesh,'" said my mother, holding up the pale, pinkish-orangish crayon, "but that's not really true. There are many colors of flesh," she went on, "white flesh, black flesh, brown flesh, red flesh, so this crayon isn't the only flesh color here, and it shouldn't say flesh. It's wrong."

I was fascinated. The crayon-makers were wrong. It was not only a lesson about race, it was also a lesson about truth in advertising and about permission to critique the written word. Years later, during seminary, I took a class on racism at the University of Pennsylvania School of Social Work. As the only white person in the room, it was an uncomfortable but challenging experience—yet the first lesson had come from my mother. It was 1959, and she was way ahead of Crayola's multicultural box.

The grace lesson came when I was about seven or eight years old. I used to like to play by a stream past the woods in back of our house. The stream ran at the bottom of two steep banks. At one point, there was a rock ledge across it to a field on the other side. My parents warned me never to try and cross the ledge because it was slippery and I could fall and hurt myself. But what did they know?

One spring day when the woods was full of fiddlehead ferns, wild violets, and may apples, I found myself at the stream, wanting to cross over to the field beyond. Climbing down one bank and up the other side was too much trouble. It was better to walk across the ledge. I got half way across and—it was slippery after all. I fell, hard, onto the rock bed of the stream below. I wasn't badly injured, but I hurt and had to climb up the muddy bank to get back home. I climbed and slipped and climbed and slipped and finally emerged, covered with mud, blood and tears.

My mother had just gotten dressed for a women's luncheon at the church. She was wearing a dress that my father considered impractical. It was the palest shade of yellow, would soil easily, and had to be dry cleaned after each wearing. As I remember, it was questionable whether it could be cleaned properly at all. When I came from the woods, my mother was standing at the back door, waiting for me to come home so that she could go to church in her beautiful, pale-yellow dress.

When she saw me, she never hesitated, but came and hugged me to herself—mud, blood and all. She never made it to the women's luncheon that day. I don't know what happened to the dress. There were no conversations about fault or disobedience to belabor the obvious. Never releasing her loving touch, she took me upstairs to wash. The Gospel of John tells of a blind man whose sight was restored when Jesus spread mud on his eyes and sent him to wash in the pool of Siloam. The bath water was my Pool of Siloam. The mud went down the drain and my child's eyes adjusted to recognize the gift of grace.

Opening Windows

My family continues to hold me close despite the mud and blood I still track back home. They keep me far saner and more centered than I would otherwise be. I can't help Ana with Latin verb declensions and, at the same time, think about whom I need to visit in the hospital at the same time. The future imperfect tense just doesn't allow for it. Going over spelling words and counting out the measures while Hans practices his trombone are equally absorbing. Book reports, science projects, baseball, basketball, volleyball, Hans's fossils, and movies with Ana exert their inexorable and wonderful pull. The pull of laundry and dishes is less wonderful, but just as unavoidable. And about once a week, Gregorio brings me flowers.

It's a lot, and for years it was more than enough, or so I thought. We had a German student, Bernd, staying here and visiting the church for two months. At the beginning, he asked me about friendships in the parish and how it worked to maintain relationships with friends in other places. I said that it was hard to do because most of our friends now lived at some distance, but that it didn't bother me at all. My work and my family were more than enough. When I said it, I believed it was true. But I remember exactly what I was doing when he asked the question. I was standing at the sink washing pesto off the dinner plates. I remember the Brillo pad in my hands, the pieces of green-flecked pasta and bits of garlic stuck to the plates, the running water. I've washed dishes countless times since then, but I can't remember one. I was fooling myself when I thought it was an easy question.

It's true that my work and my family fill my heart and occupy my days. Nevertheless, I've come to see that other things matter, too, and that I am also a person with a life beyond the blessings and boundaries of being a pastor, parent, and spouse. It was easy to become Bernd's friend because it was convenient. He was right there. When he left, I had to ask myself—am I sad because Bernd is leaving or am I sad because another friend is moving out of reach? It was both. But friendship is not always, or at least in my circumstances, not usually convenient. So, is it important or not? I decided that it was. The pain in my heart told me that it was, and is.

Sometimes the view from someone else's windows brings light into our own. It happened for me with Luz. She was almost completely blind and didn't appear to have long to live. Everything was *muy nublado, muy oscuro*—very cloudy, very dark. Her apartment was always dark; I never liked visiting her there. In any season, at any hour, the rooms were stagnant and dusky—stifling in winter or summer. Windows were closed and covered with curtains, blinds, even blankets. Luz would become agitated at any mention of air and light. I knew it, but couldn't control myself. I wanted to tear open the curtains, push up the windows. I always made the unwelcome suggestion, and Luz would say, "No! no! The light bothers my eyes." I couldn't stop: "It will make you feel better. You need some air in here." "No! no!" Every time I left, I'd go out into the street and have to squint until my eyes readjusted, even on rainy days.

Luz was depressed when I first met her, and things went downhill from there. Her husband's slow dying provided a righteous reason for her to do nothing but worry. When he died, she just did nothing. Her own health deteriorated. At every visit a new ache or ailment surfaced. Her adult daughter died. Her grandchildren ignored her. Finally, she lost her dark home and had to move into an airy, bright apartment with three strangers to share a home attendant. It was dreadful for Luz, who'd lost the power to keep the windows covered, so her eyes found a more drastic solution, squeezing out the light, becoming blind.

From the beginning, I wondered at the exquisite irony of Luz, whose given name is Spanish for "light." If Luz means light, what made Luz so afraid to be herself? What makes any of us resist being utterly who we are? When Luz began to complain of the dark, I took it as a good sign. I read her the song of old Simeon who held out against death until he could take the infant Jesus from Mary and cradle the light of his longing in his arms:

> Lord, now you let your servant go in peace; your word has been fulfilled.
> My own eyes have seen the salvation which you have prepared in the sight of every people; a light to reveal you to the nations and the glory of your people Israel. (Luke 2:29–32)

She pressed my hands and asked me to read it again, and then again. I think that Luz was finally coming into her own. She was getting ready for the light.

Proximity to death can make a big difference. It did for me. Of course, I don't know the timetable of my own death; indeed the actuarial tables give me quite a few more years, but what do they know? I used to think that I would get back to pursuits like friendship and writing when our children were grown and when I retired, but now I feel differently; I feel more urgency. The last time I felt this way was when, as a teenager, I really did believe I was dying.

It was fall, and I lay in bed watching the tree, a sugar maple, from my bedroom window. Unable to get up much, I had time to examine each leaf lifting in a breeze I could not feel. At seventeen, I was sick with a parasitic disease that was not properly diagnosed for a year. It left me increasingly exhausted and depressed. During one hospitalization for a biopsy, I overheard a mistaken diagnosis of lymphatic leukemia. As soon as I could get to a library, I figured out that I had perhaps a year or two to live.

I was stricken with grief made worse by loneliness. Since the diagnosis had been discussed among doctors who thought I was sleeping, I concluded that I wasn't supposed to know the fact that would change everything for me. Since I wasn't supposed to know it, I didn't talk about it. Presumed ignorant in the first place, I was never informed of the mistake.

Faith was no comfort because I had none. My faithful parents had taken me to church since I was a baby. It was such an assumed part of life that my mother remembers the Sunday when I was five and we drove past a busy tennis court. I watched the players in wonderment and finally came up with a plausible explanation: "They must have gone to the early service." Nevertheless, by the time I was fifteen, I lost interest in a God who didn't do what I thought should be done to make the world a better place. So I was alone with my grief.

Some days I thought I was going crazy. I could barely drag my body up and down the stairs, but my mind, like a caged animal, was charged with frantic energy. Writing kept me from going over the edge. Somehow the words held me back and grounded me. I wrote poem after poem. If paper bled, my bed would have been drenched in it. It was a safe way to let the animal out of the cage, my personal Howl. While my friends pounded the dance floor, I pounded out poems.

I read and reread the poetry of Anne Sexton and Sylvia Plath. As they circled round death, drawing closer, they were pulled in. In Plath's case, literally into the oven. But for me, the opposite happened. Word by word, line by line, I found myself reeled more deeply into life. Facing a death that seemed to offer no choice, I rebelled. I wanted life with a force I'd never known before. Fear and sorrow were fierce, but the desire to live was fiercer.

Between poems, on days when I couldn't leave the bed, I lay and looked at the trees and the sky, grateful for each leaf, each cloud, even the bugs—everything. I thought of all the people I loved and cared about and how I didn't always express my feelings very well because I was fearful or shy. It was a paradox: being sick separated me from the normal round of activities with other people, but at the same time, I experienced a profound connectedness, our human rhyme.

The other result of this experience was a return of faith. It was nothing I sought or even wanted, but suddenly God was there in the light flaring through the leaves and in the desire to live burning in my blood. Faith grew as a yearning, the way leaves lift and turn toward the sun, an ache for the bright touch that came gently as breath, stirring through me like holy wind. Why did it come? I don't know. I can only be grateful that it did. This was not yet a return to a concretely Christian faith, but it was the beginning.

After half a year, while tests continued and a true diagnosis of toxoplasmosis was finally made together with the likely promise of longer life, I made some promises, too: I would live each minute of every day to the fullest; I would value every smallest sign of life; I would seek to uphold life—especially where others wanted to crush it; I would express my love for people openly, without holding back; and I would waste no time or energy on trivia. It didn't last. The intensity of living each moment as though it might be the last, each day like the only day, always being attentive and loving—it just couldn't last. On the other hand, those promises did change me and refocus my life.

Something similar had happened before when my best friend died. Tracy was my first good childhood friend. She had a solemn, pale face with deep, black eyes and hair and a congenital disease that was slowly killing her. At the time I only knew that Tracy was sick and that we had to play quietly. It was beyond imagining that seven-year-old girls like us might die. One night, I went to church with my parents to see a movie about some missionary work in India. The people were building wells.

The film included pictures of children who were near death for lack of clean drinking water. One of them was a little girl about seven years old. My age. Tracy's age. I saw that the eyes of that Indian girl were identical to Tracy's eyes. They were unmistakably the eyes of a child facing death. I remember sitting on my metal folding chair, in the darkened room full of grown-ups, feeling very hot and very cold, seized by a terrible, forbidden knowledge. I knew that Tracy was going to die. Shortly thereafter she did.

What was born in me then was a powerful sense that something unfair was afoot in the world, both near and far, and I hated it. I hated it with a purity of will never achieved again, but it began to shape my life, forging from perfect anger at death an imperfect but persisting love for life later rekindled in my own near brush with death.

When I still believed death was close as a teenager, one of my plans was to spend the last year of my life writing letters to people to say all the important things I had never had the courage to verbalize. It was a case of now or never. I have felt it again, this need to say what I don't take time to say, to write what I don't take time to write. It is a part of myself that I am no longer willing to give up until some distant future when life slows down. Waiting for that is probably as dumb as waiting to pray until I find some perfect silence. I don't want it to be never, so it must be now—opening the window for breathing space. It's true that some windows are shut. Some limits do come with age, marriage, motherhood, and work. Some choices and experiences are closed. There are bounds to embrace as forcibly as Luz insisted on shutting her windows. But others should be refused, shattered if necessary, to let in the air.

I'm not leaving my family and church to head off for Tahiti in a midlife crisis. I just want to pray a little more and write and have an occasional cup of coffee or tea with a friend, though some days such simple pleasures seem as farfetched as the exotic ones, but I am feeling freer and more certain that I will create some space for writing, prayer and friends. There was a time when I never would have dared to put meeting a friend on a to-do list in the midst of work-related tasks. Friendship was something outside a pastor's working hours. I am slowly coming to believe that friendship is actually an essential part of our ministerial work, a vital component of healing in a broken, disconnected world.

The writing place isn't physical space, at least, not a room of my own. The space I once claimed is now where my mother stays when she visits and is the home of our only computer, which the children need for homework and covet for games. But I am trying to make room in my head and my heart. St. Teresa recognized that the cloistered nuns she wrote her books for had little space for recreation. They were hemmed in by rules and cramped quarters. "I think it will be a great consolation for you," she wrote, "in some of your convents, to take your delight in this Interior Castle, for you can enter it and walk about in it at any time without asking leave of your superiors." The space I'm trying to enter may not be an interior castle, but like the makeshift *casitas* that dot our landscape, it will have to do.

CHAPTER FOUR

SOUL DOORS—
BREATHING SPACE

These Trees Are Prayers

Silence my soul these trees are prayers.
I asked the Tree: Tell me about God—
then it blossomed.
R. Tagore

One day the big tree in front of the church fell over and crashed into my van, almost totaling it. Just a slight breeze toppled it. To everyone's surprise, the tree turned out to be completely rotten inside. The outside looked fine and was still putting out leaves.

I don't know how the tree got that way, but I can sure identify with it. Until I opened the book and saw the picture, I didn't realize I had one inside my chest, a tree, that is. There it was, clearly labeled: the bronchial tree. The delicate bronchial tree stirs with life, branching out inside the lungs to bud with tiny air sacs—or we die. For too long, I neglected the task of tending this tree. Those who study the science of breath emphasize the importance of breathing from the diaphragm rather than the chest. Shallow, rapid chest breathing is related to our "fight or flight" response. Slow, deep breathing from the diaphragm channels fresh, energizing oxygen into the far recesses of the lungs, the blossoming tips of each bronchial branch, called alveoli.

My alveoli were not flowering as they should. The tree was shriveling. I felt short of breath, my throat clenched, the tracheal trunk clogged and shrunk. It is a feeling that I get in certain dreams: I am stuck in a tight space, with a small hole out of which I must climb, but I can't get through. Fear plunders the thinning air. I was crying easily, losing patience with the children, having no resistance, walking around without skin, lost to myself. Was this the beginning of burnout? It might have been, but it wasn't. It was the beginning of this book. Writing would keep me from going over the edge again. Writing became a door to contemplation and a channel for grief.

It continues to be a struggle to tend to my inner life with its bronchial tree and be faithful to outer responsibilities. Sometimes it helps to leave the neighborhood in order better to re-engage with it. This is as true for my congregation as it is for me. In November of the same fall that the tree fell, a group of us from the church went on retreat to a Benedictine community of women in Peekskill, New York. I had already taken Lucy and Burnice from our women's group there for a brief respite. When I picked them up, they told me about the sisters. "They do everything slow! They walk slow! They talk slow! They eat slow!" "And we saw the night sky full of stars!" they added. They told me that their days were directed by a verse in Psalm 46 painted on the convent wall, "*Be still, and know that I am God.*" "How can we do this at home?" they wanted to know. Good question!

I told them about the rest of the Psalm, which, in addition to inviting stillness, is fraught with violence: "*We will not fear, though the earth should change, though the mountains shake in the heart of the sea; though its waters roar and foam, though the mountains tremble with its tumult.*" At least, these other sisters, Lucy and Burnice, who live with more than their share of heart-shaking tumult, had found a few days of stillness and stars.

Now we were back again with some others. In every room there were signs reminding us to be silent and pamphlets to explain why. Silence was a new concept for some. Others, like me, were familiar with the concept but struggled with the practice. Teresa of Avila wrote that "the mind is the cracking mill that goes on grinding." We were in the chapel to pray with the sisters. We began by sitting in silence. I was finally in a quiet space with no sirens, no gunshots, no shouting, and no Mr. Softee. But there was a foot right in my face. The foot belonged to an angel painted on the wall beside me, just at eye level. The foot had six toes. I found myself looking around the chapel counting angel toes. Some had five and some had six. What was the meaning of this?

As long as I was puzzling over toes, I began to check out the rest of these angels who watched over our chapel prayer. One of the angels there appears to be delicately stifling a burp, pressing the blue cloth of her dainty robe to her mouth. Above her is a naked seraphim demurely wrapped in six gilded peacock wings, from which she peeks slyly toward the altar. Her twin across the room does the same. What was the artist thinking? I should have been praying, but instead I was playing art critic. The clacking mill ground noisily on while the sisters' birdlike voices filled the air with morning Psalms. It took considerable effort to tear myself away from the astounding angels and plunge into the Psalms, but at last I did.

The words of the Psalms are unfailing helps to prayer when silence fails me, or rather when I fail with silence. My prayer life varies from day to day, from week to week. My friend Bernd once wrote of fasting for ten days and how marvelous it was to eat again: "From now on, I always will be conscious of how wonderful and special it is to have something to eat." But it didn't work. He concluded that an occasional ritual fast might help him to sustain the gratitude. For me, prayer is like such a fast. It is an intentional stop in the daily round, an emptying in order to be full in a different way, full of desire for all that is life and life-giving, lifting, and turning toward the source of life. Sitting quietly helps effect the stop. Sometimes that is enough, but often opening the Bible or another book opens my heart and mind to life-giving connections. So does praying for others, allowing their presence to surface in recollection, one by one. But often my heart is like a sieve, and there are many I forget. Sometimes there is a struggle that leaves me shaken, sobered, and weak. Sometimes my prayer is just grateful collapse in strength beyond myself. Often, too often, there are resistance and boredom, but even the silly emptiness of counting angel toes deepens my hunger for what really counts.

After morning prayer, we all trooped silently outside and headed off in different directions. The air was cold, clear, and silent. It was a relief to be in the woods, where there is no need to redecorate. Golden leaves stirred against the blue sky. A solitary sugar maple blazed before a cluster of pine trees, veins of light flaring through each perfect red leaf.

We met back at the retreat center for lunch, which the helpful signs reminded us to eat in silence. Rosa and Delia, both from Central America, gestured excitedly to one another, pointing to a succulent potted plant on the window sill. It had pale, green leaves with white and pink markings. I'd seen it before but didn't know its name. Rosa and Delia did. Both women are wise in the medicinal uses of herbs and plants from their native countries, Guatemala and Honduras. Both have foraged their native woods and jungles for healing leaves and roots. This plant is *tintime* to Rosa and *Pie de Niño* (Child's Foot) to Delia. Its leaves break open to secrete a thick milk that is rubbed on wounds to promote healing. This was all explained as we broke silence after lunch.

The afternoon began as all of us visited the cemetery, where generations of sisters have been buried. I worried that this might be depressing for some in our group, but we were a death-defying bunch with enough diseases among us to fill the infirmary: AIDS, cancer, heart disease, high blood pressure, and addiction. We kicked the colorful leaves and crunched them beneath our feet like children, laughing and glad. Liz, a woman in her thirties who has almost never left the Bronx, cried out, "I thought places like this only existed on TV!" I've never visited Liz's apartment when the TV wasn't on; in fact, as in many homes I visit, it always is. She has trouble sleeping without it, and so a knowing friend smuggled a small, forbidden radio into the retreat house to serve as a surrogate TV and lull Liz to sleep. Ernestina, in her eighties, thanked me for bringing the group "to such a healthy place."

Bundled against the cold, we left the cemetery and went our separate ways to forage for healing in the silent woods.

Poppies On and Off Broadway

I met Georgia O'Keeffe on Broadway one afternoon. She called out to me from the garbage, wrinkled and beautiful. O'Keeffe is one of my favorite artists. I love the way she saw and painted flowers, one at a time, magnifying and revealing unseen qualities in each petal, stamen, pistol, bloom, and leaf.

A vendor was selling art posters on the street, and I saw O'Keeffe's poppies lying in what appeared to be a pile of discards.

"Are you selling that poster?" I asked.

"Nah, it's ruined. It's wrinkled. It's got a stain."

"May I have it?"

"Just take it," he said.

I don't see wrinkles or stains. I see a reflection of my inner life. I see what unfolds in the intimate petals. In the magnified flowers, I see a Magnificat, the text I chose for my ordination—Mary's song: *My soul magnifies the Lord and my spirit rejoices in God my Savior . . . He has brought down the powerful from their thrones and lifted up the lowly; he has filled the hungry with good things and sent the rich away empty.* "Nah, it's ruined . . . wrinkled . . . got a stain. It won't sell." The Magnificat won't sell in this Wall Street–driven New York. So many that flower in what would otherwise be a barren landscape are expendable, fit for the dump, like our blossoming crabapple tree which was unable to pass muster with the NYC Parks Department.

The tree planting seemed like a lovely idea. A group of Latino immigrants meeting at the church to study English, support one another, plan cultural events, and learn their rights decided to end their first year together with a special celebration. They wanted to give something back to the community here and collected money to buy a small tree for a nearby park that was dirty and treeless. Their plan was to clean up the park, plant the tree and tend to its continued growth. They picked a beautiful flowering crabapple. Who could object? Designated class members called the NYC Parks Department and received the following list of tree-planting regulations:

1. No undocumented trees are permitted in a NYC park. Undocumented trees are subject to immediate removal.
2. Certain foreign species of trees are not permitted. [Evidently they might mess up the distinguished gene pool of Bronx trees.] A list of illicit [alien] trees can be obtained from the Parks Department. Under no circumstances will they be granted the necessary documentation.
3. Trees must be 3 1/2 inches in diameter to ensure their long-range survival. [The tree must be able to support itself and not become a charge and burden the state?]
4. Trees must have a straight trunk. [Why? Is there something wrong with a crooked tree? Gay trees? Lesbian trees? Bisexual trees? What's the problem here? We're talking about a treeless park. Are trees that are not straight unnatural and unwelcome in NYC parks?]
5. The tree must be healthy. The tree must come with a certificate of

health from an accredited tree nursery and an inspector's permit must
be issued after a site visit.

6. Would-be tree sponsors must submit a plan for tree planting that
   includes the following documentation:

   a. name of group and purpose

   b. name of park and address of where tree is to be planted

   c. photo of site [3 copies?]

   d. notarized reason for choice of site

   e. name of accredited nursery where tree is currently in residence

   f. preferred date and time of planting

   g. rain date

7. Tree sponsor must document ability to pay up to $600 in fees.

   —$300 for a tree [the group's small tree was much less]

   —$300 for transport of tree [the group was going to put it in my van]

8. A Parks Department inspector must be present at all tree plantings in
   NYC parks.

Talk about killjoy regulations. There was no way the class could plant a
tree, no room in our city for these immigrants' flowering gift of beauty. But
definitely room on my desk. Every Saturday evening, Gladys, an immigrant
from the Dominican Republic has the job of cleaning our church. Every Sunday morning, I find a single red rose in a vase on my desk.

O'Keeffe is also a good teacher of friendship and paying attention:

> In a way—nobody sees a flower—really—it is so small—we haven't
> time—and to see takes time like to have a friend takes time. If I could
> paint the flower exactly as I see it no one would see what I see because
> I would paint it small like the flower is small. So I said to myself—I'll
> paint what I see—what the flower is to me but I'll paint it big and they
> will be surprised into taking time to look at it.

O'Keeffe wrote these words in September 1939, the precise moment when
Hitler invaded Poland, igniting the horror of World War II. She compared the

attention and vision needed for her art to the attention and vision we need to make and nurture relationships. With war raging across the ocean, this could be viewed as a dangerous form of quietism, but I think it might also be seen as a way of resistance. Lifting up beauty and magnifying human connections can be a powerful protest against magnifying the differences between people and justifying their deportation, imprisonment, and destruction. It helps me to recognize this, to defend the time and space needed for the arts of writing and friendship in the face of what usually seem to be more urgent, important pursuits. It helps me to see the value in magnifying what has become too small and insignificant in the rush of my life. Nevertheless, time, space and silence remain big challenges, especially for writing.

> For it is only framed in space that beauty blooms. . . . Even small and casual things take on significance if they are washed in space, like a few autumn grasses in one corner of a Chinese painting, the rest of the page bare. (Anne Morrow Lindbergh, *Gift from the Sea*)

I've always written best when my day is "washed in space," when I have time to daydream, space to reflect. It helps me note significance in otherwise unnoticed things. Paradoxically, distance and space serve to magnify meaning. But now I need to write my best in days that are not "washed in space," but closely crowded. I must access an inner space without going through a long reflection time. This is a difficult trick, distasteful too—instant insights, like instant mashed potatoes.

> I have to be part of community and do much more, since the house I am in is just starting out. . . . So I never have peace and quiet for writing, and I have to work in snatches. I wish I had more time, because when the Lord inspires me, everything gets said much more easily and in a much better way. Then it is like doing a piece of embroidery with the pattern right in front of you.

Well said, St. Teresa! I may be a Lutheran, but if my book ever gets done it will definitely be because Teresa is cheering me on.

Her friend and confessor, John of the Cross (*Juan de la Cruz*) is another fount of inspiration, writing lush poetry in the most unpoetic places. You would think he was at some idyllic retreat:

Debajo del manzano, (Beneath the apple tree:
Allí conmigo fuiste desposada, There I took you for my own,
Allí te dí la mano, There I offered you my hand,
Y fuiste reparada . . . And restored you . . .

El aspirar del aire, The breathing of the air,
El canto de la dulce filomena, The song of the sweet nightingale
El soto y sudonaire, The grove and its living beauty
En la noche serena In the serene night
Con llama que consume y no da pena. With a flame that is consuming
 yet painless.)

John of the Cross did not write these verses in a beautiful garden, but in prison, where he wrote pages of stunning, mystical poetry. It was a very small room built into the side of a prison wall in Toledo, Spain. His own Carmelite brothers shut him in because he refused to back down on the reforms he deemed necessary for their community life. The room had no windows, no ventilation, and had been used as a lavatory by previous guests. It was essentially a tiny, abandoned toilet facility that retained sickening odors, not unlike those that emanated from the sewage treatment plant in Hunts Point. His own chamber pot was not removed or cleaned. In addition to its foul air, the cell was freezing in winter and sweltering in summer. Juan became sick. He could barely eat. When summer came, he could barely breathe. I don't like close spaces. I find the smell of dead mice in church distracting, not to mention the cold. Yet, the saint found breathing space everywhere, and his writing flowered in the furnace.

A Writer's Life

I told a friend and colleague, Father John Grange, pastor of St. Jerome's Roman Catholic Church here in the South Bronx, that I was having a terrible time finding time to write. He said, "Of course you are! It's simply not possible! The life you are living is not a writer's life!" He should know. His brother is a successful writer living what must be a writer's life in Maine. I suppose it's true that I am not living a writer's life. But what is a writer's life? A life with more leisure? A life with less clutter so that writing notes are not mixed in with doctors' bills, spelling tests, letters, crumbs, children's drawings, files and files of things to file? A life without a parish? A life without a husband? Without children? Then what would I write about? I don't know.

The academic world has come calling several times offering what might pass for more of a writer's life. On several occasions, I've gotten a phone call or a letter urging me to apply for a position at one of our seminaries. Of course, this is not yet a job offer, but it raises the possibilities and is flattering, especially since the only doctorate I have is a *doctoris causa honoris*. Each time, I pause and imagine myself as a professor sitting in my book-filled office getting paid to read and write and talk about it. I imagine the students as my new parishioners. If the seminary boiler breaks down, no one will call me. If there are budget problems, it will not be up to me to solve them. If the seminary electricity goes on the blink, no one will call me. I will not have to raise my salary, it will just be handed to me. I will not have to recruit students to come to my classes, they will simply show up. If the seminary toilets are stopped up, no one will call me. There is great appeal to this, especially since faculty committees and meetings never intrude on the fantasy. And if the roof leaks, no one will call me.

Every time I turn down one of these invitations, my choice to remain in the parish feels more irrevocable because it happens that each time I am a little bit older and an institution would be a little bit less likely to want to invest in helping me to get a doctorate, usually part of the deal. But in the end, it is always parish ministry that tugs my heart back to where I am. It feels like the heart of the matter for me. At least, I still have the book filled office.

Someone asked me where I do write. I write on a wooden table in a little cabin on the edge of a forest. The table is large enough to spread out pages when I need to rearrange and a few steps from a kitchen stove where I can boil water for endless cups of tea. When I need a break, the woods are also a few steps from the front door, with miles of paths made for walking. The only sounds there come from the birds and the wind in the pines. There are no interruptions other than the teakettle, which I sometimes forget I've turned on. That's where I write—in my dreams.

Actually, I did write there for one idyllic week as the guest of my friend Bernd's parents, who allowed me to use their vacation home in Germany. Bernd was writing too and long sessions at the table were spelled by long walks in the woods. It was a balanced and highly productive period, but alas, of brief duration. The rest of the time I write on my laptop or on a yellow pad, catch as catch can. I write on my bed, in church, in restaurants, in parks, in airports and airplanes, at my mother's house, in the car (with computer wedged between my lap and the steering wheel) waiting to pick up my children. I have even written on the subway, but that is not something I would suggest if you care to get out at the right stop.

I've probably done the most writing on the top floor of our house in a book-filled room I call my study. It is also a guest room and the place our children went to use our one computer before I had a laptop. Being on the third floor, it is also the warmest room of the house. Much of the book was written over two summers, with high humidity and temperatures of 100 degrees plus. I sat at the computer, shedding clothing until there was nothing left to shed and dripping in sweat with a towel beside me and a pitcher of ice water on the floor by my feet. It is not a scene you would wish to imagine. Occasionally, I sought relief by traveling across the Bronx River into the air-conditioned splendor of Barnes and Noble or Starbucks. I would certainly not recommend this writing pattern to anyone. It is only for the desperate. For all others, go with the little cabin in the woods.

Conspiracy

The creation of breathing space is an act of conspiracy. I have come to see "conspire" as a word with profound spiritual resonance. Like most people, I associated the word with its political meaning: to conspire in the sense of formulating secret strategies to overthrow some public power, person, or nation. But the word "conspiracy" is rooted in deeper soil. It means, literally, *con-spiritus*, to breathe together. To be of one spirit, one breath. *Con-spiritus*. Conspire. To be of one breath is to pray and to labor as one. In the Epistle to the Romans, Paul refers to such conspiracy:

For the creation waits with eager longing for the revealing of the children of God; . . . We know that the whole creation has been groaning
in labor pains until now; and not only the creation, but we ourselves. . . . Likewise the Spirit helps us in our weakness; for we do not
know how to pray as we ought, but that very Spirit intercedes with
sighs too deep for words. (Romans 8:19,22,26)

Paul makes some powerful connections here. He connects our prayer with
the sighing of the Spirit and the travail of creation itself. The word translated
as "sigh" is the same word used in the Bible for the groaning of a woman in
labor. When I was in labor, there were no sweet, little sighs coming out of me.
So here, to breathe is to sigh is to pray is to groan. The breath belongs to all
people, places and created things—in labor together, *con-spiritus.*

This is conspiracy that connects the political and the personal, the community and the congregation, the sanctuary and the streets. For Paul, we are
one *oikos,* one habitation with a common yearning, a common labor, and
a common future. This is always collaborative work. I remember the importance of my husband's hands during my own two labors. I held on tightly the
entire time. I recall my horror when a nurse suggested that, after about ten
hours of labor, it might be good for Gregorio to get himself a cup of coffee.
Good? Was she insane? It was terrible to release his hand for even a moment.
By the end, his hand was colored with slight bruises as evidence of my grip and
his steadfast love entwined with mine. I think of Lorca's beautiful lines: *"las
manos del hombre no tienen más sentido / que imitar a las raíces bajo tierra"*
("our hands have no other purpose than to imitate the roots below the earth").

The labor required to rebuild church, lives, and community needs the
steadfast grasp of many hands willing to stretch out, touch, and bear the
bruises of struggle. It is hard work. The contractions that enlarge our hearts
and minds and stretch open our systems and structures for new life produce
groaning and pain. Change hurts. *Yet,* says Paul, *I consider that the sufferings
of this present time are not worth comparing with the glory about to be revealed to
us.* (Romans 8:18)

In my own case, after eighteen hours of labor, eighteen hours of muscles
straining to open a passageway for birth, it seemed that the night's sufferings
would never end. Then I heard the welcome news. It was time to push. Was I

relieved! In all the compulsive pre-birth reading I'd done under the illusion that so many books, articles, and footnotes would prepare me for the great event, I had somehow grabbed hold of the notion that once you got to the pushing stage, birth was mere minutes ahead.

Two hours later, I was still pushing, with no baby in sight. That's when my body decided that enough was enough. My brain had no strength left to disagree. The flush of excitement and confidence that carried me through the early hours of labor was long forgotten. Now, tides of pain pulled every thought and effort into their vortex. I needed some breathing space. Forget those stupid staccato bursts of oxygen I'd practiced with my husband that were supposed to carry me through the incessant contractions. I longed for languid breaths on my own timetable. Then an actual miracle occurred. The contractions released their stranglehold, slowed to gentler waves, spaced further and further apart, until I could actually breathe instead of gasp and gulp.

I had no intimation of danger. On the contrary, drained of energy and drenched in sweat, I savored these luxurious breaths as a gift from heaven. I was a drowning person lifted to the surface, breaking free of the water's grip. So absorbed was I in this miraculous respite, that I failed to notice the concerned bustle around me. If the contractions didn't crank back up to speed soon and I didn't recommit my energy to pushing, our baby, on the threshold of birth, would suffer oxygen deprivation, possible brain damage or even death.

Something was injected into my IV to make sure my body got the message that had already shocked my brain into attention. Within minutes, my groans gave way to Ana's own cries as our newborn daughter burst into the world and filled her lungs with glorious breath. *I consider that the sufferings of this present time are not worth comparing with the glory about to be revealed to us.* And yes, the pain was absolutely nothing compared with the slippery, wet glory of our newborn daughter. A fine baby. A fine baby—like so many we receive into our arms.

During one of our Lenten healing services, a little boy named Nelson asked how Jesus knew he was God and how Jesus could be God. Our intern Anita asked him if he was a child of God, and immediately, without missing a beat,

Nelson replied, "of course I'm a child of God!" But in truth, there was no "of course" about it. Nelson is now eight. He first came to the church when he was two, along with twenty other siblings and cousins. They were all living with their mother, who had her own twelve as well as some of the cousins. The other cousins lived nearby with a grandmother. Both groups were living in shelters in this neighborhood. Nelson's mother was addicted to drugs but supposedly managing better than her sister, whose children she was raising along with the grandmother. As far as I could see, there was little managing of anything. The children lived in chaos. They slept on piles of dirty, smelly clothes, and the ones under five ran around naked, at least whenever I visited. They grazed on what food they found. Discipline consisted of screams and beatings.

Then all twenty-one began coming to church. Their mother would line them up by size, and in they would march, behind her. I thought of a mother duck followed by her brood. She would spend about fifteen minutes outside the church screaming and pushing to get them lined up like that, march in and then relinquish all control. They came in and ran wild. They had never been to church before and had no reference points for any expected behavior. Teaching them was fun—but difficult. There were a number of Sundays when I, who happen to have a high tolerance for disorder (I need it to tolerate myself), guiltily wished they would not come in so I could have some respite from the disruption they created. Some members had that sentiment more frequently. The mother resisted invitations to get help for her addiction. Nevertheless, I was really happy to see the children learning stories about Jesus and singing the songs. We made prayer books together. They did everything with gusto—whether singing God's praises or misbehaving.

After about six months, they were baptized. The waters broke and old Sarah gave birth to all twenty-one. *For the creation waits with eager longing for the revealing of the children of God.* I like the J. B. Phillips translation: *The whole creation is on tiptoe to see the wonderful sight of the children of God coming into their own.* The church was on tiptoe to see this prodigious birth drama, as each fine child left the womb of the font dripping wet, foreheads brightly anointed with the seal of their glorious inheritance. "Of course, I'm a child of God!" said Nelson, and St. Paul adds . . . *if children then heirs, heirs of God and co-heirs with Christ.* (Romans 8:17)

One week after the baptism, an abusive ex-boyfriend of the mother located them at the shelter and they were transferred to a safer apartment in Queens. They took the train back a few times, and then I lost track of them. For a number of years, they moved around Queens and Brooklyn. I often thought of them with heartache and prayed for them, but I never expected to see them again on this earth.

Last spring, Venus, the oldest sister, aged seventeen came to my office door. Their mother had gotten treatment and was in recovery from addiction and was going to school. She and her own children had just moved into a five-bedroom public-housing apartment near the church. Venus wanted me to come with her and see the apartment. There was no furniture. None. Not a bed, not a chair, not a table. They were sleeping on top of their clothes again, but this time, they were clean clothes. Members of my mother's church in New Jersey gathered enough furniture, dishes, bedding, and other items to furnish the entire apartment and hired a truck to bring it.

The family came back to church and has not missed a Sunday since. Two of the children are labeled as autistic. One is partially deaf. One week they came late to Sunday school because on the previous night, the oldest brother thought people were coming out of the TV at him, and he attacked the mother and grandmother, who almost died from the bites he inflicted on her. One nearly severed a major artery in her wrist. When Nelson dialed 911, the NYPD arrived and stood out in the hallway for a long while consulting one another about how to subdue the young man as the children and their mother inside tried futilely to restrain him.

The traumatized children still managed to come to Sunday school the next morning, excusing their lateness by explaining what had happened in their home and conceding that "they had not slept well." They got dressed and came on their own since their mother was in the hospital with the grandmother. They were shepherded to church by Venus, who also teaches Sunday school. During the week, she works as a tutor in our after-school program, helping her younger siblings and many other children with their homework, serving them a hot meal and helping teach basic computer skills that some local schools ignore. She also gets up every morning at 5 A.M. to make breakfast for her sisters and brothers.

"Of course, I'm a child of God!" said Nelson. *And if children, then heirs, heirs of God and joint heirs with Christ.* But there's no "of course" about it. Many would consider Nelson and his siblings only as heirs of a family system fraught with abuse and pain, heirs of a cycle that breeds poverty and crime, a future of dry bones. Old Sarah disagrees. At one point, it is true, her barren womb was shut, the cycle closed. Nelson and his family would have found the doors to Transfiguration locked. But after you've passed menopause and gone on to give birth to twenty-one children at a time, you tend to see things differently.

A fine baby. That's what we see in every child here, every child with an asthma pump in the pocket, with a parent in prison, every child labeled as an alien, born HIV positive, every child who is worth more to the economy locked in prison than learning in school, every child for whom so many statistics spell disaster. *A fine baby.* That's also what Moses' mother saw when she held him in her arms for the first time: *She looked and she saw that he was a fine baby.* (Exodus 2:2)

The story of Moses' birth as told in the first two chapters of Exodus is a great conspiracy story. Certainly, the statistics were against Moses. The demographics doomed him. It was open season on Hebrew baby boys, all slated to be drowned in the Nile River because the ruling pharaoh had determined that the economy and security of Egypt depended on their elimination. But when Moses' mother looked at her newborn child, she didn't see an impending tragic statistic. She didn't accept what demographic probabilities might say about her son's chances of making it. Instead, she wove a little basket of papyrus reeds and plastered it inside and out with bitumen and pitch to keep the water out.

Moses' mother built a breathing space for her fine baby, as so many mothers and grandmothers seek to do. She did it in a holy conspiracy with others —the two midwives, Shiprah and Puah, who resisted Pharaoh's orders to kill the babies on the birth stool, and his own daughter who showed defiance by having compassion on the infant's cries. It was a conspiracy of women from different classes, different positions in society, different races and resources. Moses' mother and sister were at the bottom of a society that wanted to sacrifice them. The midwives were slightly higher on the social ladder, having gained the position of civil servants of sorts, required to maintain the sacrificial system. The princess, of course, lived at the top, in the Trump Tower of Egypt. Together they conspired against the death-dealing Pharaoh so that the child Moses might grow up and come into his own.

Without these women of Exodus, Moses would have been a victim, but with them, he became a liberator. We seek to follow in their footsteps forging alliances, conspiring and organizing with other churches and people of good will. It is the way our bones come together and stand up as Ezekiel envisioned: *and the breath came into them, and they lived and stood on their feet, a vast multitude . . .*

On tiptoe, as Paul says, *to see the wonderful sight of the children of God coming into their own.* Yes! Children of God—fine babies created for life, freedom, and the pursuit of happiness. For them we build, we labor, we pray, and we conspire. For them we needed to build an extension to our church. We needed more room for the family to grow, more breathing space for the children of God coming into their own.

Enlarge the place of your tent, and let the curtains of your habitations be stretched out; hold not back, lengthen your cords and stengthen your stakes. (Isaiah 54:2) We printed this quote from the prophet on the fund-raising brochures for our building campaign. I should have remembered the painful contractions that stretched open the curtains of my own baby's habitation, but perhaps it was best that I didn't.

TWO

Construction

CHAPTER FIVE

GATHERING RESOURCES

Potholes

Some pastors have framed diplomas, awards, and certificates of appreciation hanging around their walls, bearing witness to proud accomplishments. I had a sewer permit, an irritating reminder of construction setbacks and personal inadequacy. We had already gone through quite a few starts and stops with several contractors and architects before we'd hit on the right combination. Our plan was to build an extension to our existing building in the adjoining parking lot. With the changes in our congregation and community over time, only a few of our members now had cars, and there was plenty of room for parking on the streets of this neighborhood where contrary to stereotypes, the poor usually do not own cars. We needed room instead for the children, the teenagers—for women and men, for people, not cars. We called the project "Space for Grace."

Before any digging in the parking lot could commence, we needed a sewer permit. This being my first venture into the world of construction, I was shocked to discover that such things take time. Months passed while the paperwork sat on someone's desk. It got to the point where the entire congregation vowed to stop in its tracks every day at noon to pray for this paper from the Sewer Division of the Bronx Department of Buildings, an office where Space for Grace evidently had no priority.

I remembered a story from St. Teresa's building travails. She constructed a group of small hermitages only to have the local water inspector claim that "the shadows cast by the hermitages would chill the fountains in winter and freeze the water supply." Bureaucratic idiocy prevailed, and her carefully built retreats were torn down. But Teresa promptly found a new site and planned to rebuild. We held our ground and grappled with our own local inspectors.

As it turned out, the sewer permit was the least of our problems. By the time it arrived, other roadblocks had come up. We started to raise money for the construction in 1988 and began well. Our congregational goal was $15,000. We raised $30,000 and had the first $10,000 matched five to one by St. John's Lutheran Church, the congregation in which I had grown up in Summit, New Jersey. (This suburban church that nurtured my faith as a child continues to follow and support my call to ministry as an adult, for which I am deeply grateful.) The Mission Investment Fund of our national church body agreed to loan us the rest. It was spring of 1991 when we first broke ground, in a manner of speaking. (How do you break ground in a parking lot where there is no ground? This is New York. We did it in a pothole that had opened during the winter.)

It was an exhilarating day as we gathered outside—children and teen-agers, old members and new members, Black and Hispanic, visitors from St. John's in Summit and several Lutheran churches in Long Island who'd given significant donations at the recommendation of our bishop. Everyone wanted a turn with the symbolic shovel, on which we'd all written our names in per-manent marker, and we dug up our dreams in the pothole. We joined hands and asked God's blessing on the land and longed for work of construction.

Then the promised loan was delayed because it was not clear how we would repay it. We worked on alternatives. Time went by, and the sewer per-mit began to turn yellow and curl at the edges. It was going to expire. Three years later, with the loan newly secured, we went back to the pothole for an-other try. Our national presiding bishop at the time, Herbert Chilstrom, was in New York for the second ground breaking. We dubbed it "Ground Breaking: Part Two" and did it up big, with several bishops present and articles in the local paper. We got the first loan installment, $80,000, and the foundation was laid.

Then we hit another bump in the road. Second thoughts set in, or third thoughts, over at the Mission Investment Fund. We were informed that no fur-ther monies would be forthcoming unless we could show where every dollar of repayment would come from. This occurred, despite the assurance of our bishop that he would back the loan and help us to raise the money. Evidently, mission in the Bronx was viewed by some as a poor credit risk. It was depressing that this was the view within the church, considering that it was on precisely such poor credit risks that Jesus built his church. Evidently the Mission Investment Fund was looking for the kind of rock Prudential has to offer, but there aren't any of those here on Prospect Avenue.

Where was Jeremiah when we needed him? Jeremiah is the prophet told by God to buy a field at Anathoth. The curious thing about this directive is that Anathoth was under enemy attack at the time. There was blood on the streets, and people were going hungry. Jeremiah himself was in prison. The field didn't seem like a particularly wise investment under the circumstances. But Jeremiah jumped at the chance to own a stake in a future only God could guarantee. Jeremiah bought the field. He wouldn't have lasted long over at the Mission Investment Fund.

This is not to say that we didn't take the responsibility of repaying the loan seriously. We had already identified sources committed to donate half of the money we needed to borrow, and I was confident that we could manage the rest with support from the bishop. I believed it, but I couldn't prove it.

Two more years passed while our foundation sat beside the church, inviting ridicule or defying it, depending on one's mood. A visiting expert in both funding and foundations came, stomped around on the foundation, pointed out irregularities and told me to sue. Then he told me to write proposals. I was angry with those who went back on the loan and even angrier at myself for not being able to raise more money more quickly when others raise millions. If I wrote more letters, made more calls, spent time at the Foundation Center in Manhattan and days developing proposals, I would probably be much more effective. Thinking about it was only more depressing.

Once again the whole congregation stopped to pray each day at noon. I was reminded of a great sermon by the Reverend William Watley, "Giants Keep Coming." The successful battle of David against Goliath is well known, but Goliath was just the beginning. Lesser-known giants followed: Ishbibenob, Saph, and several other nameless but equally fierce giants. Watley points out that the young David was able to slay Goliath on his own, but as the years went on, he needed help from other quarters to keep up the fight. As the years of this building project dragged on, we needed help from any allies we could find.

For weeks I'd been trying to contact Gaylord Thomas of the Evangelical Lutheran Church in America Hunger Fund who was laid up with a bad back. Gaylord has always been an ally and is one of the most dedicated advocates and tireless workers for justice in our church—probably in any church—and outside of the church, too. When I finally reached him, he offered to assist us with a no-interest loan of $75,000, with the stipulation that we match it. Somehow, by day's end, we had commitments of $80,000.

I was briefly elated by this sudden rush of progress but immediately checked my emotions. I didn't even trust myself to tell the congregation the good news. After all the times I'd stood there and said, "This time it's going to happen!" and then proven wrong, I didn't know how I could say it again. I think they all felt the way I did—we'd believe it when we could see it.

When I called the lawyer who had helped us find the second architect and the third contractor, and had made a generous donation to the project as well, he suggested that we have "a great big, rousing, ground-breaking celebration." I told him that "rousing" and "celebration" were not the operative sentiments. This was probably the only construction project in history that already had two ground breakings and no building. There would be no enthusiasm over Ground Breaking: Part Three. I certainly didn't have any. How many times could we dig around in that pothole? We needed to build, and that would be rousing enough. By then it was June of 1996, eight years after we'd first begun raising money.

Walk-a-thon

In the middle of our "Space for Grace" fund-raising, the roof on our present building gave out. How did I ever come up with the preposterous idea that we should have a walk-a-thon to raise money for our roof? Don't other churches have walk-a-thons? Don't other groups have successful walk-a-thons? We needed another $10,000 and a walk-a-thon could get us off to a good start. Planning the route was easy. It was just the right distance from Transfiguration to Immanuel Lutheran Church on Lexington Ave. and East 88th Street in

Manhattan. The five miles were a challenge but not an impossible one. The good people at Immanuel were prepared to welcome us with plenty of cold drinks and the makings for a hearty lunch. And we could take the subway back home. Everything proceeded without a hitch. About fifty enthusiastic people signed up to walk, and on that day the weather was great.

Of course, the point of a walk-a-thon is to raise money. It was definitely our point. This entails signing up sponsors. Here is where we encountered our first glitch. There was Jack, a mostly-in-recovery alcoholic. He showed up bright and early, eager to walk, doing his all for the church walk-a-thon. Where was his sponsor sheet? Well, virtually all of Jack's acquaintances are men from soup-kitchen lines, people who do not tend to invest their spare change in walk-a-thons. "I didn't really sign anyone up," Jack told me, "but I'm here to walk!" His story was repeated, with variations, by about two-thirds of the walkers, who ranged in age from five to eight-five.

Which brings up another point—the physical condition of our entourage. When eighty-five-year-old Ernestina came down the street, I wondered what she was doing. Had she come to wish us bon voyage? Of course not. "I'm here to walk, Pastor," she informed me in no uncertain terms. Ernestina sports a pacemaker and is not in the best of health. Not by a long shot. On the other hand, it didn't seem right to turn her away, an opinion with which her adult sons strongly disagreed, as I later discovered. In any case, we would have the van to drive along beside us if anyone needed a lift. The van also carried plenty of water and energizing snacks.

In spite of her age and general frailty, Ernestina was in better shape than many of our walkers, whose ranks included a number of people with AIDS, cancer, high blood pressure, and asthma. Several of the walkers had their canes. Whatever was I thinking? Surveying our group, I no longer cared about the money. I only hoped that everyone would live to complete the walk. Just as we were heading down the street, Enid called out, "Wait for me!"—Enid had a bullet lodged in her foot from a drive-by shooting. The year before, she was going to the corner store, when shooting broke out. She described freezing in fear and then shaking off her paralysis to run. When she ran, she was hit. The doctors said it would be better to leave the bullet in, but it often hurt. Nevertheless, she spent her Saturdays for several months walking all around the community with voter-registration forms, during a voter turn-out campaign the church participated in. Instead of then putting her foot up in front of the TV and taking it easy, Enid was out and about, walking the streets, urging folks to vote—the South Bronx on its feet! And now, she'd turned up for our walk, hobbling to catch up as fast as she could.

Our route took us down Bruckner Boulevard, tramping over broken bottles and empty crack vials. We crossed into Manhattan at the Willis Avenue Bridge and went down Second Avenue passing bodegas and bakeries. Every few blocks, I suggested that Ernestina might like to get into the van. Every few blocks, I was told "no thank you." Finally, after the fourth mile, several of the younger women with canes climbed into the van. Ernestina decided to keep them company. When we reached the last stretch, they disembarked. We trudged up the last few breathless blocks together and collapsed into the hospitality of Immanuel.

When the results were tallied, we'd raised $196 and lost no walkers. A few days later, the total came to $10,196. So how did this absurd walk-a-thon bring in $10,000? A homebound, elderly member of Immanuel read about the event in her church newsletter and made out a check.

As I child, I was not even permitted to sell lemonade or Girl Scout cookies because, according to my parents' logic, friends and neighbors would feel compelled to buy what they might not want. Perhaps this is why I now find the fund-raising part of my work so unappealing, even though it is very different from selling lemonade and cookies. I really do wish we had more friends and neighbors who would feel compelled to invest in this work, and I know that I ought to be out on the road more often, courting them.

For about ten years I was relieved of raising monies for our social programs until our church council voted unanimously to pull out of the organization through which most of them had been funded. There were many good reasons to do this, including the organization's debt (we alone were owed $14,000), which habitually left workers multiple paychecks in arrears. We'd put off pulling out because some money seemed better than no money and some job better than no job, but everyone finally reached their limit.

I was the only one not completely relieved by the decision. I knew it was absolutely right and should have been made far sooner, but that now I was going to have to find funding for after-school, youth, AIDS-prevention, and domestic-violence programs just at the time we needed construction funds. It became a fund-raising marathon, and I had no idea how I would ever complete it.

Table Dancing

I decided to hone my skills at a conference about fund-raising attended by *Ms.* magazine, among other groups. Someone from *Ms.* was waxing eloquent on the esteem-enhancing effects of "Taking-Our-Daughters-to-Work-Day." What did this have to do with women's needs in economically devastated neighborhoods? I got home more frustrated than when I'd left for the conference. At 11 P.M., the doorbell rang. It was Crystabel, a five-year-old girl, recently moved to the block with her mother and seven-year-old sister. She wanted to know if Hans could play. As I said, it was 11 P.M. I told her that Hans was asleep and asked where her mother was.

"She's at work," said Crystabel.

"Oh? What does she do?"

"She dances on tables."

She dances on tables. I wondered where *Ms.* would wax on that—table dancing in the wee hours in Hunts Point behind the windowless walls of the Dream Girls Bar (handy to all the truck traffic around the wholesale food market) so that in the morning, a mother can fix her two small daughters a proper breakfast and send them off to Catholic school with backpacks and white blouses under their blue-and-gray plaid jumpers.

Business must have been good at the Dream Girls Bar. Despite protests and legal challenges from the entrepreneurs of erotica and the connoisseurs of their establishments, Mayor Giuliani at the time was determined to banish money-making sex to the far fringes of the city. There is no doubt that Hunts Point qualifies as the far fringes to those who began to whine because they wanted their fun without having to travel into neighborhoods with bad air where you cannot buy the *New York Times* or a cup of Starbucks coffee. (Sometime they should try the much better Spanish coffee here, at a fraction of Starbucks price.)

All whining aside, the law to divert sex traffic joined the no-jaywalking law as part of the clean up of the quality of life in the city. But table dancing is something else. I'd already sat at the polished, oval table in city hall itself and watched the seductive dance of unaccountable wealth. It wasn't the meager bills tucked into her G-string that bound Crystabel's mother to the bar, undressing before men who tossed her their table scraps. It was the billions tucked into stock portfolios with an obscene gesture of apathy.

One of the more encouraging points the fund-raising conference made was that funders like boards who represent the community engaged in the proposed program. This sounded good, since all the members of our board, basically our church council, had South Bronx zip codes, and most lived right in the neighborhood. Soon after, a proposal that I wrote for our after-school program was rejected, and I asked the director of the foundation in question for the reason. He began by telling me that there was a problem with our board of directors. What was the problem? "What I'm going to say will probably sound offensive to you, but the problem is that your board is a group of nobodies. You need names with clout at the table, you know, movers and shakers." Table dancers who know whom to wink at?

Nobodies! No movers and shakers! He should have attended the walk-a-thon. Cheryl has a saying that puts our money troubles in perspective: "We may not have any money, but we're sure not broke!" She should know. She's climbed back from addiction, gone back to school, gotten a job as an organizer through South Bronx Churches, and now she is gaining skills in fund-raising herself.

Feeling Rich

"I felt rich!" That was the pronouncement from one of the children in the choir, "I felt rich!" A group of young people from our church were invited by St. John's Lutheran Church in the Bronx to sing Christmas carols on the main floor of the New York Stock Exchange. We were there before the bell rang at nine o'clock sharp. But before the usual business of the day, something unusual happened: our children stepped out onto the floor and sang. They sang in six different spots around the Exchange, and when we looked up above the big computer screens mounted on high, we saw our name in lights: "The children's choirs of St. John's and Transfiguration Lutheran Churches in the South Bronx will be singing on the floor of the Exchange." The message was repeated in moving, electronic glory throughout the huge expanse. We sang, and the traders listened, smiled, and put money in a basket.

Afterward, we were treated to an elegant breakfast. There were linen tablecloths and real silverware. The children at my table were counting glasses. Each had one filled with water, one filled with juice and then the waiters came bearing silver trays laden with goblets of chocolate or strawberry milk—take your pick, or have both. The waiters returned to serve scrambled eggs and crisp bacon, toast and butter and three kinds of jam. The golden fixtures in the bathrooms were another source of wonder.

"I felt rich!" I felt rich, too, but not because of this taste of wealth at the Stock Exchange. True, it was an amazing juxtaposition to see the name of Transfiguration up there in lights surrounded by the big computer screens tracking trillions of dollars. But those trillions do not belong to us. There may have been lots of money trading hands there, but it wasn't passing through the hands of the children who sang. Precious little is being diverted to the South Bronx except to build prisons. As soon as the bell on the floor rang, our singing was over, and the lights with our names went out. Business as usual got underway without us.

In the days immediately after September 11, Con Edison and Verizon workers were feverishly laying cables and wires so that Wall Street could return to some semblance of "business as usual" on the following Monday morning. I wish another phrase had been chosen. Of course, there is some security in the idea that Wall Street is on its feet and our economy is not in total collapse. My husband's family in Argentina is suffering dreadfully because of the instability there. But with all our wealth, we could do much better in our inner cities and other places where the poor congregate. I can't believe it is a lack of resources, so I can only imagine that it is the absence of value being placed on the treasure we brought that morning to the Stock Exchange. I felt rich to be in the presence of the children who got up early to sing about the unusual business of Christmas. I felt rich to be on their side of the Bethlehem exchange in which we actually believe the story of heaven kicking up a storm in a poor teenager's womb and power bared in the thin, downy arms of a baby, whose growing strength will one day turn the tables—a day that can't come soon enough.

I wish some of the folks who work on Wall Street could sit at the table and have lunch with Danielle. Her mother, Deena, died from an asthma attack brought on by smoking crack. She's ten and has eleven sisters and brothers. Some are older and on their own, and some of them went to live with a relative down South. That left five parentless children in the home. An uncle, known to be a compulsive gambler, moved in. Rumor had it that his main interest was in using the children to get money for his habit. I don't know if that is true, but there's little affection or attention shown to the children at home, except what they offer each other, which is considerable. Three of the youngest were in our summer program.

One hot day when a swimming trip was planned for the afternoon, Danielle was brought to my office in tears. It turned out that she didn't own a bathing suit. We decided that it would be all right to skip the morning math lesson and go out to get a suit. The trip took us out over lunchtime, and so we stopped at a nearby McDonald's, where Danielle ordered a Happy Meal. She got up and came back with some extra napkins. Then she began divvying up the small bag of fries into five little piles, each on its own napkin. I asked her what she was doing. "My sisters and brothers will feel sad that I got french fries and they didn't," she explained. "I'm taking them home to share."

Sitting there in McDonald's with Danielle, I felt rich.

What if the investment bankers and Danielle really could sit down together? My bishop, Stephen Bouman, posed the question when he called me out of the blue and asked me to consider being a candidate for a pastoral position at a church in Manhattan, Trinity Lutheran Church on West 100th Street and Amsterdam Avenue. The call did not come as a complete surprise. About six months earlier, one Sunday on vacation, I had stumbled into this church by accident, when a subway delay caused me to miss worship with a different congregation. I went in and found out that their pastor had left and that it was to be their interim pastor's first Sunday.

Somewhere in the Bible it says that the word of God is a two-edged sword.

It struck a blow that day when the gospel was read and I heard Jesus calling
Peter to get out of his boat. Actually, what I heard was Jesus calling me to get
out of my boat. I was seasick in my pew, overcome with *malabarriga*. Could
God really want me to get out of my boat? Could God really want me to leave
Transfiguration? Surely not. And then the bishop's call came.

In the past, whenever the possibility of another pastoral position was presented to me, I never gave it serious consideration. I never even bothered
to pray about it. I politely declined without a second thought. But this time, I
felt that at least I had to be open to the possibility. The church is located on a
corner facing a large public housing project. On the other side, there are condominiums and co-op apartments. In addition, numerous immigrants, especially Mexicans, live throughout the neighborhood. Columbia University and
Union Theological Seminary are not far either. What a rich mixture of people
surround the church!

Gregorio was quite open to the possibility of a change. I agreed to meet
with the church call committee, the group of people selected to interview
potential pastors, but not without much trepidation and reluctance at the
thought of leaving here. Our children shared none of my ambivalence. They
were not going to move under any circumstances. One evening we were playing a new Monopoly game with a New York City theme. They noted with disgust that the cheapest property on the board was the Bronx (the NYC version
of Baltic Place). "What a dis! What's wrong with the people who made this?" I
nodded in agreement with my children, who turned on me as one: "You
should talk! You're just as bad! You're a traitor! You want to leave the Bronx
yourself!" I couldn't convince them that I didn't really want to leave the Bronx
but that I was trying to follow the proddings of the Holy Spirit. In truth, I was
still trying to convince myself.

I had several wonderful meetings with the call committee which induced
further *malabarriga* as I felt the day of stepping out of my boat approaching.
Then a letter arrived telling me that they had decided I was not the right pastor for them. It hurt, but the sting of rejection was washed over by waves of relief at not having to leave here after all. Perhaps I'd misunderstood. It wasn't
about leaving the boat, just making the boat bigger, a process which was unsettling enough.

CHAPTER SIX

SUMMER CONSTRUCTION REPORTS

Theophany, Part One

Theophany is the technical word for the presence of God breaking into conscious human experience. It comes from *theo* (God) and *phaneia* (to show); literally, "God's showing." In the Hebrew Scriptures, a theophany was often associated with attention-grabbing earthquakes or mountaintop thunderclaps. The powerful shaking and trembling of the Earth signaled the presence of the all-powerful Creator. It happened on Mt. Sinai, which "shook violently" amidst clouds of smoke, thunder, and lightning right before Moses received the Ten Commandments.

According to St. Matthew, it happened on the hill where Jesus was crucified:

> The earth quaked; the rocks were split . . . the centurion, together with the others guarding Jesus, had seen the earthquake and all that was taking place, and they were terrified and said, "In truth this was the son of God." (Matthew 27:51ff.)

And it happened in the summer of 1996 on Prospect Avenue and 156th Street in the South Bronx. The earth shook, rocks split apart, and clouds of dust filled the air. An orange and brown backhoe set to work, sounding the power of God breaking through, theophany! At last, construction resumed on Space for Grace!

I was giddy with excitement, but not for long. In addition to theophany, we now had dead phone lines, severed mistakenly in the sacred commotion, and we were also trying to run our annual summer program. We thought we could manage eighty children and a construction site at the same time because the initial work would all be outside of the building. By the time the outer wall came down, we would have to leave to spend the week at a church in White Plains. In addition, we planned a lot of trips to get away from the noise. The program itself was a space for grace in the summer, when youth have a lot of time on their hands. We didn't want to cancel it.

The stupidity of this decision was quickly apparent. The construction crew had neglected to mention that they needed to build a temporary wall inside before the outer wall could be knocked down. It was becoming clear that before we would have more space, we would have to make do with a lot less. In fact, we had to move all activities into the sanctuary, which quickly became jammed with furniture, boxes of supplies, bookshelves, cartons of pantry food, and lots of nesting places for displaced rodents. More trips were added to get the children out of the building.

Rise and Shine

Rise and shine and give God your glory, glory!
Rise and shine and give God your glory, glory!
Rise and shine and give God your glory, glory—
Children of the Lord!

Jay was standing in the back of the church, bleary-eyed from having to get up before the ungodly hour of 9 A.M. to be at work, singing "Rise and Shine" along with the children during the morning's opening song and prayer time. Anything to avoid his assigned reading. We don't have enough money to pay people to work all day for seven weeks with the eighty kids in our summer day camp, so we also serve as a site for the city's Summer Youth Employment Program, which provides jobs for teenagers. We can choose most, but not all, of the youth who will work with us. We usually have jobs for about twenty-five. Working with them, giving them job training and experience, is part of our summer ministry. Sometimes working with the teenage staff takes more energy than working with the children. Fortunately we have our wonderful, indefatigable youth worker, Ms. Debra Simmons. Debra is the mother who first came to the church looking for help with her two young sons. Over the years, passion for her own children's welfare spilled over into a passion for hundreds of young people who come to her for counsel and support.

After making it through the first week of orientation, Jay, who was new to us, was arrested for robbery and assault over the weekend. He got out on bail, but we didn't want him working with the children. On the other hand, it seemed counterproductive to leave him at loose ends, with nothing to do all summer but sit around waiting for the outcome of his case. Debra had her hands full shepherding the other twenty-four teenagers, many of whom were more interested in each other than in the children they were hired to teach and care for, so I volunteered to come up with a plan for Jay.

At the time I had been reading *Makes Me Wanna Holler* by Nathan McCall, a book about his experiences growing up, getting first into trouble, then into prison but finally ending up as a reporter for the *Washington Post*. Time spent reading and reflecting was the key to what made such a change possible for him. Perhaps, I thought, this might be helpful for Jay. Instead of working with the kids, he would spend the time on various reading and writing/reflection assignments.

Jay was far from enthusiastic. Reading and writing were not what he had in mind for a summer job. On the other hand, criminal behavior was not what we had in mind for a summer employee, and no other job prospects loomed on Jay's horizon. This seemed to be a way to build a temporary wall to hold Jay up until something stronger was in place. We went to the library to pick out some books. Jay had trouble concentrating on the reading, and the construction racket provided a ready excuse. After a few days, however, he seemed to get into the writing assignments. One of the first he did was titled "My Life in Five Years." In his essay, Jay expressed a desire to graduate from high school and get a job as a car mechanic. He preferred to live in a house, but would settle for an apartment at first. He hoped to get married and have two children, a boy and a girl. Then Jay concluded, "But I have to see what will happen from 5 years from now. Maybe it will happen. I want it to happen. If it do my life will be great."

At seventeen, Jay's goals were good, but he had no idea of how to reach them. He would simply "see what will happen." He didn't have confidence that he could actually do things to make his goals more likely to happen. It wasn't surprising. The world he lived in hadn't given him much hope of power to take his own future into his hands and shape it effectively according to his dreams. His family didn't help. I don't know what happened with Jay's own parents, but he was currently living with his alcoholic sister-in-law and his brother. It provided little more than a place to come in off the street and lie down.

Jay made lists on what he was doing that might help him realize his goals and what he was doing that would hinder them. I wasn't able to find an ongoing mentor, but I did find a few older and wiser African-American men willing to meet with Jay on several occasions. Before each meeting, he was incredibly nervous. I think to him it felt as though he were appearing before the judge. But each time he came back clearly pleased. The men encouraged Jay to begin attending church, and on their word he did.

Another assignment for Jay was to create a monthly budget for himself and his future family. He had to first determine how much money he would make as a beginning car mechanic—his stated goal—and then figure out his expenses. After doing the dreaded reading, he visited some garages and got salary quotes. In order to come up with a realistic grocery bill, Jay planned imaginary weekly menus. There was much missing from the list—no snacks or sweets, for instance, items I couldn't imagine him giving up, but I let it go. I suggested that he begin with one child rather than two and include items needed for the care of a baby. Jay blithely added "Baby Stuff" to his list. Jay was becoming proud of this project and talked with some of the other teenaged boys about it. The summer job was turning out to be less of a bore than he'd anticipated. Several of them asked if they could go with him when he went to the supermarket with the list and a calculator. Before they left, each one looked at the list and tried to estimate the total. I promised to treat the one who made the best guess to lunch. After about an hour and a half, the boys came back, all worked up—"That baby stuff is mad expensive!" I hoped they'd remember that.

* * *

I had my own budget problems and spent the afternoon with our lawyer going over construction finances. To pay off everything we would owe, we still needed to raise $100,000. Some of it would come from friends of our church in Germany and some from a church in Manhattan and still others around the city—but not all of it. I left the lawyer to complete the last bit of paperwork needed by Gaylord for the loan. When it was finally signed, sealed, and mailed, I knew that I should have felt grateful and relieved. Instead, I was worn down. My energy felt diverted from where it should be in ministry. I felt like shouting along with Jay, "This construction stuff is mad expensive!" And money is only one of the costs.

We had a women's meeting and made plans for some relaxing summer activities—Bible studies in my backyard garden, a visit to the Bronx Botanical Garden, lunch at their favorite air-conditioned restaurant (an all-you-can-eat Sizzler), and a trip to Bear Mountain to ride paddleboats in the lake. In spite of these plans, there was a feeling of discouragement that too few people were doing too much work. I realized that the woman in the group who felt worst had the same issue at home, shouldering all the responsibility; nevertheless, it left me feeling like a bad pastor, unable to maintain high levels of energy and enthusiasm.

Whom was I kidding? I felt like a bad mother, too, stressed out, lacking patience. "I didn't see you smile yet today, Mommy," said Hans, and worse, "I asked you not to look at me like that, Mommy. Why don't you listen to me?" My eyes mirrored dissatisfaction at my children, when it was mostly myself with whom I was dissatisfied. The ups and downs of the construction pulled me up and down as well. Soon after the backhoe began work, we were informed that the permit file for our project had been lost by the building department. My heart sank. Then the contractor came to pick up his set of keys. He must expect to need them soon, I thought. My spirits rose. Rise and shine. Rise and fall.

Not sleeping well didn't help. Even when we turned on the air conditioning to mute the sounds of the street, which increase by many decibels in the summer, I would awaken to every shout and gunshot. Gregorio can usually sleep through it, and even if not, he can return to sleep with ease. I can't. My whole system goes on red-alert at the sound of gunfire, and even if I'm lying down, I feel like I am on the edge of my seat, ready to spring. I wanted to take the damned guns and bury them at the bottom of the sea, but the problem was not the guns. You can't drown the grief and the anger. The violence is a fever and not the sickness itself. It is the fitful reaction of a body that seeks to throw off disease. Biological warfare spreads deadly pestilence; economic, racial, and spiritual warfare promote this sickness and this fever. Many hands pull the trigger of every gun, and most of them live somewhere else. These thoughts don't promote sleep, either. I wondered if the breathing disciplines of yoga would help. I should take yoga classes, I thought . . . but when? The thought of the yoga classes I should now take only made things more stressful.

Because of the construction, we couldn't take much vacation, but we did spend a week at my aunt and uncle's house in Florida. It was a wonderful week of lazy living. The slow tide of light that swept the beach to brightness each morning washed through me as well. But too soon it was over and back to the Bronx.

As we drove from the airport and hit Bruckner Boulevard, Hans cried de-lightedly, "We're home, we're home! I can tell by the drawings on the build-ings." "That's graffiti, Hans," said Ana. We came into the house and found the door to our bedroom locked from the inside. How this ever occurred remains a mystery. For an hour, we tried various keys, an awl, a screwdriver, a hammer. At one point, Gregorio accidentally pushed against a chest in the hall piled high with discarded mystery books. They toppled down, frightening the cat, who scratched Gregorio's bare feet right down the line of a big vein. Blood spurted all over the floor and into the kitty litter. The box of Band-Aids was locked in the bedroom. Sometime after midnight, we gave up, broke down the door and fell into bed. Rise and shine. Rise and fall.

The next morning I went to church for Sunday worship and found a mess. The contractor had needed some more closets emptied, and everything had been dumped in the sanctuary, which had become our only catch-all space. There was no other room big enough. I went to the altar and found the white linen covered with mouse shit. They must have smelled crumbs and wine from

Communion. It was so bad that I had to take it off and leave the bare wood. The extra linen was in the laundry and hadn't been returned.

It didn't matter. Another tide of light washed through our lives and brightened our shore. Nina, who had recently been hospitalized for a collapsed lung, came in with her six children, four of her own and two in foster care, all ready for their baptisms. Her lungs were weak, her breathing labored, and she needed a cane to walk, but she was all smiles surrounded by the shining candles held by her newly washed and anointed brood. Rise and shine.

Gates of Heaven

Our building efforts in the summer of '96 were not limited to our own block. The same year we celebrated Ground Breaking: Part One, in the pothole, we were breaking ground with our group of ecumenical partners in South Bronx Churches to build the first Bronx Nehemiah homes. The housing takes its name from the prophet Nehemiah, who took action after the Babylonian Captivity to realize his vision of a reconstructed Jerusalem:

> "You see the evil blight in which we stand: how Jerusalem lies in ruins and its gates have been gutted by fire. Come, let us rebuild the walls of Jerusalem, so that we may no longer be an object of derision!" Then I explained to them how the favoring hand of my God had rested upon me, and what the king had said to me. They replied, "Let us be up and building!" And they undertook the good work with vigor. (Nehemiah 2:17–18)

Already a desolate, desperate corner of Brooklyn had been transformed into a thriving community through the construction of 2,300 single-family Nehemiah homes built by East Brooklyn Congregations, a sister organization to South Bronx Churches (SBC). Leaders from SBC, fired-up after our successful Sign Up and Take Charge Campaign, which listed housing as a top priority, visited Brooklyn and were inspired to adopt the Nehemiah plan to build similar homes and renewed neighborhoods on our own rubble-strewn tracts of land. The ground breaking took place in the pouring rain, but everyone was too happy to care. We just stood outside in the mud as the backhoe went into action and the words of Scripture were read: *How awesome is this place ... this is the gate of heaven.* (Genesis 28:17)

In the first round of construction, 224 single-family homes and 288 condominiums (required by the city for reasons for density) were built, sold and occupied. These homes have the lowest minimum-income requirement ($20,000) of all new housing in the Bronx and the lowest carrying charges ($350–$475 a month). The money to begin construction came from an interest-free loan pool of ecumenical contributors, including $500,000 from the Evangelical Lutheran Church in America. Roman Catholic loans totaled $250,000. The other major financial partners were two Episcopalian churches in Manhattan that have each loaned $800,000.

In June of 1996, we held our dedication. I'm sure that Nehemiah himself would have been pleased. The street was no longer *"an object of derision."* Thirty-five square blocks were transformed by the homes, and now a central area was transfigured for the party. The street became a dance floor surrounded by tables covered with white cloths. Salsa Caterers was there to dish out heaping portions of rice, chicken, plantains, and salad. Thousands of homeowners, friends, children, those who helped with initial loan monies, church leaders and members who couldn't afford even these low-cost homes but who worked for their neighbors who could, all were there admiring, eating, talking, laughing, and finally dancing in the street.

Twelve years before, this had been a dim vision. Now we could see it for real. Bricks were raised by a people, not for Pharaoh, but for themselves. *How awesome is this place ... this is the gate of heaven,* we had read at the groundbreaking. Now many of the gates by these homes were entwined with roses or morning glories. At Christmastime they are lit up like Las Vegas. Maybe our own vision of space for grace would one day flower, too.

In his essay "The Street Is for Celebration," Thomas Merton discusses the question of what makes a street inhabited: "The quality of a city depends on whether the streets are inhabited or just occupied ... when a street is not inhabited it is a dump. A street may be a dump for thousands of people who aren't there. They have been dumped there, but their presence is so provisional they might as well be absent. They occupy space by being displaced in it." This is a good description of city planner Robert Moses's dumping of poor families in the South Bronx in the late fifties—and of the inner city in general as a dumping ground for toxic despair. Merton speaks of the alienation found on such streets, where people either submit or become violent. But he suggests an alternative: "Instead of being formally and impersonally put in their place by the street, people must transform the street and make it over so that it is livable. A street can be inhabited if the people on it begin to make their life credible by changing their environment. Living is more than submission; it is creation."

In the end, Merton says that what makes a street truly inhabited is "when it becomes a space for celebration." He wrote of the early Mayan cities of Guatemala and of Monte Albán in Mexico, built in 500 and 300 B.C.E. He observes that these were the first cities on this continent and that their primary purpose was neither economic nor military; rather, they were built as grand celebratory spaces.

I watched six-year-old Elena dancing the *punta* with brazen grace, a dance from her native Guatemala. Instead of the quetzal feathers that adorned the heads of celebrants in those earlier cities, her hair was arrayed in a rainbow of plastic barrettes. Our streets were once joyless deserts, but they are surely inhabited now.

In 1996 our homes won the National Excellence Award, and Henry Cisneros from the Clinton administration came to town. Cisneros's advance team was pretty comic and amazingly disorganized. At least it was amazing to me as a member of his hosting group. His security people told us that he would have his own van. He didn't, and instead was assigned to go in the van of a local church. His security chief was in another car, but he forgot where he parked it. The church van ended up hitting another van. When the driver stopped to check if there was any damage, Cisneros's team, glancing at their watches, said, "Oh, don't stop, just keep driving—they don't look bothered." Fortunately, there wasn't any damage to the other van.

We showed Cisneros around the homes, and then we went on to the high school, our other major building accomplishment, the Bronx Leadership Academy. It had just moved into a splendid, newly renovated space. Six million dollars can do marvelous things with an old warehouse. Imagine how much could be accomplished with $100 million! According to a *Daily News* report, that was the amount misplaced by those charged with school renovation: "The School Construction Authority is scrambling to account for $100 million it received in state aid to repair schools over the past five years."

When I was leaving the house to attend a meeting with other leaders from SBC and sister organizations around the city, Ana asked me what the evening's agenda was going to be. I told her about the missing millions. "Wow!" said Ana, "That's a lot of money! How can anyone lose that much money?" The Reverend Johnny Ray Youngblood from Brooklyn also took up the theme, "That's a lo—tta of money!" and soon the entire assembly was shouting the refrain "That's a lo—tta of money!" A lot of money not going into the education of our children.

On the other hand, we could be proud of our stewardship. The science lab was ready for experiments. The gymnasium was ready for exercise. The computers were up and running. The classrooms were filled with teenagers (including Rakita and Latoya, church members who waved shyly when they saw me) sitting more attentively than any high school group I'd seen in a long time. The school simply shouts pride and shows what parents, churches, educators, and administrators on the board of education are capable of at their best.

Understanding that housing itself does not build a community, the education of children was a major priority for new homeowners and for all of us who organized to build the homes. In addition to developing the Bronx Leadership Academy, parents began to organize for improvements in elementary and junior high schools. A group from our church decided to approach the school across the street:

The four young mothers praying in Transfiguration Lutheran Church were nervous. They had been preparing for weeks, but they were still nervous. They asked God to help them and to melt a heart of stone if necessary. Their children would be entering school in the fall for the first time, and the mothers had arranged a meeting with the local elementary school principal as part of the South Bronx Churches parents organizing project. The mothers were eager to put the training they had received from SBC and the Public Education Association to work—they planned to survey nearby schools, interview the principals, visit classrooms, and evaluate which school would be the best place for their children. (*Signs of Hope in the City*, chapter by Lee Stuart)

The meeting was a failure because the principal cut it short after refusing to answer their first, respectfully framed question: "My child is going to enter the first grade in this district next year. Can you please explain your safety and security policies so that I can be sure that my daughter will be safe if she goes to this school?" Simultaneously, the meeting was a success because the women left with rekindled anger on behalf of their children fueling their motivation to work with others for educational reform in the South Bronx. We worked in two areas. The first was to encourage and assist parents in becoming more informed and engaged in their children's education. Obviously, moving from that basic premise to significant change in the public school system was going to take a long time. The second project we undertook, with the guidance and tenacity of organizer Lee Stuart, was the formation of the new public high school.

In the early nineties, then Schools Chancellor Joseph Fernandez invited community organizations to establish small, thematic high schools in collaboration with the Board of Education. We were excited by the possibility of creating a smaller school, a school that would prepare young people for college without restricting admission only to those with the highest test scores. It would be a school that would give students tools for community leadership now and in the future.

It was a daunting challenge. For two years, already tired parents, pastors, organizers, and educators went to interminable meetings and met with intractable problems but still believed and worked to come up with a proposal acceptable to the Board of Education. Naysayers abounded. At some points the process felt to me like a blur of meetings, allegations, lies, conflicts, stress, headaches, heartaches, shouts and whispers, slander, frustration, and delays. But it was worth it, and it became my privilege to speak at the dedication.

I recalled the story of Daniel, Shadrach, Meshach, and Abednego. When they refused to bow down to King Nebuchadnezzar's golden statue, he threw them into a furnace of blazing fire. That is where we had spent a lot of our time back when the school was still a dream. Because we refused to bow down to low expectations and Board of Ed business as usual, the furnace was stoked way up, and some of our leaders were burned, lives were threatened. Even then, we kept on walking through the flames like Shadrach, Meshach, and Abednego, and like them, came out of the furnace in triumph into this dream-come-true public high school.

Cisneros was duly impressed with the school. On the way back, I had a conversation with him about the Lutheran Church and theology. He said he had always thought of it as a "very white church" and wanted to know what Lutheran worship was like in the South Bronx and what the rest of the U.S. Lutheran Church thinks of us. We talked about Martin Luther and incultura-tion and worship, something I did not expect to be discussing with the U.S. Secretary for Housing and Human Development. I explained that while the Lutheran Church was brought to the Americas by German and Scandinavian immigrants, it slowly began to attract people from many different ethnic groups.

Our early heritage is both burden and blessing. Our past continues to shape our present to a large extent and the U.S. Lutheran church still remains very white. But our theological heritage has growing appeal for a wide range of persons and Luther's belief that the church's worship should reflect the lan-guage and culture of the people has undergirded many changes. For Luther, it meant translating the Bible into the sixteenth-century German vernacular. Today, it means that in the metropolitan New York area, Lutheran churches worship in twenty-two different languages.

Theophany, Part Two

The real wonder of our high school became clear to me on Pentecost. A small group of young people gathered at church very early in order to fill one hun-dred red balloons with helium and tie long red ribbons to them for our Pente-cost celebration. Pentecost is the day we celebrate the storied coming of the Holy Spirit to Jesus' disciples after he was no longer physically present. A rush of wind and tongues of fire rocked the room in which they were gathered, like lightning on Mt. Sinai, another instance of biblical theophany. Everyone there was zapped, and *they began to speak in other languages, as the Spirit gave them ability ... and at this sound the crowd gathered and was bewildered, because each one heard them speaking in the native language of each.* (Acts 2:4,6) Others decided that it must be the babbling of a bunch of drunks, which is how many of our best ideas for the high school were greeted. We consider Pentecost as the Church's birthday, the beginning of a new community, a new Spirit-filled and powered people that embraces not only all nations, but all ages and classes:

I will pour out my Spirit upon all flesh,
And your sons and your daughters shall prophesy,
And your young men shall see visions and your old men shall dream
    dreams.
Even upon my slaves, both men and women,
In those days I will pour out my Spirit; and they shall prophesy.
(Acts 2:17–18)

One ribbon got taped to the end of every pew, and the balloons rose high above us, a host of joyful heralds. When the Pentecost story was read, the children whirled in with the sound of wind whooshing from their lips and a theophany of red and yellow streamers flaming from their hands. I thought of Abba Joseph, one of the fourth-century Desert Fathers: "Abba Lot went to see Abba Joseph and said, 'Abba, as much as I am able, I practice a small rule, a little fasting, some prayer and meditation, and remain quiet, and as much as possible I keep my thoughts clean. What else should I do?' Then the old man stood up and stretched out his hands toward heaven, and his fingers became like ten torches of flame. And he said, 'If you wish, you can become all flame.' "

That afternoon, a young woman named Passion did just that and spoke out for justice. Whoever named her was a prophet. She was one of the youth chosen by her peers to speak at an assembly of South Bronx Churches. We had gathered from about twenty-five churches and a local mosque to identify future issues and formulate preliminary strategies. We were joined by a spirited group of students from the Bronx Leadership Academy. Sherri Perry was a

classmate and friend of Passion's. Like Passion, Sherri was an honor-roll student at the high school. She dreamed of becoming a pediatric nurse or doctor.
One spring day, while walking home from school, Sherri, age fifteen, was
dragged into a nearby building and strangled. More than a month later, there
were still no suspects, and no apparent progress had been made on the case.
The students and their families had felt secure that this was a safe school, but
now, only a few blocks away, one of their own was murdered.

Passion gave full voice to the students' fear and anger over what had and
had not happened. The impressive thing is that she didn't stop there. She presented a plan of action developed by the students themselves. They wanted to
meet with the Police Borough Commander within ten days to get a report on
the investigation into Sherri's death. They wanted police patrols in the area
when school was in session. They wanted to meet with the HPD Commissioner to demand that the abandoned building where Sherri was taken be de-
molished. They wanted the renovation of a second, neighboring building that
appeared salvageable. They wanted the Bronx borough president, Fernando
Ferrer, to attend these meetings as their ally. They wanted him to put up
$100,000 of his discretionary funds as a reward for the arrest and conviction of
Sherri's murderer. They wanted one hundred leaders from our congregations
to stand with them at these actions. This was their list of wants—not more
CDs or designer clothing, but justice. This is what the school is about—intelligent analysis, planning and action, young people taking charge of their lives
and their community.

Instead of being overwhelmed by their grief, becoming cynical, numb or
exploding with frustration and turning their anger against each other, these
young people were modeling a better way for the adults around them. It was a
superb example of what we mean when we say that action is the oxygen of our
organization. In the very act of speaking before this group, Passion became a
towering current of energy, electrifying the room, a pillar of fire to blaze our
way through the wilderness, a one-woman theophany. Most Sunday after-
noons, having been up since 5 A.M., I am ready to fade, but not that day.

Molech's Throat

You must not hand over any of your children to have them sacrificed to Molech.
(Leviticus 18:21)

The biblical prophets unequivocally denounced the god Molech to whom human sacrifice was made, especially children. Molech was also associated with uncontrolled greed and economic gain. Isaiah condemns those who bring offerings to Molech: *You journeyed to Molech with oil and multiplied your perfumes* (Isaiah 57:9). Evidently an investment in Molech was good for one's net worth, but Molech's thirst was not satisfied with oil. Molech exacted a higher price: *You that slaughter your children in the valleys and under the clefts of the rocks ... you have poured out a drink offering ... your children's blood.* (Isaiah 57:5–6)

In the 1990s, while we were building Space for Grace and organizing with others for the construction of Nehemiah homes and the Bronx Leadership Academy, there was one other major investment in the youth of the South Bronx. Nineteen ninety-eight brought the dedication of a state-of-the-art facility that had been in the works. This one was topped with barbed wire, twisted coils of cynicism that glinted and winked in the sunshine. It was "New Horizons," a new prison for youths aged ten to fifteen, built on the edge of the "Hub," a major South Bronx shopping district at 149th St. and Third Ave. You have to pass it on your way to buy shoes, jeans, T-shirts, earrings, or toys. A Burger King, complete with play station, is directly next door, leading my children to comment on the cruelty of the incarcerated kids having to smell unattainable french fries day and night.

This prison has the capacity to "serve" thousands of youth annually, but it's not big enough. It was built, along with a second one in Brooklyn, to replace the dilapidated Spofford Juvenile Center in Hunts Point, not far from the church. Spofford was built in 1957 as a home for runaway boys, not as a juvenile prison. In 1978, it was "retrofitted" as a juvenile detention facility with secure locks, bars on windows, and razor wire but "programming for children remained difficult." Programming for children?

According to a report by the NYC Department of Juvenile Justice (DJJ), until now the city had never built a prison for "youngsters charged with the commission of a criminal act." Now we're catching up. Two new prisons were built to replace one old one, but the need for prison space was underestimated even by the most cynical. The overflow of youthful offenders had been held on a floating jail barge once used for adults until the old Spofford unit was renovated as Bridges Juvenile Center. Plans are already under development to expand the two new facilities as well.

These bridges to nowhere are good business. It is lucrative to keep these children trapped inside the system. The layout for educating youth around here who are not imprisoned is about $6,000 per child a year. What goes into the coffers for incarcerated youth is $130,670 for one child for one year. The facilities here serve the entire city of New York, but the assumption is that most youth who will not be kept at the twin facility in Brooklyn will come from our neighborhood, so it has been built here to keep transportation costs down. Money had to be cut from the city budget for education and other youth programs, but evidently, it was no problem to find funding to build two new prisons and renovate a third. Where there is the will, resources appear. Molech has deep pockets and prefers to spend it on keeping the kids behind bars.

The New York City DJJ has an annual budget of $53 million, most of which (65 percent) is used to run the three "secure facilities." A mere 3 percent is used for prevention and after-care. Contrary to what one might expect, the recent growth in the city's juvenile prison population is not due to an increase in violent criminal behavior among young people. The numbers have swelled with the incarceration of youths charged with low-level, non-violent offenses. In fact, only 10 percent of the jailed youths are charged with violent crimes. Other cities (Portland, Chicago) have had success by investing in alternative programs that have proven to be more effective in the long run—and in the short run. Such programs are less expensive and the youth show a better rehabilitation rate than those who find themselves behind bars at an early age. Nevertheless, NYC has no plan to expand the Department of Probation's Alternative Detention Program which costs a mere $22 a day, compared with the $358 daily incarceration expense.

The DJJ's report is quick to pitch the economic advantages of the new Bronx facility under the heading: "DJJ as a Neighbor Provides Economic Revitalization." We are told that the prison houses a "specially designed community room" with a kitchenette, TV/VCR and a movie screen. Community groups can rent out the space for their "affairs." Local merchants can look forward to increased business round-the-clock: "Operating in three assigned shifts per day, DJJ employees will become consumers at many area businesses in the community."

Of course, the true cost of this great revitalization might put a damper on all the fun affairs and financial boom, but not to worry: "Safeguards were built into the design of the building that prevents youth from viewing members of the community and vice versa. . . . The facilities have been designed so that there will be no verbal or visual contact between detained residents and passersby on the streets." What you see is the landscaping around the prison, a beautiful, well-tended oasis that it is hoped will draw your eyes away from the barbed wire on the roof, which was selected from an array of choices that include Maze, Supermaze, Detainer Hook Barb, and Silent Swordsman Barbed Tape—all sounding like the names of video games.

When it comes to prisons, the South Bronx is certainly not a place of second-rate leftovers. Here, it's nothing but the best, top-of-the-line, state-of-the-art, first class. The in-depth research of Eric Schlosser in his seminal essay for the *Atlantic Monthly* in 1998, "The Prison-Industrial Complex" elucidates a few innocuous looking names on the DJJ's Bronx Facility Fact Sheet: Kaplan, McLaughlin & Diaz of San Francisco are named as architect and CRSS, named as contractor. These are among the bigwigs of prison construction, regulars in the trade newspaper *Correctional Building News*. According to Schlosser,

the prison-industrial complex now includes some of the nation's largest architecture and construction firms, Wall Street investment banks that handle prison bond issues and invest in private prisons, plumbing supply companies, food-service companies, health-care companies, companies that sell everything from bullet-resistant security cameras to padded cells available in a "vast color selection." A directory called the *Corrections Yellow Pages* lists more than a thousand vendors.

In choosing a firm from San Francisco, the DJJ went straight to the top—
to California, where the state system alone is 40 percent bigger than the Federal Bureau of Prisons. Schlosser's research shows that California jails hold
more inmates than France, Great Britain, Germany, Japan, Singapore, and
the Netherlands altogether. Plenty of practice for the architects at KMD.
We're adopting other West Coast designs as well.

The tremendous expense to build new prison space has left little money
for less costly programs within the system, such as drug treatment and proba-
tion. Unsurprisingly, this failure only increases the need for further incarcera-
tions—and the need for more new cells.

While this is a vicious cycle for some, it is a windfall for others. Prisons have
become a multibillion-dollar industry. One private firm has annual revenues
of more than $1 billion. Prisons are big business on Wall Street and, increas-
ingly, in the global marketplace.

A block away from the "New Horizons" prison is an intermediate school.
The school is in one of the city's educational "dead zones," defined as areas
where less than one-third of the children are reading at grade level. All of the
dead-zone schools, comprising approximately 70,000 children, are in predominantly poor, Latino and African-American communities. At this school, as at
several others near our church, fewer than one in five students is performing at
grade level. This is no secret to school and city administrators. The failure had
been identified by the State Education Department for more than a decade.

As parents from our congregations began looking into the issue, we were
horrified. While the persistent failure of these schools may have many sources,
it has clearly been fueled by greed and by an utter lack of accountability on the
part of those entrusted with the task of educating children. I sat with church
members listening to the testimony of local school-board members. The
board treasurer admitted to purchasing a $250 platinum-and-gold pen with
school monies. When asked how she could justify this expenditure in a school
district that lacked money for basic textbooks, she answered that she had a lot
of documents to sign. Another board member claimed that his frequent trips
to Puerto Rico financed with school money were part of a project to investi-
gate "ethnic breakfast food." A third found that he needed to buy a $650 elec-
tronic organizer with public funds. He probably needed it to keep tract of his
travel itinerary.

The *Daily News*, in an article entitled "Livin' High off Kids" documented more of the dirty details. The same district aforementioned spent 43 percent of its entire budget on travel, hotels and meals, compared with the citywide norm of 8.6 percent. In order to improve education in the South Bronx, they somehow found it salutary to attend conferences in Orlando, St. Thomas, and Honolulu. Spring finals saw them off to Santa Fe and Albuquerque. All this travel must have required considerable refueling, as they ran up bills of $29,500 in food expenses. To top it off, with money from the special education budget, one member bought a $625 blue-leather chair for her home. Meanwhile, teachers were reaching into their own pockets for things like paper and pencils. It has never been unusual for children in our after-school program to line up to make copies of classmates' copies of readers, stapled-together sheets in black and white. The children had never laid hands or eyes on the colorfully engaging originals. A fourth-grade class attended by some of our children had only dog-eared first-grade reading materials. The new, grade-level books were "missing," yet $917 was spent on doughnuts.

That was in the 1990s before Mayor Bloomberg took over the Board of Ed as the 2002 school year came to a close. The jury is still out on what changes are in store, but hopefully not a jury of justices like Alfred D. Lerner. Upon hearing testimony that the schools are often limited to seriously out-of-date books (and often not a sufficient supply of even those), Lerner responded, presumably with a straight face: "surely a library that consists predominantly of classics should not be viewed as one that deprives students of the opportunity to a sound basic education." A surfeit of Shakespeare? Justice Lerner must have overdosed on those over-priced doughnuts.

In the same week that the "Livin' High off Kids" article appeared in 1994, an editorial in *El Diario*, the Hispanic daily, ran a long article about the unprecedented number of asthma cases in the South Bronx. According to *El Diario*, "the air the area's residents breathe is some of the most lethal anywhere in the United States." The children here couldn't read or breathe; but nonetheless, quality-of-life crimes were down, according to Mayor Giuliani.

Parents felt rightly that their children were being treated like dirt, and there was no difficulty in organizing a group to gather in the park outside city hall after the mayor and chancellor Rudy Crew refused to respond to requests for action. The problem was not limited to the South Bronx, so we joined with fellow IAF organizing groups from around the city. Our leaders spoke out to challenge the chancellor and the mayor on their continuing renewal of contracts for principals and superintendents who persisted in failing to educate the children in their trust. We demanded that they recruit and equip new principals for the job and meantime support more alternative schools.

It was two days after Palm Sunday, and I couldn't help but think of Baby. Baby was the donkey who for several years led our annual Palm Sunday procession around the block. In order to dramatize the celebration, I came up with the idea of making a papier-mâché donkey head and attaching a gray sheet to it, creating a costume children could wear when we went around the block singing songs and waving palm branches in memory of Jesus' entrance into Jerusalem. The children took it a step further and decided that it would be even better to have another child ride on top of the "donkey" as Jesus. This was great until their backs gave out, about a few yards from the start. The next year, I spotted an ad about ponies to rent for birthday parties. There was a stable in the Pelham Bay area of the Bronx and, sure enough, they rented out ponies. When the woman who answered the phone asked me the age of the children at the birthday party, I explained what Palm Sunday was. This was unnecessary, as she turned out to be an active Roman Catholic. "Would you like a donkey instead of a pony?" she asked.

The donkey's name was Baby, and she delighted the children who were allowed rides during our usual Sunday school hour before the formal procession, which could only accommodate one Jesus. The men on the corner, who had been up drinking most of the night, looked up in amazement from their morning beers in paper bags and thought they were hallucinating the first time Baby approached, but after that, they seemed to enjoy her yearly visit.

For five years, Baby showed up on Palm Sunday in her trailer, good to go. Then, in year six, Baby balked. She refused to have any children on her back. She refused to walk. Baby wouldn't budge and had to be forcibly shoved back into her trailer. I had a dispute with the owner because I refused to pay for a donkey that had refused to do that for which she had been hired. After that we had to settle for a pony, but come Palm Sunday, Baby is ever on my mind.

And so it was at city hall. After all, we were there because of some others who didn't want to budge, who didn't want to bear the weight of responsibility for educating the poorest children of New York City. These donkeys didn't want us on their backs either. Why should they be paid when they didn't want to carry our children forward? When it was my turn to take the microphone and make these clever connections (at the last minute I graciously decided to scratch the biblical term "ass" as the august King James Version puts it: *Behold thy King cometh unto thee, meek, and sitting upon an ass.* [Matthew 21:5] and use the less inflammatory "donkey"), a uniformed policewoman went slithering on her stomach through the bushes behind me. Her mission was to pull the plug. I didn't see her and was surprised when the sound went dead. I tried fiddling with the mike, which didn't work. The cop had cut the connection.

I stopped fiddling and spoke louder. This was not Central America where people have had their tongues cut off for daring to speak out. This was New York City. This was a public park. We had a permit for our gathering and a right to speak. At least, we still had our tongues, and we still had connections that couldn't be cut. Stopping the power flow between our message and the microphone was a pathetic ploy. What they really wanted to do was to sever the connection we were making between bureaucratic greed, corruption, racism, and the classrooms of the South Bronx, Harlem, Washington Heights, and East Brooklyn. I should have stuck with King James.

A month after our visit to city hall, it was time for school-board elections. The *Daily News* came out with an article on District 9: "Though the court feels that the reinstatement of Mr. Saez [school-board president of a board charged with unmitigated failure and corruption] is not in the best interest of the students or parents of the district, nor does the reinstatement serve the interest of good government, the court is nonetheless compelled and constrained at this time to reluctantly reinstate the entire board." The court is compelled and constrained to uphold failure and fraud? Our school-board elections had become a joke. On the day of the elections, we marched, singing and chanting, down the Grand Concourse—more than a thousand parents, grandparents, children, clergy and friends, Muslim and Christian. We marched to the Bronx Courthouse steps and gave our testimony about this farcical election and our vision for education here. Ana, who went with me, was very pleased afterward to see herself on TV.

The Sunday before this march happened to be the day that a youth group

visited us from a suburban church. We were anticipating the upcoming education action, so I preached on the biblical witness against child sacrifice to Molech, citing several texts condemning the practice. The passages about Molech
are left out of our weekly lectionary. Perhaps they're not deemed fit for Sunday
morning consumption. I disagree. We need to hear Leviticus' warning, and we
heard it on that day:

> If the people of the country choose to close their eyes when children
> are handed over to Molech, I shall turn my face against them. (Leviti-
> cus 20:2)

The Hebrew Bible refers frequently to temple sacrifices as part of worship,
but these are never human sacrifices. The only time God seems to speak in
favor of a human sacrifice is when Abraham is told to sacrifice his son, Isaac.
In that case, a lamb is provided at the last minute and Isaac is saved. Whatever
God wanted of Abraham in this difficult passage, it was not his child's death.

The grim words from Psalm 106 seemed especially appropriate for parents who'd felt trapped in the system, with no choice but to accept a substandard education for their children:

> They found themselves trapped into sacrificing their own sons and
> daughters to demons. They shed innocent blood, the blood of their
> own sons and daughters, offering them to the idols of Canaan. (Psalm
> 106, vss. 38–39)

The majority of people living in the United States and attending our
houses of worship would probably say that child sacrifice is a thing of the
past—certainly not a matter of public policy critical to our national and global
economy, as the flow of children's blood was vital to sate Molech's greed. I
don't think it is an exaggeration to say that there are many neighborhoods in
our nation and in this city where child sacrifice is a daily event. The school
boards aligned themselves with Molech by demanding the sacrifice of children
to feed their greed. By their manipulation of the educational system, they
effectively had people trapped into sacrificing their children's future to the

demons of corruption, incompetence, and failure. The school across the street from the prison feeds its graduates into high schools where one in four of all students will drop out. That's at the "better" schools. At nearby Morris High School, only 3 percent of entering students graduate on time. Only one of every ten who enter graduates at all.

Dropping out of school often means dropping out of the legal economy and turning to crime, which in turn will often lead to prison or death. The city is well aware of this. In fact, the public-affairs office of former Mayor Giuliani's Department of Juvenile Justice published a handout with the relevant facts and figures citing the poor academic skills of "the youngsters admitted to secure detention." So the city that did not take significant steps to turn failing schools around, stepped up a solution for the young people with academic failure on their horizon—"New Horizons." Like so many schools in poor neighborhoods around the nation, the school across the street from the prison is a "feeder" school. It feeds children right into the prison, right into Molech's razor-sharp, goldcapped teeth to be swallowed alive down his insatiable throat.

I appeal to you therefore, brothers and sisters, by the mercies of God, to present your bodies as a living sacrifice. (Romans 12:1) That was actually one of the designated texts for our Sunday worship, and it contrasted well with the deadly sacrifice of children. I urged the congregation to present their bodies to walk down the Grand Concourse two days hence. After the church service, a few leaders and I met with our suburban guests for lunch and conversation. The visitors, particularly the adults, were shaken. Their pastor explained that they had never heard a sermon like it; it was so "political." One of the adults with the group suggested that if there existed a problem of school board corruption and lack of participation by parents in the voting process, then this would be a job for the League of Women Voters. Actually, he asked, "Where is the League of Women Voters?" Not here. No one around here besides me had ever heard of them. He felt they should just be called in from wherever it is they operate to fix things.

The League of Women Voters solution represented two big misconceptions—underestimation of the power of evil and underestimation of the power of people who live in the South Bronx. The LWV fan saw the problem as somebody having stolen a little money—a crime that civil due process could take care of. It was hard for these visitors to understand that what was actually at stake was a matter of life and death, that we were not talking about ousting a misguided politician, but unseating Molech, that we are in a contest with powers beyond flesh and blood.

Nobody other than the guests considered my sermon "political." It was not politics that informed my preaching but biblical theology. Our Muslim sisters and brothers had just celebrated their high holy day of Id al-Adah remembering Abraham's near sacrifice of his son Isaac, which God did not allow to take place. The imam of the Bronx mosque had spoken of this at a recent SBC meeting. It got me to thinking on the many biblical injunctions against child sacrifice. I remembered Gordon Lathrop's talk to our ministerium, a gathering of Lutheran pastors in the metropolitan New York area. Gordon is the professor of liturgy at the Lutheran seminary in Philadelphia. He's more interested in first-century worship patterns than Bronx politics, but it was his words, in large part, that inspired my sermon.

Gordon told the gathered clergy about the mosaics in a sixth-century church in Ravenna, Italy. The image on one side of the altar table shows Abel and the priest Melchizedek. Abel offers the first-born from his flock, foreshadowing the offering of Jesus as the lamb of God. Melchizedek holds an offering of bread and wine. On the facing side of the table, Abraham, Sarah, and Isaac sit at another table that mirrors the real one. Three angels have come with a kid from the flock. In the corner, Abraham, Isaac, knife and lamb complete the imagery. Gordon summarized by saying that these mosaics invite the worshiper "to eat with the One who ended the slaying of our children and ourselves." Amen!

Some of our adult guests found my sermon sacrilegious, but I think that it would be a sacrilege to ignore the realities that threaten our children's future. How can we offer First Communion classes, welcome children to the table and then meekly send them out into the killing fields?

Fortunately, we have new allies in our battle against Molech. By 2002, our high school, the Bronx Leadership Academy, under the extraordinary administration of Principal Katherine Kelly, was rated second in academic achievement among all Bronx high schools behind only the selective Bronx High School of Science. Because of that success, South Bronx Churches was asked by the Bronx Superintendent of High Schools to serve as a lead partner to create more small high schools in the borough. Besides planning our own school, Bronx Leadership Academy II, we helped to design eighteen more new, small Bronx high schools to open over the next several years (beginning with ten in the fall of 2002). Three major foundations have funded this work with $7 million. It is the largest effort to improve high schools in the nation. And it all began with a block of concrete plunked down in the middle of a group of angry parents, back when our first organizer, Jim Drake, told us to "be concrete."

"I baptize you in the name of the Father, and of the Son, and of the Holy Spirit!" Thanks mostly to Trevor, I got to say it twenty-one times one Easter. Trevor was about to turn fourteen. On Sunday mornings, he got himself and his younger brother and sister up and dressed for church while his mother slept off the highs and lows of the night before. He called or knocked on the doors of several neighboring apartments and woke up his friends, pestering them to get ready for church.

On the day of Trevor's own baptism, his mother promised to come, and I believe that she meant it at the time she said it. Throughout the service, Trevor kept one eye on the door. I did too, but his mom never made it. I asked Trevor if he wanted to wait for another Sunday, but he wanted to go ahead. Trevor bowed his head over the baptismal font and listened to the voice of love that washed over his broken heart: *You are my beloved son with whom I am well pleased.* (Luke 3:22b) These were the words spoken at Jesus' baptism. We read them for Trevor.

A year later, thirteen of our Easter baptisms were of children and teenagers brought to the church by Trevor, who was not yet confirmed. Confirmation is the rite that signals a full, mature participation in the life of the Church. We also call it a reaffirmation of baptism. In Trevor's case, it would be an outward sign of what was already true. Not yet confirmed and certainly not ordained, Trevor was the bishop of his block, leading his flock of youth down the street to the pool of living water like a good shepherd.

"Do you renounce all the forces of evil, the devil, and all his empty prom-ises?" These words are also part of our baptismal liturgy. It is impossible to pronounce these words and send the children out like lambs to the slaughter. It is impossible to anoint their foreheads with scented oil and rich promise: "You have been sealed by the Holy Spirit and marked with the cross of Christ for-ever," and do nothing as they go off to substandard schools that virtually seal their failure to survive in today's economy. We put a lighted candle in each waiting hand: "Let your light so shine before others that they may see your good works...." Why must the church fight and work for better public schools? There is no better reason than the baptism of these children. Are we going to stand by and allow Molech to snatch them from us as so much prison fodder? Once we've said no to the devil, we need to keep saying it: Hell no!

Because of his effective crime-control strategies, Mayor Giuliani received many guests from police forces and city governments in Europe, who came to see what they might learn. These visitors were treated to glowing displays of statistics that signaled lower crime rates, safer and cleaner streets and, until the devastating collapse after September 11, 2001, economic upswing. But these statistics never documented those who were being sacrificed. It is absolutely true that Giuliani restored Manhattan as a tourist mecca, boasting a Dis-neyfied Times Square where the Lion King rules. But all the while that African animals were drawing sell-out crowds on Broadway and wowing visi-tors at the Bronx Zoo, more sinister cages were prepared for the poorest African-American and Latino children. To say that crime is down depends on how you define crime.

Like virtually everyone else, I could not have wished for a more compas-sionate leader in the wake of our city's trauma, but that does not change the hidden costs of our city's progress. "Stone within stone," wrote Neruda, "and man, where was he? ... did you lift stone above stone on a groundwork of rags? / Coal upon coal, and, at the bottom tears? / Fire in the gold and in the gold, the red, trembling drop of blood?" Neruda was writing his great poem on Macchu Picchu, an Inca city high in the Peruvian Andes built in the fifteenth century, but his questions are crucial for any urban renewal and reconstruction.

There is a chilling verse of Scripture tucked away in 1 Kings chapter 16, verse 34: *In his days Hiel of Bethel built Jericho; he laid its foundation at the cost of Abiram his firstborn, and set up its gates at the cost of his youngest son Segub.* Hiel's children were killed and buried as the foundation sacrifice in order that the splendid walls of Jericho might rise up.

Boom Chica Boom

Pam was outside taking attendance and ushering a line of children into the bus that would take them to Trinity Lutheran Church in White Plains to spend the final week of our summer program. Pam was assisting the program director, Debra, and had developed enough of a résumé here to begin full-time work in the fall as a teacher's assistant in a special-education class. She was about to start night school, too. We have had five young women in college studying to work with children because of their work with children here.

Pam lost her mother to drugs and grew up with an aunt. Now her arms are full of children, her own daughter, and all of these in our program. After leading songs in the bus, Pam led the children into the parking lot, which members of Trinity had turned into the Jordan River. Volunteers were there to provide music, arts and crafts, snacks, lunch, games, and Bible stories. They put a lot of creativity into the stories—on this day, Joshua and the battle of Jericho.

The children carried a papier-mâché Ark of the Covenant into the river, where they lifted papier-mâché stones bearing the names of Israel's twelve tribes. After they crossed to safety, the children readied for the battle of Jericho by making colorful trumpets of cardboard, feathers, and glitter. At the appointed time, seven priests blowing seven trumpets marched in a circle around someone's Suburban Ranger that had been transformed into Jericho's city walls. The rest of the tribes followed Joshua's instructions to remain in absolute silence (no small feat) until the city was circled seven times on the seventh day, and then it was time to make noise.

Pam led the kids in their favorite song—"I SAID A BOOM CHICA BOOM!!! I SAID A BOOM CHICA BOOM!!!" Joshua would have been proud of the earsplitting volume as the city walls fell down flat—also, I hope, some walls between White Plains and the South Bronx.

After the fall of Jericho, it was time for lunch, always a big hit. Naturally, the homecooked meals in White Plains beat the ketchup-as-a-vegetable lunches provided by the summer school lunch program in the Bronx, but that day a serious problem surfaced with two of the children, Edwin and Juan, who are brothers. One never stopped eating, but the other had to be cajoled into taking even a few bites. Both were rail thin and wan, with long bangs hanging over their eyes. Juan picked at his arms and legs constantly and refused to talk in public. Edwin told one of the women serving food that only the dogs got to eat dinner at their home. He slowly consumed the entire rind of his watermelon slice. She told Pam. Pam told me. Another home visit to be scheduled immediately.

Back in the Bronx there were no trumpets or shouts, but another wall was tumbling down. In some ways, this was more exciting than the theophany of the backhoe. It signified real structural change. The outer wall of the church on the side of our construction site was coming down at last! The top was being dismantled by hand, while the rest would be done by machine. The end of the wall meant the end of the mural painted on it. In the center, Jesus stretched out very black, muscular arms under a rainbow the width of the wall. The words, "Come to me," "Ven a Mí," floated in clouds over his head, words he spoke to welcome children in blessing. City buildings filled out the background and the largest portion of the mural was crowded with children of all shapes, sizes, and colors, some represented with bodies and some with only big, smiling faces.

Years previously, the children in the summer program had spent excited mornings painting themselves on that wall. We'd miss the mural, but not the wall. For as the wall came down, the mural came to life. We broke the wall to build space for Jesus to bless God's children. Pam was only ten when the mural was done, so before it came down, she rushed over to have her picture taken beside the painting of herself she'd made as a child.

After everyone went home, I couldn't leave. I just couldn't tear myself away from the progress I was witnessing. Vito, who was working alone on the backhoe, asked if I would come out and help him for a while. He was going to ask one of the teenage boys who was hanging around, but they'd all left. From his seat in the backhoe, he couldn't see to lower the dry well bottoms to the right position in the big hole he'd dug out. I got a quick lesson and signaled directions to place the huge concrete rounds.

I enjoyed it. Out there in the back, it also became obvious that with a big section of the building's outer wall missing, anyone could climb up and in. It would be a miracle if no one did. The dry wells were now in position to hold water and prevent flooding, but there were no watchmen to prevent theft. Fortunately, the miracle held and by the end of the next day, the temporary wall was sealed in place. The rainbow lay in painted chunks of concrete on the ground. I pocketed a piece of rainbow and headed home.

Hans and Ana were outside in front of the house playing with some children on the sidewalk. After a while, Ana came in and Hans stayed out playing. I was in our living room just feet away from the sidewalk. Within half an hour, Hans came back crying inconsolably and unable to speak. After checking for physical injuries, all I could do was hold him. Finally, I heard the story. A boy I'd never seen, who turned out to be another child's visiting cousin and who looked much younger than his fourteen years, had grabbed Hans and held him upside down by his feet over the iron fence bordering stairs down to the intern's apartment, a drop of about fifteen feet. He told Hans that he was going to let go and drop him on his head. Eventually, Hans told us that he thought he was going to die. Hans was no lighter than the boy who held him and could easily have been dropped by accident if not on purpose. It was Burnice's daughter, a year older than Hans, who came by and said, "Put him down, that's the pastor's son!" Hans credits her with saving his life.

The boy insisted that he was "only joking" and wasn't really going to hurt Hans. Of course, he did hurt Hans, probably in the same way he'd been hurt by someone. I've known a couple of children who've described being held out of an apartment window by an adult threatening to drop them as a punishment. For several years, at odd moments, this memory resurfaced for Hans, bringing fresh trauma. On that day, after being hugged for a while, he wanted to go back outside to play. I let him go, but sat on the stoop to watch, the rainbow still in my pocket.

On Sunday, people spontaneously began picking up pieces of the wall, as

I had, to take with them. I collected enough of these mementos to fill the window sill in my office. I planned to wrap some up and mail them out to our supporters—at least to the ones who wouldn't mind getting a piece of painted concrete in the mail.

The breaking down of walls to build up community is part of the calling I feel as I move between different worlds in this ministry. The tragedy suffered by our country, and most particularly by this city on September 11 has brought us together as a nation and a church, but we have a long way to go. Lucia, a six-year-old girl from my congregation was in McDonald's with her mother a few weeks after the attack when another woman gave the child dirty looks, got up, and spit at her. The mother's anger flew out in her native Spanish. "¿Qué está haciendo? ¿Está loca?" "Oh. I didn't know you were Spanish. I thought she was one of those ... Arab people." "¿Qué importa? What importance has that?" "Well, you know this is a war." Yes, we are more united, and no, we are not.

All over the city we saw photos of the missing with names and stories. Day after day they were printed in our newspapers so that everyone might see all the faces, learn the names and mourn the losses together, the loss not of statistics but of beloved individuals with unrepeatable and irreplaceable lives. Their loss tore open and ravaged the hearts of those who held them nearest and dearest, but the grievous wound has also been collective. Here in the South Bronx, we have our own memorials. Day after day, I pass them—colorful graffiti memorials spray-painted on walls for teenagers slain on our streets in the prime of their life. I have yet to see a single one remembered and mourned in our city papers. The statistics of this violence are filed away, but not the loving details of these children whose Creator has counted every precious hair on their heads. We have a long way to go. Going north to the Bronx, after 125th Street in Harlem, I am almost always the only white person in the subway.

Literally within minutes of becoming aware of the terrorist attacks, people began clamoring to get to Ground Zero in New York City—to come in person and to send all kinds of resources, material and spiritual, for rescue, comfort, support, and the rebuilding of life. This stampede of generosity was wonderful. And yet Auschwitz survivor Elie Wiesel, no stranger to the geography of terror and loss, has said that wherever human life is trampled, wherever the suffering of human beings goes on unchecked, there must become for us "the center of the universe." In this case it has been, but more often it is not. The daily ravages of injustice are less eye-catching than the events of September 11, but no less devastating in their human toll. Millions of dollars have been raised to ensure that every family facing financial hardship or displacement because of this terrorist attack can be helped, but what of the greater numbers of those already poor, starving, sick, and homeless?

After September 11, people began calling the church wanting to be connected with a family they could help. Besides Felipe's, I didn't have a personal relationship with any family that seemed to fit what they wanted. The callers were especially interested in orphans. I told them other places to call, and I thought of Trevor. A few days after September 11, his mother's boyfriend shot her dead. Trevor was sixteen, his oldest sister Janice was eighteen. She had a baby and there were two younger sisters and a little brother. They moved in with an aunt, but when someone gave her money to buy the children clothes for the funeral, she took it all for herself. When they found out what she did, they left and were finally able to rent a small apartment, supported by Janice's low-paying job. Trevor now spends some days home from school babysitting and will have to go to summer school in order to graduate from high school this year. The first time I visited, they had no furniture. When people called me wanting to help orphans, I thought of Trevor and his siblings. I finally mentioned them to a family who sent a check, and to a teacher, whose class of children sent a money order.

Martin Luther King Jr. wrote something akin to Wiesel in his "Letter from Birmingham City Jail":

> I am cognizant of the interrelatedness of all communities and states. ... Injustice anywhere is a threat to justice everywhere. We are caught in an inescapable network of mutuality, tied in a single garment of destiny. Whatever affects one directly affects all indirectly.

I sit on the Nehemiah Trust, which oversees our loan monies for the Nehemiah housing. Some of our meetings have taken place in the office of one of the Episcopalian senior loan partners. When I get out of the subway to walk to his mid-Manhattan office, near Fifth Avenue, I pass by some stores and buildings: Fendi, Asprey, Trump Tower, Prada, Tiffany, Bulgari, Mercedes-Benz, Cartier, Mikimoto, Piaget, Merrill Lynch, Disney, Reveillon and Christian Dior. After the meeting, I go tunneling back to the Bronx and come out of the subway at Longwood Avenue. I pass by some other stores and buildings: Mama's Fried Chicken, Holy Care Discount, Checks Cashed, Pop's Candy Store, Dinero Express, Alex Wines and Liquors, Mexico Unisex Beauty Salon, Mi Jesus Fruits and Vegetables, Botanica La Caridad, La Esperanza Grocery, Diamond Cleaners, and Illusions 99¢ Store.

My guess is that there are not many people gazing into the windows of Tiffany's and Illusions 99¢ Store on the same morning. It's an instructive view. Will we ever bridge the distance between Mi Jesus Fruits and Vegetables and Cartier? Mercedes Benz and Pop's Candy Store? Between those who shop at one and those who shop at the other? Traveling between worlds to build homes is so much easier than bridging this distance, which cannot be measured in subway stops. The trip from Longwood Avenue to Fifth Avenue makes clear that the problem is not a lack of the resources and ingenuity needed to produce a decent education and jobs for the children of Longwood. It is pure lack of will. It is a wound that tears open the "network of mutuality" in our city, our nation, and our world.

Father John Grange, the pastor of St. Jerome's Roman Catholic parish here the Bronx, told me of spending the night at Ground Zero performing a gruesome liturgy—blessing body parts—piece after piece after piece. He told me that he didn't sleep well after that. Who among us was not horrified by the knowledge of dismembered bodies in the rubble? But the dismembering of our human family has ceased to horrify many, who easily sleep right through it.

On the other hand, there are many good-hearted people who do care and try to close the distances between us. It seems to happen in spurts, and Christmas is always a season of largess. Wealthier suburban churches amass Christmas presents for the children here. And these are beautiful presents, much nicer than what gets donated in an average gift drive. St. John's in Summit, New Jersey, requests a wish-list from the children. A family in that church then selects a name and a wish and goes shopping, often with their own children in tow. The gifts that subsequently arrive are obviously selected with attention and care. For instance, a child who requests a basketball may get the ball as well as a book about the NBA, a related sweatshirt, T-shirt or pajamas, etc.

We receive and distribute upward of 500 gifts from different churches. Those who buy the gifts are happy to give, and the children are happy to receive. For some, this will be their only present. Others will get toys that break easily, unlike the sturdy Tonka trucks that ride to us across the George Washington Bridge in St. John's van. But there's something in the nature of this Christmas bonanza that makes me uncomfortable as well. One year, the element of discomfort was shared.

Since most of the gifts that come are for young children, we decided to ask St. John's if we could submit wish-lists primarily from the teenagers. They agreed, but in the end, this caused some understandable discomfort. The desires of adolescents are not so warm and fuzzy, even though a few of the girls wanted stuffed animals. In general, teenagers are more overtly materialistic. Should this be a surprise? Asking for their wishes was asking for trouble. After all, the Hip Hop style now popular with many suburban youth originated here. Style's not cheap and the teenagers probably figure that money in the suburbs grows on trees anyway. While this assumption may be annoying to our donors, it is likely shared by many of their own teenagers. Their lists included jewelry (gold only, please), CD players, CDs, radios, Walkmans, and name-brand clothing. The younger children's requests for baby dolls, Barbie dolls, action figures, cars and trucks were snapped up quickly. At first the teenager's lists went begging.

In the end, most of them got their wish, or something very close. The gifts were presented to us at a St. Nicholas program held at the church in Summit, along with legends about the saint. We brought a choir of children to sing in Spanish during worship. The brightly wrapped gifts were carried by children to the altar at the offering. We stayed for lunch and took the presents home.

Two of the St. Nicholas legends seemed particularly appropriate. The first tells of a poor farmer with three daughters. Having no money for their dowries, he was planning to give them over to a life of prostitution. St. Nicholas heard of the girls' prospective fate, and so he secretly went to their house by night as each daughter neared adulthood and tossed her a bag of gold through the open window.

St. Nicholas also gave the gift of new life to three boys who had been murdered and hidden in a pickle barrel. He pulled them out and miraculously resuscitated them. What strikes me about these stories is that the young people were not small children. They were youth, like our teenagers, with futures at risk, or in the case of the boys, no future at all.

No one pretends that toys and clothing bear with them the promise of a better future. This is not to say that making the present more pleasant is a meaningless act; nevertheless, once the feel-good moments of giving and getting are over, what will really have changed? Remembering the less fortunate as an enriching part of one's holiday experience before returning to post-holiday life at best fosters an illusion of goodwill. The ornaments are packed up, the tree comes down, the cookies are finished, and the poor are forgotten. This is what triggers my discomfort.

The church in Summit does not fall into this unfortunate pattern, nor do several of the other churches that send gifts our way. These congregations are engaged in a genuine struggle throughout the year to use their resources for the benefit of others. What they do with us is only a small part of their outreach, and what they do with us is significant. In addition to their contribution toward our building program, they provide ongoing support toward our afterschool summer and youth programs, college scholarships, and donations for our pantry and clothing closet. Many of the members recognize and honor the work of people here and some seek to build relationships with them, but the balance of material resources is still way out of wack.

In the summer of 1997, a group of boys from the church had an invitation to attend the Simba Camp. The camp is a two-week experience developed by the Lutheran Church under Gaylord Thomas for African-American boys between the ages of ten and eighteen who participate as "simbas," a Swahili word that means "young lions." The boys are guided by "nation-builders," African-American men in their twenties and thirties who go through intensive training to become mentors. A group of older men form the "council of elders"—role models both for simbas and nation-builders. The stated mission of the Simba Circle is to be "an Afrocentric community grounded in the gospel of Jesus Christ that creates a space for listening, teaching, and responding to the needs of young African-American males. We are determined to rescue their gifts, release their potential and restore their promise."

The camp uses a facility in Strawberry Point, Iowa, and mostly attracts boys from Chicago, Milwaukee, Cleveland, and Detroit. We were anxious for some of our youth to participate, but didn't know how to get them there and back. Our seminary intern at the time, Chris Kinney, offered to drive. His father, Larry, drove to New York from his home in Minnesota with a van so that more boys could travel. They then drove to Iowa, went back home to Minnesota, and two weeks later, with Chris's mother, Vonne, along, went back to the camp in Iowa, drove to the Bronx, and then back home to Minnesota. Talk about going the second mile!

It was understood that Larry and Vonne were loving parents who wanted to support their son's internship ministry, but that wasn't the whole story. Chris is long gone as an intern, but they have repeated this trip every summer since, for five years. On the last trip, they got a late start because Chris first went to accompany one of the boys, Danielle's brother, Dashawn, to the Bronx Family Court. The boy's father was nowhere to be found, and his mother was now dead. A month before the scheduled trip to Iowa, Dashawn got into a fight with his uncle, who held a knife to his throat. Dashawn hit him, and the uncle called the cops. Orders of protection were issued. Dashawn came to the church wondering what to do. He could no longer return home because he and his uncle were forbidden to be near each other. His brothers and sisters wanted to tell the police of his uncle's part in the fight, which they had seen, but Dashawn was troubled at that. He reasoned that if the police found out about his uncle's behavior, the children might be taken away from him and put in foster care—and thus be separated from each other. Dashawn was willing to sacrifice his own record for what he saw as the greater good—the unity of his sisters and brothers. He wanted to know what to do, and I didn't have a good answer. We prayed. Dashawn stayed with friends for a week and wrote a letter to his uncle. He went back home and had the court date, to which Chris, just arrived from Minnesota, accompanied him. They left court, picked up the other boys and hit the highway for camp.

Last year one of the other boys took Larry aside and asked, "Mr. Kinney, why do you do this?" Before Larry could answer, Lonny went on, "Why do you like us so much?" Lonny's own father was killed in prison. Kids tease Lonny. He's overweight and has a lisp—all fodder for his peers' cruel jokes. "Why do you like us so much?" Larry could have talked about the love of Jesus in a general way or quoted Scripture. Instead Larry answered by talking about Lonny in a specific way, mentioning all the good and unique qualities that Larry sees in him. "You noticed all that?" Lonny said, amazed. "You noticed all that? . . ." Larry noticed. Larry took the time to notice. There is a world of distance between the lives of Larry and Lonny, but now there is a world of connection as well.

For he is our peace, in his flesh he has made both groups into one and has broken down the dividing wall. . . . (Ephesians 2:14) Walls have indeed come tumbling down, but the overall complex structures of class and race that divide remain firmly in place. The arrival of wonderful Christmas presents that most families could never afford becomes one more reminder of what unites us and of what has rent us apart. It's complicated. It's uncomfortable. It hurts. Perhaps it is perverse, but I'm glad that some of the discomfort was shared over the teenagers wish-lists. It's better not to become comfortable as long as these divisions dismember our human family, as long as Herod, who sought to kill the newborn king born to break down walls, goes about his grisly work. Infant mortality here is now at 13.2 percent.

This is how God's children from the Bronx sang in Spanish to the children of God in Summit:

Montes y valles habrá que preparar,
nuevos caminos tenemos que trazar.
El está ya muy cerca, venidlo a encontrar,
y todas las puertas abrid de par en par.

(Mountains and valleys will have to be prepared
new highways opened, new protocols declared.
Almost here, God is nearing, in beauty and in grace!
All clear every gateway, in haste, come out in haste.)

Building these highways is backbreaking work. In a passage that speaks to my heart and ministry, Thomas Merton wrote:

> As long as we are on earth, the love that unites us will bring us suffering by our very contact with one another, because this love is the resetting of a Body of broken bones.

There are many questions without easy answers for a white pastor working in this community. Often, for me, it comes down to one: Is it better to be here or not to be here? Given the realities of the church, the context, and myself, it seems better to be here. Nevertheless, it is nothing to assume or take for granted. To be allowed into people's lives is always a sacred trust, made more so by the painful history that afflicts us. It is a challenge to remember always to remove my shoes, to be vulnerable and defenseless, to remember the blood-soaked ground on which I stand and to honor the relationships extended to me. Of course, I don't do this perfectly, not at all, but I give it my best. In some moments, the answer to my question is clearer than in others.

Michelle's eyes were covered with gauze protection because she had lost the ability to blink. She had a feeding tube down her throat and was hooked up to a respirator. She was awake enough to feel considerable discomfort. Her hands were hot and limp, with no strength left to squeeze. As I softly sang to her, her most-requested hymn, the one she had asked for when she still could speak, the one we'd sung together countless times, *Precious Lord, take my hand, lead me on, let me stand* . . . I don't believe she cared about the color of the hand holding hers. It was the skin contact, the touch, the tenderness, the human hand that mattered most.

I've read that it's offensive for a white person even to sing that hymn, "Precious Lord," written by Thomas Dorsey, who is considered the "Father of Gospel Music," and I respect the righteous anger in that statement. Dorsey spoke of gospel music "as meaning a message of good tidings expounded by one who has walked the path of trouble and hard times." He wrote "Precious Lord" after the death of his wife and baby in childbirth. I imagine that those who would find offense in my singing would say that you haven't known my trouble, so don't sing my song. On the other hand, in that particular moment with Michelle, it was the only thing I could have sung. I also recognize, with gratitude, this hymn as one of Michelle's gifts to me. Lifted up from deep waters, the music has poured through the channels of my heart with the force that all great music has to engulf us. If I am ever in a similar state, I hope someone will come to sing the song to me.

I remember a day when Michelle was stronger, able to sit up in a chair, alert and communicative but unable to speak or write. By gestures I could tell that she was glad her hair has been washed and braided; she was pleased with her newly painted peach nails. She wanted to talk and was trying to do so, painstakingly forming words without sound. The problem was that I couldn't read her lips well. I couldn't figure out most of what she was saying. At first, I acted as if I could understand her—and I could a little—but then I knew she was trying to tell me something very important to her. I didn't have a clue as to what it was, and we both knew it. She took my hand and began to pat it, comforting and ministering to me.

An old lesson repeated itself. It is always better to recognize what you don't know and not pretend that you can understand what you can't about another person, another race, another life experience. In fact, it is the only way that the network of mutuality can ever be repaired. I think that one of the reasons Gregorio and I continue to grow in our marriage is that with so many differences between us, we don't make many assumptions about one another. There are always mysteries that remain to be explored and respected.

It's a particularly humbling experience to preach in a language not one's own. You give up any last vestige of assurance and control. Preaching in English, I like to imagine that I have a firm handle on the words that "strain, crack and sometimes break," as poet T. S. Eliot said, but there's no illusion of that when I preach in Spanish, no matter how fluent I become. It is a good reminder that in the end, we are all just stuttering. Luther said that the Word made flesh was laid in a straw manger, which gives hope even for the most mealy-mouthed preacher! But music is something else; the music sweeps us all up in its power. Dr. Anna Julia Cooper, an African-American educator, theologian and social reformer at the end of the nineteenth century described God as a "Singing

Something." I definitely believe that music has divine power to shape and build community across cultures.

When we worship bilingually, as we do about once a month, the African-American and Latino members of the congregation find deep enjoyment in one another's musical traditions. The rhythms are often entwined because of a common African influence. The drums echo a distant heartbeat we share, no matter what language we speak and the divine Singing Something draws us together.

There is an Ashanti drum in the Metropolitan Museum of Art that has two large, protruding breasts. A heart is carved between them. The label identifies it as a "Breasted Drum" and says that the Ashanti people view every drum as the "mother of the assembly." The drum is heartbeat—pulse in the music and life in the veins. Some of the early Christian missionaries to Africa forbade the use of drums in worship, considering it far too emotional. Pipe organs were substituted as soon as possible. I have nothing against pipe organs, but surely something vital dies with this arrogant homogenization.

As a pastor in this place, every worship experience has an ecstatic element, pulling me out of myself into relationship with the Singing Something in the people here. When Luther spoke of worship reflecting the language of the people, he was really talking about the doctrine of incarnation, God enfleshed, God with us. I'm sure that Luther himself would have loved the wedding of Cheryl and Burt.

The first time I met the groom, he was covered in soot after their apartment burned up in an accidental fire. Cheryl had spent months getting it just right. She was doing the same with her life—graduating from a drug-recovery program, getting her children back from the sister who'd kept them during her rehab, taking college classes, and beginning work as an organizer in apartments rehabed by South Bronx Churches.

The church was at the heart of this renewal and we had recently blessed their apartment on 169th Street. I can still taste the feast of fried chicken, macaroni and cheese, Cheryl's special broccoli and cauliflower salad, and chocolate cake. Then everything went up in smoke. Replacing the lost clothing, kitchen things, and furniture was relatively easy with generous donations from other churches. Rebuilding hope was something else. Holding on to her job of organizing others helped in the midst of chaos. Burt's holding on helped even more.

They wanted the wedding to reflect their African-American heritage and asked me to join them in researching African and African-American wedding traditions. The big day began with African drums beating like wild hearts as dancers flung their gorgeous bodies from side to side down the aisle, around the church. The dancers, the wedding party, many guests, and myself were sheathed in multicolored swaths of African cloth. My robe was red, peopled with proud, dark couples, etched in gold. Cheryl picked it out. Before the service, the bride herself pulled me into the bathroom and insisted on wrapping my head.

The dancers slowed and stood aside as the wedding party swung in, followed by the bride on the arm of her son. Cheryl and Burt were decked in gold-embroidered white, with regal head dresses. *"Love is strong as death . . . many waters cannot quench love, neither can floods drown it."* (Song of Solomon 8:6–7) God's word for the wedding echoed the message of the drums. When slaveholders recognized drumming as a source of power for enslaved African people, the drums were ripped away, but their beat rose up still, a rhythmic resurrection through the feet that beat on the drumskin of the earth, in the clapping of hands, and even beating on pots and pans—the pulse of life that many waters could not quench, not even the waters of the Middle Passage.

Choosing a custom that is growing in popularity among African-American couples, Cheryl and Burt "jumped the broom." When in slave times official marriage was denied to African-Americans, some used an alternative rite—jumping the broom. The broom is an African symbol of shared home life. While a drum was beating (until drums were outlawed), a couple would jump over a broom—drums beating, hearts beating—jumping the broom into their life together. Cheryl found a suitable broom decorated with cowry shells in Harlem's African market.

During the prayers, our intern, now Pastor Andrea Walker, poured libations to the ancestors as a connection to personal history and the corporate history of a people who survived many floods and many fires. She brought this custom to Transfiguration from a Chicago congregation that has embraced many Afrocentric traditions, led by her friend Pastor Sean McMillan. The pouring of libations fits well with our understanding of baptism, uniting us as one people of God, past and present. As petitions of prayer were voiced, Andrea poured libations into a plant by the baptismal font.

When it was over, we danced back down the aisle to the drums. During the rehearsal, it took a while for my Teutonic hips to catch the beat. In terms of humbling experiences, this ranked up there even a bit higher than preaching in Spanish! It was the first wedding rehearsal I've conducted where the pastor had to practice more than anyone else to get it right. As I said, I'm sure Luther, without having to forgo what he loved, would have loved this too.

Coming back to the Bronx after a few weeks away in Germany for a conference on urban ministry, I realized again how much I love being here and worshiping here and how privileged I am. One Spanish Eucharistic prayer we use contains the words *"¡Toda la tierra se estremece con gozo incontenible!"*—"All the earth shivers and shakes with uncontainable joy!" I couldn't detect any shivering or shaking across the ocean. While in Germany, I visited the Martin Luther Church in Rotenburg an der Fulda. It was the church attended by my friend Bernd. We led a service with songs, slides, and reflections about the Bronx. I was asked to give the final blessing, which I did, but immediately I sensed something was amiss. I raised my hands and said the words, but felt no flow of energy between myself and the congregation. They just sat there. That was it.

I know that the congregation's muted response is the norm for many places, but I discovered that it no longer felt normal to me. At Transfiguration, I don't feel that I am "up front" and the congregation is "out there," even though our space reflects that arrangement. Instead, I feel a contrapuntal exchange of energy, back and forth, in and out, through and through, a power circling around the room. I used to be much stiffer when conducting worship, stiffer in general. The congregation has shaken me loose and made me shiver in places I didn't know were there. I am blessed.

This experience seems closer to the original sense of blessing. The Hebrew letters for blessing—brk—are the same as for kneeling and for a spring of water. In ancient Arabic, the words for blessing, kneeling, and raining are the same. In these languages, the kneeling association derived from the posture of camels drinking at a watering hole in the desert. A blessing was a water spring in the desert, a gush of life, power to live. I think a connection can be made between the kneeling of the camels and the attitude of the community or individual toward blessing and being blessed. Not that we are like camels—although at times we may be!—but rather that we can see a position of humility in the posture of kneeling, and experience the openness to receive an indispensable and irrevocable gift.

Early in the history of Israel, the cultic blessing was mutual. The leader would bless the people, and at the conclusion of the celebration, the people would bless the leader. Only later was this changed so that the blessing of the assembled people came from the priests alone and was not reciprocal.

Once, we tried to rearrange the sanctuary with the altar in the middle and the pews all around it to better reflect the reality of a community at worship, but the room is so long and narrow that the new arrangement didn't work right, look right, or feel right. In any case, most Sundays, the placement of furniture almost ceases to matter.

The mutuality of blessing is particularly vital when community is broken by the curse of racism. It would be a bad arrangement indeed for blessing to appear to flow from a white pastor to a passive African-American and Latino congregation. In addition, I would say that no worship leader in any context should be in the role of controlling the flow of life for others—then blessing becomes a curse, promoting the breakdown of community and relational power. Every church should seek arrangements that lead the community to a "hush harbor" space like the one in the woods described by Toni Morrison in *Beloved*, a genuine Space for Grace that has nothing to do with furniture position or liturgical appointments, a place where people can be wholly themselves and therefore holy:

> It started that way: laughing children, dancing men, crying women and then it got mixed up. Women stopped crying and danced; men sat down and cried; children danced, women laughed, children cried, until exhausted and riven, all and each lay about the Clearing damp and gasping for breath. In the silence that followed, Baby Suggs, holy,

offered up to them her great, big heart ... "O my people they do not love your hands. Those they only use, tie, bind, chop off and leave empty. Love your hands! Love them. Raise them up and kiss them. Touch others with them, pat them together, stroke them on your face; cause they don't love that either. You got to love it, you! ... More than eyes or feet. More than lungs that have yet to draw free air. More than your life-holding womb and your life-giving private parts, hear me now, love your heart. For this is the prize."

Love your heart. Baby Suggs's sermon was preached to a secret gathering of slaves in the woods, but like any great text, it extends its blessing far beyond the original context. Racism is a central curse on our humanity, our nation and our church, but it is not the only curse that divides and damages. The hypocritical way our church treats gays and lesbians is a curse—being blessed by their many gifts while pushing gay seminary students and ordained clergy into hiding places of denial. Sexism and stereotypes of beauty are curses. It has been sickening for me as a mother to watch the pain such stereotypes inflict as a baby girl grows into adolescence and womanhood. Then there are the twisted ideals of manhood that face a teenage boy. Poverty is a curse and so is *curses* wealth. The curses are many and those that lack a public name are no less real for the private heart. Morrison's vision affirms that blessing is not in a preacher's hands, to be received by a passive congregation. Blessing is in the clearing, seeing what's already there. Blessing is life beheld, shared, and celebrated through the power of God alive in our midst, the divine pulse beating in every heart. Love your heart!

The day came when Michelle was able to speak again. After many months in the hospital, and a long period of radiation and chemotherapy, her tracheotomy was removed. She had no clear memory of the visitors who had come as she was lying near death, no recollection of the prayers, songs, and handholding. But then she smiled and said, "You know, Pastor, I felt there were prayers and hands pulling me back to life."

In the wake of September 11, there is no question in my mind about the power of many prayers and many hands pulling us all back to life. Ours was just one of many churches and places that was flooded with cards and letters and offers of support. One group of church women in Oregon sent hundreds of beautiful, handmade cards which helped us through the unbearable days. A congregation in Nebraska made a banner for us featuring a rainbow of hope printed by hundreds of thumbs dipped in bright paint. The Sunday school children of All Nations Lutheran Church in Jersey City made cards cut out in the traced shapes of their own hands, with prayers inside for Felipe while he lay in the hospital trying to recover from the burns he received when the explosion caught him in the Tower 1's basement where he'd gone to get stock to fill the vending machines. So many hands reaching across the miles and through the walls! So far we have come, but so far we have to go. Boom Chica Boom!

CHAPTER SEVEN

FALL CONSTRUCTION REPORTS

Cracks

The foundation of one of the Nehemiah homes cracked because it was poured on top of garbage. According to the paperwork, the land the city gave us to build on was certified to be "clean land," construction-ready land. When city contractors tore down abandoned buildings on and near the site, the broken-up bricks, concrete chunks, and other garbage was supposed to be taken away and disposed of properly. That is the law. It was easier to ignore the law and just bury the junk right there. It came back to haunt us.

Building something new on top of our old buried junk just never works. I resented the extra money we had to spend before pouring the foundation in our parking lot. The contractor found a lot of unexpected junk under there, too. It seemed like we were just pouring money down a hole, which of course we were. Now I see that it was worth it. Time spent in prayer is worth it, too, even when it seems useless.

Thirty spokes share the wheel's hub;
It is the center hole that makes it useful.
Shape clay into a vessel;
It is the space within that makes it useful.
Cut doors and windows for a room;
It is the holes which make it useful.

Therefore profit comes from what is there;
Usefulness from what is not there. (Lao Tsu)

I was trying to be useful at the Bronx Criminal Court. This court for those who have broken some rules has posted some rules of its own, just begging to be broken. "No Eating! No Drinking! No Talking! No Sleeping! No Reading!" The last is the one I cannot abide. Especially when the average wait is for anywhere from four to six hours, despite whatever optimistic time is printed on the docket. "Well," I told myself, when I visited this purgatory with a parishioner, "perhaps they mean no noisy reading, no page rustling, no newspapers, no gossipy magazines." So on this day, I came prepared with a small book steeped in silence. A book about prayer.

I sat down with the mother of a young man arrested for possession of drugs and opened my book, careful not to make a sound. I would have preferred to spend some time talking with the mother, a new member of the church who'd requested my presence on this difficult day, but that was impossible here. I got through about three noiseless page turnings when the guard appeared. "Can't you read the sign?" he demanded. I wanted to tell him, loudly, that to read the sign seemed to be a violation of the law, but instead I quietly closed my book and feigned compliance.

After another thirty minutes of "No Eating! No Drinking! No Talking! No Sleeping! And No Reading!" I could stand it no more. My fingers were itching to open my book. I gave in to the itch and began to read. This time, I kept the book low on my lap, half-hidden in the folds of a sweater. I rationed my reading to brief glances down and then looked up innocently to adopt the vacant stare of those who had already been here for hours. I alternated the vacant stare with the surreptitious glance. But the guard was good. "I will have to have you removed from the court if you don't put that book away!"

I had joined the squirming children and their desperate mothers in this courtroom where reading is a prohibited activity. The courthouse is situated in the heart of a school district in which four out of five children are unable to read at grade level and four out of five teenagers who enter high school will drop out, making their mandatory appearance here most likely. The court would do better to hand out books and make reading here a required activity.

Disney products however, are welcome everywhere. One little boy sitting nearby began to play with his Aladdin figure. Those of us lucky enough to be in the right line of vision were instantly mesmerized by Aladdin's flight through the air. We watched him soar to imaginary destinations where we would all prefer to be. In time, the child tired of this distraction, and we were deprived of ours. Now I was left once more with my annoyance. I was annoyed that I could not talk! Annoyed that I could not drink a cup of coffee! Annoyed that I had to waste time! And most of all, angry that I was not even allowed to read my silent little book about prayer!

Well, the joke was on me. The sign did not say "No Praying!" Here was a stretch of unencumbered time, the very thing I complain that I need. It was relatively quiet, too,—an indication of the lack of legal investment in these cases is that even the lawyers have little to say. Chagrined, I began to pray, one by one, for those with whom I shared the room—the guards, the judge, the lawyers, the children, the mothers, those in handcuffs—invariably young and male. My eyes remained open. I dared not appear to sleep; but it was more than that. I was seeing my companions in waiting for the first time.

Prayer is not a magic-carpet ride carrying us off to some utopia. It is an act of attention grounded here, alert to connections wherever we wait. The root of the word "attention" is "to stretch toward" and comes from a word meaning to stretch thread as on a loom. The connections of prayer weave their own sacred carpet, joining the variegated threads of our lives one to another and to all things. The threads take color from the stains of our blood, sweat, tears, dreams, and disappointments, creating a design we cannot fully discern, but stunning even now. It is a weaving seen from the back side.

I am a slow learner, appalled by those who seem to bask in spirituality as though it were a vacation from reality, especially the anguished realities so evident in that courtroom, but there I was, eager to escape into my book. Better to read about someone else's prayer than face the far less interesting reality of my own. St. Teresa's interior castle seemed much more inviting than my own untended hovel. I was not so unlike the lawyer who came into the court without having ironed his clothes. Evidently, it was too much of an effort to make. I found his carelessness deeply insulting to the people there. Well, so was my own. Slowly I began to see.

For the first time, I noticed the grandfather in his pale green guayabera sitting immobile beside his wife. Holding hands, they stared ahead and away from each other's eyes. I saw a little girl slumped in her seat, clutching a subdued Barney toy in her lap. She'd had practice for this wait, because squirming would have been impossible during the long hours it took to fix the beautiful, intricate braids and beads in her hair. When the guard was looking elsewhere, her mother popped small candies into the child's mouth. Another mother had been wiping her eyes and blowing her nose with a single tissue that eventually gave out. I began to search through my bag for a package of Kleenex, but she had already drawn a long red scarf from her own purse. It was stamped all over in gold letters bearing a glittering message: Jesus Loves You. I was not sitting close enough to read it (if reading were permitted), but I knew what it said because I have a drawerful of identical scarves in assorted colors at home. They have all been given to me as gifts—an obvious choice for women clergy—soft, silky, and sanctified! Soon the Jesus Loves You scarf was damp with tears.

Among the changing mix of lawyers in the room, two were up front at the moment. One was young, wearing a dark designer suit, pearls, and high heels—dressed for success in the Bronx Criminal Court, not a strand of blond hair out of place. The other suit was gray and wrinkled since, as noted, ironing was too much effort for this crowd. He began by getting out the wrong file on his first client of the afternoon, creating an uproar in the boy's family. But his tie was from Disney—Mickey on a navy-blue background.

A few of the boys who had entered through the side door in handcuffs lit up the moment they spotted some friends or family sitting in the court. Most adopted a mask of cool, but all managed some small gesture of acknowledgment to those who sat and waited. My parishioner nudged me. At last, her own son had come through the door. He searched the room until his eyes found ours. It was just possible to make out the trace of a smile. For this we had come, a brief meeting of eyes to say, "You are not forgotten." This is all we were allowed. Then he turned to face the judge. We spent a few moments with his lawyer. I hadn't even had time to pray for each person in the room.

* * *

When I first saw the framework for the roof of our extension, I really did feel like I was up there with Aladdin. The flying buttresses of the new roof arched high, creating a wonderful, airy, inside sky. The height made the room seem more than twice its size, and looking up made my head spin. Sadly, a drop ceiling had to be installed because we could not afford to heat such a large space. If I could have raised more money, we would be filling our lungs in the midst of those lovely, vaulting ribs. We would be a cathedral on Prospect Avenue.

Well, it was not the height that made the cathedrals. It was the cathedra, the chair where the bishop sat. The cathedra was the seat of power. This raises an important question: Where is the locus of real power, authority, and change for the church? Is it in the bishop's office, or here? It is a question for myself as well: Where do I want to sit? The answer is always: here. More and more, it seems to me that the congregation is the real seat of transforming power for the church.

I remember one year when we celebrated Christ the King Sunday, the crowning feast of patriarchal imagery, but things are not necessarily as they seem. Sometimes I think that scriptures slip into the midst of our worship like a Trojan horse. No one is startled by their presence. The words are familiar and expected. Then they open up and out springs revolution. It's definitely true when the Christ the King gospel is taken from the 25th chapter of Matthew, as it was the year when I noticed the discarded chair. It was an old, metal folding chair that had been spray-painted red. After being sat on by so many children in after-school and Sunday school classes, by teenagers in youth groups, and adults in Narcotics Anonymous meetings, ESL classes, Bible studies, domestic violence support groups, HIV and AIDS prevention workshops, council meetings, and coffee hours, the chair was bent, broken, and ready for the scrap heap. Someone had put it out with the garbage. I brought it in and placed it in front of the altar.

"For I was hungry and you gave me food, I was thirsty and you gave me drink, I was a stranger and you welcomed me, I was naked and you gave me clothing, I was sick and you took care of me. I was in prison

and you visited me." ... "Truly I tell you, just as you did it to one of
the least of these my brothers (and sisters), you did it to me." (Matthew
25:35–41)

That chair was a throne. The new space has room for many such thrones.
More space than many cathedrals. The night after I'd had my first glimpse of
our flying buttresses, impossible architectural spaces rose up in my dreams.
The floors, ceilings, and walls were all painted the same deep, luminous blue,
so that it was impossible to distinguish between them—up, down, and around
were all the same. Bright Calder-like mobiles floated in the air. I soared
through tides of blue space like a bird.

For the third time in a week, I arrived at the church to find old mattresses and
broken furniture and a stove on the sidewalk in front. This oversized trash is
not dumped by local residents. Companies hired to collect it drive to the South
Bronx in the middle of the night to make their deposits rather than pay a fee
for legal disposal at a licensed dump. Making things worse, if we do not dispose
of the junk immediately, the city sanitation department will ticket and fine the
church. Someone else's garbage becomes our headache. One Sunday we had
to delay worship while a few members struggled to remove the door of a re-
frigerator left out front so that small children arriving for Sunday school, or
any children for that matter, didn't get stuck inside.

Inside the church, the reality of construction was more nightmare than
dream. Part of the old roof had been taken off over my office for some reason,
and the section was left unfinished on the afternoon before a big rainstorm.
The next morning I found soggy pieces of the ceiling splat on top of my desk,
soaking into unfiled papers and unanswered letters. Even worse, all of my vest-
ments had been hanging there. My Pentecost chasuble, made from a beautiful
sari I got in India, was ruined—the red silk, embroidered with golden flames
and flowers, was splotched with ugly water stains. A white Easter stole covered
with flowers and butterflies embroidered with bright woolen thread by an old
woman in Peru as a gift to me was also wet, the dyes running together. The
same problem had occurred with the ceiling in the kitchen, but it was relatively
easy to clean up dishes and countertops.

* * *

Sunday-morning construction—building up the body of Christ—is just as subject to unexpected cracks, collapse, and disarray. The first Sunday of our fall worship schedule everything went wrong. To begin with, I arrived at the church to discover that it had not been cleaned the evening before. I found out later that the person who was supposed to clean it had a severe asthma attack and was rushed to the hospital. It was probably brought on by all the construction dust. I was away and hadn't gotten the message. The trash cans were all overflowing. The front sidewalk was strewn with garbage. Old bulletins and papers lay crumpled and scattered about the sanctuary; likewise, paper towels on the bathroom floor. Brown-edged flowers in stinky water sagged in their vases.

In addition to that mess, somehow when I had been away the week before, the worship booklets for the English service had been thrown out or misplaced. It was hard to find anything anymore, given all the displacement caused by the construction. When I tried to make new bulletins, the paper jammed and the copy machine shut down. Then it turned out that the wrong English service times had been announced, and as it was the first Sunday following our summer schedule, scarcely anyone showed up when it was time to begin. The musicians did not arrive, either, since they'd heard the same erroneous announcement.

Just as we were about to begin, in walked a visiting pastor from Chicago. She was so excited to visit our church because she'd heard so much about it. She had wanted to come for the Spanish service, but didn't check about the times. The Spanish service was over, and we were now about to start this less-than-exemplary English service in a dirty church with no music, no worship books, and hardly any people. The mice, however, were making their presence known, running across the chancel in front of the altar. So much for showing off! Surely there are pastors whose spiritual maturity leaves them unconcerned about making a good impression on out-of-town visitors, but I'm not one. Worship numbers in particular command my emotions which go up or down depending on the score. I might as well be standing before the tote boards at the Stock Exchange on Wall Street popping antacids. That Sunday the scoreboard did not look good. Our visitor was polite when she left but clearly confused as to why this would be a church that anyone would want to go out of their way to visit.

Yet on another level, everything went right. It was the last Sunday of the sermon series that had begun in the summer. Each week had raised the question, "Where is God when … ?" This Sunday was, "Where is God when I'm hurting—from domestic violence?" That was to be the focus of the day's readings, preaching, and prayers. I had gone to church early to pray but instead found myself frantically rushing around trying to tidy up. I was fuming about the copy machine when in came Amelia with her two beautiful children, Tamara, age three, and two-month-old baby Felix. Last week, she had requested that we do a special blessing for Felix. It's a pre-baptism tradition in the Hispanic community. I was warned by a previous pastor never to do this because it was a misleading kind of superstitious insurance against evil assaults on an unbaptized baby. I don't agree. I see it is a joyful presentation of the baby coming to church for the first time. It seems natural and good to pray in thanksgiving for the baby—and for the child's health and well-being. Those who refuse to do it remind me of the grouchy disciples who warned off the parents bringing their children to Jesus to be touched and blessed. How can there ever be too much loving touch? Too much blessing?

As soon as Amelia saw me, she fell into my arms and burst into tears. "Look what my husband did to me," she sobbed, and I saw the lump on her forehead where he'd whacked her with a broom handle. Welts burned on her back, and thumbprint bruises circled her neck. It had happened before. She'd been to the police and now brought the paperwork to show me as if she needed proof. No action had been taken. I know that if the same man had done this to me in the street, the response would have been immediate. She said that his "episodes" were getting worse now as he drank more beer and used more drugs. He told her that if she were to go to the police, he would kill her. He had filed a lawsuit against the police over some other incident and was expecting to get a windfall, which further complaints against him might obstruct.

Many women would be too terrified to leave, but it seemed that Amelia was ready. I was relieved and glad that she felt safe enough to come in unafraid of judgment, but it looked like she needed the hospital more than the church. She explained her plan to move in with a cousin until she could find an apartment, and she absolutely refused to go to the hospital.

As other women entered the church, Amelia found more of the tender embraces she needed—and some nursing care, which she accepted from their hands. She said that she still wanted to present Felix. Both he and his sister were beautifully dressed. How had her trembling hands managed the tiny white buttons down the front of his little blue suit? He smiled and gurgled in my arms through the whole thing. Who could refuse a blessing to this child?

I wondered if the sermon was going to be too much for Amelia. "Where is God when I'm hurting?" Well, that was our question for the morning, and it was surely Amelia's question, too. One of many. I'm sure she didn't find any really satisfying answers, but I hope she felt less alone with the questions. A few women took her and the children out for lunch. Later that evening, after her husband left for his work as a taxi driver, we planned to load the van with Felix's crib, boxes of clothes, toys, and other items. I mentioned the hospital again. After having quoted statistics in my sermon, such as that, for every twenty shelters for battered women, there are fifty animal shelters, I was thankful that Amelia had the hospitality of her cousin. In the end, it was a great Sunday. Great pain. Great strength. Great trust. Great love. The visitor from Chicago had no idea.

The next morning, Amelia was waiting on the sidewalk outside the church when I came back from taking Ana and Hans to school. She had returned home to get more of her things, expecting her husband to be asleep, but he wasn't. This time, she was ready to go to the police, so I took her immediately, thinking that they would escort her to the hospital. We were sent to a special domestic-violence unit. They appeared to be well-trained in their area, sensitive and smart, but there was one problem. That particular unit had no direct access to squad cars. They depended on other police to drive them around. They were ready to leave and arrest Amelia's husband, again thought to be home sleeping, but no car was available. At first I assumed that this was some kind of lame excuse, but then I overheard the officer's urgent phone calls and conversations, begging for a car. I couldn't believe it. An ambulance came and took Amelia to the hospital, but the police said that they couldn't leave to make the arrest because there was no car.

"Is that really the only issue," I asked, "no car?"

"That's it."

"Well, I have a car."

"Oh? OK, fine. We'll go in your car."

I was incredulous. We got into my minivan and off we went. I was wondering what was going to happen when we arrived at the apartment. I wondered if they were really going to arrest this violent man and bring him into my
van. I couldn't believe that it would be legal, but since I wanted him arrested
ASAP, I didn't dare to wonder out loud and interfere with this progress. When
we got to the address, the cops explained the procedure. Once he was arrested,
they could call for a car, which would come immediately. As it turned out, he
was arrested and imprisoned because it was the third reported offense. Amelia
was treated, released, and moved to begin her new life.

When I picked up Ana and Hans after school, Hans inquired from the
back seat, "Mommy what's this doing here?" It was an NYPD hat with its
shiny shield, left behind in the van.

Rats 101

A brochure arrived in the mail inviting me to a "Rat Summit" cosponsored
by Columbia University and the *Daily News* to address the city's intractable
rat problem. According to the brochure, Rats 101 would be held in the morning, followed by lunch. The afternoon was for more advanced studies and
proposed solutions. I was unable to attend, but if I had, I think I could have
skipped the morning session (and lunch). Most of us in the South Bronx have
more experience than we would like. What I didn't know, but read in later information about the summit, was that the rat population had been under far
better control during the 1970s when New York's rat program was considered
a national model of effectiveness. It was in 1981, when President Reagan
began major budget cuts in federal aid to cities, that the Centers for Disease
Control's support for New York's program fell away and the rat population
proliferated. The trend continued. Under mayors Koch and Giuliani, the Department of Health's allocation for pest control dropped from $18 to $5 million (later in Giuliani's administration, it was increased to $13 million, but the
rats had wasted no time in taking advantage of the lull).

The most disturbing bit of new information for me was a statement sum-
marizing the consequences of lessened attention to the rat problem: "The

result . . . is that rats have now escaped the 'defined border' areas where they were permitted to live (the South Bronx, Central Brooklyn and other poor, communities of color), creating the political agitation that will get control programs expanded." I shouldn't have been surprised. If this community was expected to be a dumping site and transport point for a large part of the city's garbage, it is only natural that we would also host a disproportional share of the city's rats, and that they could live within our "defined" borders with full impunity.

Nehemiah Condo Four had a major rat problem. I was on the condo board at the time. The rats had multiplied because of the inadequate containers for garbage disposal. Rodents were running rampant in broad daylight, so much so that the exterminator wanted to use the site to make an instructional video. I could have volunteered to bring it along for Rats 101. And this was our model housing! Actually it was, and is. What is "model" is not the absence of problems, but the concerted dedication to solving them. The garbage containers were immediately changed, and at the following meeting we had a rat update. The pest-control company was proud to announce that we had embarked on a successful "rodent abatement program" that "will power dust all open rodent burrows, runways and travel ways . . . rodent carcasses will be removed at each visit." I wondered why there would be carcasses to remove at each visit if the rodents were abating, but I wasn't an expert.

Every month, I was attending these meetings devoted to subjects about which I had no expertise. In addition to the early condo-board stint, which was eventually taken over by the owners, I have been the official Lutheran Bronx presence on the Nehemiah Housing Trust, watching over our $500,000 loan investment, along with the $2.5 million from the Episcopalians and Roman Catholics. This has taken a lot of trust, considering that I can't balance my own checkbook, but I've learned a lot. And with the other Bronx clergy on the Trust, I bring a local perspective that provides a certain counterweight to the corporate lawyers. We had to learn to trust each other.

We were now entering into the second phase of Nehemiah housing, which aimed to build an additional 250 homes. The new construction was held up because an archeologist received a grant through the city to study early Bronx settlements. He had located the latrines of Dutch settlers on the property and wanted to study the contents of the old latrines to collect information about these seventeenth-century immigrants' diet. The city was paying for this while hot breakfasts were being cut out of the school menu and in their place out- dated, spoiled food was taken from warehouses and served to the children to save money.

Such skewed priorities are not unique to the Bronx. The construction of Nehemiah homes in Brooklyn was held up because a rare breed of mice were making their home on the land. Much hoopla and major concern were raised over the mice. Meanwhile, in many city-owned apartments, poor conditions breed asthma and lead poisoning that damage children permanently. No hoopla for that.

Not infrequently at these meetings one thinks of other ways to spend the time. Why do I attend such meetings, where the subjects range from rodents to retaining walls and requisitions? For the same reason we were trying to build an extension to the church. The rebuilding of lives is facilitated by the rebuild- ing of bricks and mortar. When Isaiah says: *they shall repair the ruined cities, the devastations of many generations* (61:4), he is referring to concrete as well as spiritual reconstruction, as was Jeremiah when he told the exiles to build houses and plant gardens:

> Thus says the Lord of hosts, the God of Israel, to all the exiles whom I have sent into exile from Jerusalem to Babylon. Build houses and live in them; plant gardens and eat what they produce . . . seek the welfare of the city where I have sent you into exile, and pray to the Lord on its behalf, for in its welfare you will find your welfare. (Jeremiah 29:5ff.)

When I began this ministry in the Bronx in 1984, I picked this chapter of Jeremiah for my installation ceremony, so I shouldn't have been surprised to find myself in meetings about rats. You can't build houses or plant gardens here without them. Some would agree that this is the church's job, but not the pastor's job. It is true that as an ordained minister, I ought not to have rat con- trol at the top of my agenda, but it is on the page. In the sixth-century Rule of St. Benedict for monks, even the abbot is expected to take his turn at kitchen duty.

In my case, kitchen duty meant going home at lunchtime to fry bacon, just right—for the rats. I should explain that the congregation has long since given up expecting their pastor to cook for potlucks. It is not that I don't like to cook. It's just one of those things that I have trouble making time for. I'm always happy to bring anything that can be bought—coffee, milk, soda, bread, doughnuts, cake, pizza, chicken from KFC. Or else Gregorio will cook something wonderful, as he frequently does. Just don't ask me to cook. Then came the day when I was—dare I say, baited—into cooking for the rats. It was bad enough with mice everywhere when construction commenced. But that fall we discovered that rats had made nests inside the heating vents of my office and in the organ, which had not been working properly. The organ repairman delicately informed me that "rodent water" was corroding wires and seeping into the wood. "Rodent water?" "Are we talking about rat pee?" I asked. Well, yes we were, but that seemed a bit strong to say in church. I felt like saying something stronger.

Our treasurer, Manny, who also saves us money by doing all kinds of needed maintenance and repair work for the church, bought rat-sized glue traps, and I came in to find them chewed up. Manny went out and bought rat-sized snap traps and suggested that we set them with bacon. "We should do this right away, Pastor." He said that the bacon should be cooked not too crispy (because then the rats could break it off), but just enough to produce a nice, enticing odor. So there I was, frying bacon to perfection for the rats—our own rodent-abatement program with power bacon instead of power dust. I am no good at preparing bacon for my family, and there I was doing it for the rats. As long as I had all that bacon in the pan, perhaps we could have the leftovers for dinner? On second thought, we went out for pizza. The perfectly cooked bacon netted us four fat rats that night.

Rodents may not be high on my list of God's creatures, but being a pastor and a parent one has to make all kinds of accommodations. My mother gave Ana a hamster for a birthday gift. I looked in the cage at it, and it was bad enough, but manageable. Then, an hour later, one hamster had morphed into six. Unbeknownst to us, she was pregnant and gave birth to five babies. Unfortunately, Ana had already finished reading the hamster-care book. There was an entire chapter devoted to the care of pregnant hamsters. The owners of pregnant hamsters are given specific instructions of everything that must be done to ensure that the new mother will be in a good mood. This is vital, since anxious hamster mothers have a tendency to eat their offspring. Not realizing the gravity of the situation, we did none of the proper things. Ana couldn't sleep. Every time she heard a noise from the cage, she imagined that the mother was eating her babies. In the morning, I found Ana sleeping on the living room couch with a pillow over her ears.

In the end, even I had to admit that all rodents are not created equal. I was becoming attached to our still-hairless babies. Their survival became a family project. One day, when I checked in, one of them appeared dead—curled up and grayish. Gregorio wasn't home, or I would have called for him. When it comes to dead rodents, I retreat into traditional gender roles. But Ana couldn't bear to be in her room with the dead baby. Maybe the mother would get hungry. I would have to deal with it myself. I made elaborate preparations to remove it, finally deciding on tweezers. After an embarrassing number of false starts, I positioned the tweezers around the dead baby and took a deep breath, readying myself to take it out. It was a walnut. The babies were all alive. What relief! What joy! It seemed that my own maternal fantasies and fears had kicked into high gear. Ana put in fresh water, and I bought pumpkin seeds as gift for the nursing mother. Hopefully, they'd keep her stomach full until hair could grow on the babies. According to the book, hair decreases the cannibalistic instincts of mother hamsters. Later when they had all grown up, we took them back to the pet store pronto, before more babies were born. I actually felt a twinge of sadness at letting them go.

I never expected to feel anything approaching separation sadness over a rat. It began with sorrow over Margarita and her son Pablito who both died in the crash of American Airlines Flight 587 on its way to Santo Domingo a month after September 11, 2001. The plane went down minutes after takeoff in Queens, killing all 255 people on board, including nine-year-old Pablo—a buoyant, chubby child, ever eager to show off his arm muscles, and excited about preparing to receive his First Communion on Christmas Eve. His mother, Margarita, sold pastellillos and alcapurrias from her truck across the street from our church. People came from all around to buy these Dominican specialties that funded her trip with Pablo to visit his grandmother. His body was found but hers had to be identified through DNA taken from the hair of her comb. Pablito's brother, six-year-old Angelo, and his father had stayed behind.

The first time I visited the family after the crash, Angelo told me that he wanted to go to the Bronx Zoo. The family found this strange and inappropriate in the midst of their trauma, but Angelo kept repeating that he wanted to go to the zoo. It was a cold and rainy time of year, and I thought it would be far better to visit the zoo in the spring, but there was an urgency to Angelo's wish that I couldn't ignore. We set a Saturday for the outing, and I invited Felipe's two children, Leonel and Rosalina (still dealing with the trauma of their father's fiery brush with death in the World Trade Center), to join us. Hans had just turned twelve and came along to help. I didn't like the idea of sending the small boys to the bathroom alone, or leaving them unattended when I took Rosalina.

It was actually a great time to visit the zoo because nobody was there to block our view of the more popular exhibits. From the moment we arrived, Angelo began to talk about the Mouse House. "Eeewww," said Rosalina. I didn't say anything, but felt the same way. Looking at the map, I decided the best time to visit the Mouse House would be on our way back to the car at the end of the day. Angelo did not let us forget it. So the kid likes mice, I thought. We got to the Mouse House and Rosalina reached for my hand. We were walking about in the shadowy building where lights are kept dim when Angelo stopped before a particular cage. "My mother took me here with Pablito," he said. "We stood right here. We looked at this mouse." This was the closest he'd been to his mother and brother since they disappeared. It was the last outing they'd shared together. For Angelo, this was no trip to the zoo; it was a pilgrimage. The final exhibit in the Mouse House holds a large, sleek, familiar-looking specimen. It was a Norwegian rat, the kind that thrives in NYC, as a helpful sign tells the world. "We saw this one, too," he said. It was time to head home, but Angelo didn't want to leave this sacred space. "Why don't we say a prayer here," I suggested. Rosalina was still holding my hand, and the others joined in. And so we prayed, surrounded by rodents imprinted with remembered love.

Pillars of the Church

In spite of all the construction mess, *Strength and beauty are in God's sanctuary* (Psalm 96:6), and so they were at the church council meeting as we began with this Psalm. I hear many colleagues complaining about council meetings, but I usually love ours. In some churches, these meetings drag on for hours, which would drive me crazy, too. When I was an intern and the meetings began at 7 P.M., I used to request that my report be put on the agenda before ten o'clock so that I might still be awake enough to give it. Our meetings are never more than two hours, although we shoot for one-and-a-half hours. This means there's not a lot of time for discussions that go nowhere. One meeting lasted one hour and forty-seven minutes on the dot, which was the total time allotted for our agenda. The times given to each item were not exact, but it all added up precisely. Ironically, this punctuality has never extended to worship, as folks arrive throughout the service, but some punctuality is better than none. It is a discipline based on SBC community-organizing training that many members have participated in. This training has also led us to end every meeting with an evaluation of what went well, what didn't, and what we might do better next time. It seems like an obvious thing to do, but we'd never done it before the training.

The precision at our meetings gives people pleasure. What gives me pleasure is the privilege of serving among such people. By any standards, most of them are poor. Zora Neale Hurston described one side of poverty far better than I could:

> There is something about poverty that smells like death. Dead dreams dropping off the heart like leaves in a dry season and rotting around the feet; impulses smothered too long in the fetid air of underground caves. The soul lives in a sickly air. People can be slave-ships in shoes. (*Their Eyes Were Watching God*)

They surely can, but these folks aren't—and not because the air isn't sickly enough. The Psalm that begins with beauty and strength in the sanctuary ends in the fields with dreams of different trees: "*let the field exult and everything in it, then shall all the trees of the forest sing for joy!"* Because the people gathered at our council table have taken on these parish streets as their field of action, they enable others who were sunk in rot to leap up and join the song. These on-time council members are veterans of many dry seasons and dropped dreams. Their own souls are sometimes filled with fetid air, which comes out in the same petty jealousies and conflicts you find any place, but rooted in ruins, they continue to draw forth new life for this congregation and community. Strength and beauty are at the table—with clout to spare (despite what some funders may think). I'm honored to sit there, too.

The meeting ended with the song that has become our mantra, "Thank you, Lord," "Gracias, Dios." Even after hard meetings, the infrequent ones that do leave me feeling slightly sick in the stomach, gratitude puts things in perspective. What meeting is more fraught with disaster and futility than the pediatric intensive-care unit where Lucy, a council member, sat each day beside her eighteen-month-old goddaughter, Laurie, who lay unconscious in the crib? During a visit to Lucy's apartment, the toddler pulled over the table holding the TV. The big television fell on top of Laurie, crushing one side of her skull. Lucy spent each day sitting beside the hospital bed singing softly, "Thank you, Lord." When I visited, I wondered exactly what she was thankful for. "She's alive—and I can't remember anything else to sing." After a month, Laurie woke up and slowly recovered.

A friend, recently moved to a house by the sea, wrote me that he is blessed to live in a place of such "stunning beauty." So am I, although sometimes I don't know how the pillars of our church manage to stay standing upright.

I came home from an all-day conference on Latino ministry to a message that Burnice's apartment had been broken into and trashed by police—not just any police, but the elite corps known as the NYPD Street Crimes Unit—out on a drug bust gone berserk. It's true that they had the right to break in since no one was home at the time, but that is where legal force ended and another force took over. Burnice was at church helping with the after-school program when she got the news through a neighbor. She sent her children to stay with a friend to spare them some of the trauma. When I arrived, there was not a single free spot of floor space in the entire five-room apartment. From the threshold forward, the floor was covered with several feet of debris. To enter, I had to walk over clothing, photos, blankets, bills, books, magazines, food, plates, toys, pots, pillows, knickknacks, towels—everything torn, broken and tossed in chaos. The mattresses had all been cut up. The VCR and TV were gutted, with their insides hanging out. This wasn't a search. A gale of vicious fury had whipped through these rooms.

Burnice was shaking in shock. Her eyes refused to focus, rebelling against the scene of destruction spread out on every side. This apartment had been her dream-come-true after leaving her old rat-infested building for a shelter. With more scrimping, saving, and sacrifice, it was furnished and filled. I remember the day we blessed it. If this had been "an act of nature," the government would step in to help, declaring it a disaster zone. But this disaster was an act of human nature gone awry, a hurricane of hatred, racism, and prejudice wrought by the NYPD Street Crimes Unit*, with its pumped-up slogan, "We Rule the Night!"

Burnice's night had been shot to hell and the thought of clean-up was too much for her. It was impossible to imagine reordering this chaos. At that point, it was too much for me, too, but before I left, near midnight, I promised that a crew would be there in the morning to make some order. I went home and called the church council, of which Burnice was the president. As I lay in bed, waiting for sleep to come, I remembered the two handsome men who smiled and greeted me that morning as I'd walked by Burnice's building on my way to the subway. They had been standing on the sidewalk and appeared to be expecting someone to join them. "Cops," I thought, "I wonder what they're up to?"

Earlier in the day, at the conference, the difficulty of having various ethnic groups work together in a church had been a topic of discussion. But the next morning our multiethnic crew assembled. It didn't matter if we spoke the same language, ate the same food, or liked the same hymns. We arrived, a dozen strong, and spread out two or three to a room and began sifting through the ruins. We separated clothing and linens to wash and mend and folded what

* The Unit was later disbanded following pressure brought on by the death of Amadou Diallo, shot forty-one times by the SCU.

seemed salvageable. We filled bags with garbage and with what had become garbage. We filled so many bags that we had to run out to buy another box of them. We gathered hangers, rescued toys and photographs, and repaired broken furniture. After five hours, with a dozen of us working nonstop, it wasn't the same—it would never be the same—but it was better. We stood together on the newly swept living room floor, held hands, and prayed. Then we made sandwiches, broke open the soda, and ate.

Later I found out that the destruction was worse than I thought. The day had in fact not begun with our arrival, but with Burnice's husband screaming, "Get up and clean up this shit!" He blamed it all on her, the mother of a son in trouble. This beloved's betrayal was far worse than the faceless violence, wrecking havoc in her heart.

I wanted Burnice to fight back. I wanted her to kick this man out who put her down. I wanted her to confront the police and demand reparation. She would not have been alone. She would have had the whole church at her back, and others, too. But she didn't want to, and I had to respect her choice. It was her life and her decision of how to use her resources and her strength. Nevertheless, I was worried about Burnice, who had only been drug-free for a few years, worried that in the shadows of this merciless valley, she would go back to the illusory high that ever beckoned from a vial of crack.

A few days later, I found Burnice still shaky but doing better. She still didn't want to confront the police, and she didn't want anyone else to, either. She said that she was getting up early, making coffee, and just sitting quietly looking at her plants and thanking God for another day. She told me that she always used to do this in the kitchen, but now she had moved her routine to the living room window where the plants were. She'd sit staring at the plants and feel a measure of peace and the ability to keep on keeping on. "I don't know why," said Burnice. I think I do. The plants were the only thing in the apartment that had not been violated. Why did they leave the plants rooted in their pots? They offered as good a hiding place as any. Only God knows. Burnice contemplated the plants, an untouched mystery—pure, green, growing, tranquil, beautiful, luminous, and strong. I think they mirrored a hard-to-reach place in her heart—her interior castle, her Space for Grace.

In the spirituality of the Orthodox church, icons play an essential role. According to the *Byzantine Book of Daily Worship*, "the underlying idea of the icon . . . is the manifestation of the hidden. . . . . The icon is not a picture. . . . The icon is a grace and a life. . . . A saving truth is not communicated by the word alone but by the fact of awakening vital forces of life, through the presentation of beauty." The group of icons at the entrance to the orthodox sanctuary is called the iconostasis, drawing worshipers into the embrace of heaven and earth. The plants on her window sill had become Burnice's iconostasis. She was fighting back the best she could.

When Jim Drake, the organizer we hired for South Bronx Churches through the Industrial Areas Foundation, first visited me to talk about his vision for community organizing, he emphasized the key work of identifying leaders. He broke it down into recognizing primary, secondary, and tertiary leaders. The last category was people who showed leadership skills among family and close friends. Secondary leaders were those who moved beyond that inner circle, demonstrating leadership in their interactions with neighbors or coworkers. The top level would be people like Minerva, an elementary-school principal who used her passion for educating children to help organize the South Bronx Leadership Academy.

This was all well and good, but I sat there thinking about many people I had met who did not readily fit into any of those categories, people whose battered lives left them disconnected from family and neighbors, work and community. People who were depressed. People who were addicted. People who were too sick and weak or too sick and tired to do much of anything. What about them? Jim sensibly pointed out that such persons clearly are not in a position to lead anything and that there would be no real role for them in our community organizing efforts. Moreover, to the extent that our efforts were successful, our community would be a more humane place, a place with fewer social ills and therefore fewer people like the ones I'd been thinking of who fell outside the categories of functional leadership.

It made perfect sense, but it left me deeply troubled because basically it dismissed a large group of adults as beyond hope for the foreseeable future. According to this model, Burnice would never have risen to leadership as the president of our church council, a Sunday school teacher and women's group leader, a woman who eventually organized with others and, among other vicories, got the drug dealers banished from her block. If I, as the pastoral leader, had looked at her and thought, she's a crack addict and she's a mess, and left it at that, then the church and the community might have missed out on a great leader. On the other hand, without the outstanding leadership training provided by Jim and later on, by our second IAF organizer, Lee Stuart, Burnice and others would not have known what steps to take to better their community. They never would have developed powerful muscles in the fledgling legs of their newfound hope.

There is a riveting picture in the book *Children in Danger; Coping with the Consequences of Community Violence*. It is a copy of a drawing made by a little girl when asked to draw a picture of herself. The child who drew the picture, Sheila, was five years old at the time, living in a Chicago housing project. Her short life was filled with the sights and sounds of violence and death. She herself was struck by a stray bullet but had physically recovered. Most five-year-olds can draw figures with recognizable forms to indicate a face, arms, legs, and often hands with fingers sticking out like sunrays. Sheila pictured herself as a rough, ovalish shape with no eyes to see, no ears to hear, no mouth to speak, no arms to hug, no fingers to touch, no legs to walk anywhere. Sheila's self-portrait is simply an empty blob. One colleague I showed it to said it looked like a body bag. There is no mistaking her loud message, even if she did draw herself without a mouth. This is what the mirrors held up before Sheila had shown her.

I have met many adults who've looked into the mirrors held up to them and seen the emptiness and powerlessness that Sheila saw. We need to shatter those mirrors, but until that happens, we need to hold up a different one, the one described by the psalmist when he writes: *Keep me as the apple of your eye* (Psalm 17:8). In Hebrew, "the apple of the eye" is literally "the little one in the pupil of the eye." It is an image of profound intimacy, looking into the eyes of God and seeing oneself as in a mirror, cherished and held close. It is this sacred mirror that we need to hold before each and every person we possibly can, no matter how messed up they seem to be. We need especially to hold this mirror steadily before those who appear most disconnected and unfit for leadership. Maybe that's one of the gifts that the church can bring to community organizing.

Of course, there's a difference between being a pastor and being a community organizer, although we share the belief in identifying, training, and nurturing leaders. For us, it is a theological mandate. We believe that all human beings are created in the image of God, without exception. In the book of Genesis, our human prototypes are told to *"have dominion,"* to use their God-given power to care for the world around them, not as oppressors but as lovers seeking the well-being of all creation. Everyone therefore is born into the world as a natural leader. The forces that go counter to the goodness of creation and distort this reality, lifting up other mirrors that reflect all sorts of false and destructive images: these things are unnatural—sin and evil.

Over the years I've learned that while certain people are easy to identify as strong leaders, you can make a real mistake by writing others off too soon. There are many surprises. Obviously transformation doesn't always happen—every addict doesn't beat his addiction, everyone who has been beaten down will not rise up, at least not on this earth, but you never know. Our job is to hold up the sacred mirror, the possibility, the hope. Some future pillars of the church arrive in ruins.

Milly's life was a wreck. In her own words:

From the age of seven to fifteen, I was being sexually, mentally, and physically abused by my mother's boyfriend. Every time before he would have sex with me he would force me to drink hard liquor and sometimes beer. He also would force me to smoke marijuana with him. If I refused, he would beat me so of course, I did what he said. By the time I ran away from home as a teenager, I was an alcoholic and a pot head. I didn't like myself at all at that time and I started hanging out in bars. This is where I was to find my best friend, or so I thought—it was cocaine and later, crack.

I was using crack for a year when I couldn't afford it anymore so I started to dance at a Bronx topless bar. I hated myself. I often owed money to drug dealers who threatened my life. I became homeless. I was alone. I felt that God had abandoned me. I was angry at God and angry at everyone. I got into constant fights and I almost got killed many times on the street.

When I was twenty-two, I had my first child. When I looked at her

I realized that I had to stop. I didn't want her to go through the hell that I went through as a little girl. I stopped using crack just like that. I just stopped. But it took more than ten long years before I could stop using everything else.

I visited Milly in the hospital after she had suffered a nearly fatal asthma attack. She had just begun coming to the church, and I didn't know her well. When she saw me, she became very excited and declared, "For the first time in my life, I was able to put something on the hospital form that asks what religion you are! I put Lutheran, and it felt so good!" She also told me that she was four months clean.

We were about to begin training for our TLC campaign—Time to Listen to the Community. Our plan was to train a dozen leaders to meet individually with a combined total of fifty people from the community each week (each leader meeting with two or more persons). Our goal was to do this over the course of eight weeks that fall, meeting 400 people and trying to develop relationships with them. The people we planned to meet with were parents and family of children in our after-school and youth programs, people who came to our food pantry, or GED classes as well as friends and neighbors identified by our own leaders. The individual conversations were expected to last thirty or forty minutes. We called them one-on-ones, a term adopted from our community-organizing training. We wanted to listen to those we didn't yet know in order better to understand their hopes, angers, hurts, and vision.

The main church growth we were interested in achieving through this campaign was to expand and deepen our network of relationships in the community. It was also a way to nurture the leadership capacity of those doing the work, and it was a way to encourage and honor others by taking their voices seriously. It was not a membership drive per se, although we would certainly be glad to welcome anyone interested in becoming part of the church.

We began by practicing our listening skills with each other. We emphasized that the point of the conversations was not to scavenge around in the intimate details of one another's lives but to get to know another person in a public way. We were guided by the Spirit of Pentecost that had raised Passion up as a leader in her high school: *I will pour out my Spirit on all flesh . . . sons and daughters and even slaves will prophesy, the young shall see visions and the old shall dream dreams.* (Acts 2:17) When Peter quotes these words from the prophet Joel on Pentecost, he's not referring to private communications but to passionate messages entrusted to a wide range of human beings that need to be heard for the sake of the whole community. Marvin Calloway, an organizer with South Bronx Churches at the time, led us through the training. Such training is one of the benefits of belonging to a group like SBC. It is a valuable tool not only for increasing the network of relationships with people who are previously not connected to the church, but also for deepening communication and rapport among church members. After the training, each person was asked to make a written commitment of how many people he or she would meet with each week. Milly, just out of the hospital and the only person in the training who was not a member of the church, signed up for ten. I was skeptical. Milly had only just begun to come to the church. She was invited by Cheryl, who in turn had been invited by Burnice. Cheryl and Milly were in the same drug-recovery program. Milly had already told me about her volatile anger and inability to get along with other people, and I had seen signs of it. Her recovery seemed fragile, and from a few incidents in the church she was very defensive and sometimes offensive. In addition to her shaky emotional health, I learned from the hospital that, besides asthma, she simultaneously suffered from diabetes, heart problems, osteoporosis, and ulcers. None of this would appear to add up to prime leadership material in most books.

Milly also told me how grateful she was for the acceptance she'd felt and the change she was beginning to experience in her attitude and impulse control. Everyone needs to be given a chance. Besides, in this place, for a person with so many health problems such as Milly, the window of opportunity for a person to use their gifts is often small. When it's now or never, now is always better.

Milly became the only person who met her full goal of one-on-ones, completing the eighty she committed herself to. It became the focus of her life for those eight weeks, and she loved it. Her enthusiasm was contagious, and a number of the people who did end up joining the church were folks who met first with her. Altogether we did not meet our goal of 400 individual meetings, however we did manage to do 304, which wasn't bad for a first attempt.

* * *

Milly herself was still not a formal member of the church during the campaign but decided to join right afterward along with others newly connected through the one-on-ones. I went early to church to pray. I like Zora Neale Hurston's description of Nanny's prayer in *Their Eyes Were Watching God*:

> There is a basin in the mind where words float around on thought and thought on sound and sight. Then there is a depth of thought untouched by words, and deeper still a gulf of formless feelings untouched by thought.

The last is the place to which I like to sink in prayer. I like to spend some time like this before the busyness of Sunday morning sets in, but this time, as soon as I settled down, a car alarm activated and wouldn't quit. I tried to let it wail on the surface while I dove below to some deeper space, but I couldn't shake the noise, which was like having a supersized, mutant mosquito in my ear. Finally, I turned to the morning's Psalm and shouted the words in the empty room. Then I turned on the sound system. We'd need it if the alarm kept going.

It should be noted that the sound system itself has betrayed us. One Sunday during Communion in the Spanish mass when the church was blessed with a rare, rich silence, an earsplitting blast erupted from our amplifier, followed by shouts of the police making an arrest, all at the same excruciating volume. Somehow, the frequencies had gotten mixed. I almost dropped the chalice. Someone unplugged the sound system, but the delicate membrane of silence had been ruptured like an ear drum. I could feel a collective wince of pain. And it has happened again from time to time.

On this special new-members Sunday, Kenneth was to be our lector. Kenneth is everything a lector and liturgical leader should not be. Past drug use and present psychiatric medication have affected his mental processing and speech. To entrust Kenneth with the public reading of Holy Scripture could be a major liturgical goof. Does not God's Word deserve the most gifted readers: those of resonant voice and clear pronunciation, those who do not halt and stutter? That's what the manuals say. Kenneth's gifts are different, but they serve us just as well. Perhaps better.

When Kenneth stands up to read, the church falls silent. This should always be the case, but it is not. Children take time to settle in their seats. Teenagers flirt. Over and under the Word, we hear the shushing of adults, the rustle of papers. But when Kenneth approaches the lectern, even the papers are still. Young children, familiar with their own reading struggles, sit quietly, silently urging him on. We all sit on the edge of our seats straining at attention, collectively willing each word forth.

The wilderness and the dry land shall be glad,
the desert shall rejoice and blossom; . . .
like the crocus it shall blossom abundantly . . . (Isaiah 35:1,2)

The words pushed out through Kenneth's lips, little by little, like shoots breaking through desert crust.

Then the eyes of the blind shall be opened, and the ears of the deaf unstopped, then the lame shall leap like a deer and the tongue of the speechless sing for joy. (Isaiah 35:5–6)

The words unfolded like petals in slow motion, syllables in time lapse. Mary watched over us from the sanctuary wall—a lovely black Mary robed in bright orange, hugging her baby boy. Kenneth did this painting during a psychiatric hospitalization and brought it to the church as a gift. It reminds me of the traditional icons of St. Luke that depict him as an artist painting an icon of the Madonna and Child, an icon within an icon. What strikes me in these images is the small cup at Luke's feet into which he dips his paintbrush. It is a chalice filled with blood-red paint. Kenneth had labored through his suffering, and now the Word became Flesh through his lips.

When he said, "This is the Word of God," it was over, and we all took a deep breath. Grinning and triumphant, he returned to his seat.

Milly came forward with the other new members, including those she had irst met with. Francis was typical. She came with her son, Rafael, who was soon to be baptized. Rafael was bound to a wheelchair because of his cerebral palsy. He attended our after-school program. After she and Francis spoke, Milly told me that Francis would also like a call from me. This was part of the time-consuming follow-up that we had not planned for. In the end, I abandoned most of my own new conversations to do follow-up visits with people identified by the other team members. When I called Francis, she was so pleased to talk, that she burst into tears. She told me that she wanted Milly to be Rafael's godmother. Milly and her two daughters joined the church along with the others. She said that she hadn't joined before because she'd felt unworthy, but she was beginning to like what she saw in a different mirror. "Milly" is short for Milagros, Spanish for "miracles." She is now one of our pillars serving on the church council.

> So then you are no longer strangers and aliens, but you are citizens with the saints and also members of the household of God, built upon the foundation of the apostles and prophets, with Christ Jesus himself as the cornerstone. In him the whole structure is joined together and grows into a holy temple in the Lord; in whom you also are built together in the Spirit into a dwelling place for God. (Ephesians 2:19ff.)

Of course, not every story has a happy ending; in fact, all too many don't. Speaking through a crack haze, Deena left a message on the church phone: "Don't call, don't write, don't visit." I chose not to pay attention and went to see her anyway. Her son, Dashawn, was in the confirmation class, and it was the final meeting before they'd be confirmed. She had punished Dashawn by keeping him locked inside, unable to attend class or church. (Odd as it may sound, forbidding church attendance as a punishment is not unusual in this community. For children who exhibit their joy in going to church, denying their participation is part of being "grounded.")

I remember when he first began to attend church, invited by Trevor, another of our young pillars. At the time for making announcements, Dashawn stood up and said in a quiet voice that God had given him an announcement to make. Since it was only his second Sunday at church, I wondered what announcement God gave to Dashawn that wasn't on my list. I put him off while the planned announcements were made. He kept nudging me, reminding me that he wanted to speak. When his turn finally came, he proceeded to talk about a fight he'd had with a friend. Where was this going? I wondered. He'd hit the friend and hurt him, and his friend had hurt him back. It looked like neither would back down because that would mean losing respect, but now Dashawn had decided to let it go. "That friend is here this morning," said Dashawn, "His name is Trevor. Trevor, will you come up here?" Trevor went up, and Dashawn spoke again, "I'm sorry." The boys hugged, and the church gave them a standing ovation. They had everyone's respect.

I went to Dashawn's home knowing that the door might not open, but it did, and Deena immediately informed me that she had nine puppies and eight children and was overwhelmed. She had no time to talk, but I could talk with Dashawn. He asked me if I would like to see the puppies. He pointed to their eyes, which were not yet open. Dashawn is skinny, but by sitting on the floor, he managed to get all nine snuggled on his lap. The puppies' mother was nowhere to be seen. He tenderly patted the puppies while we heard Deena cursing at her children in another room. When the screaming died down, I went and convinced her to let Dashawn leave with me and come to the class. It was virtually impossible ever to have a real conversation with Deena: she was either high or angry and paranoid, because she wanted to be. When we left, I felt overwhelmed, too, by sadness. A few years later, Deena died in her building's stairwell.

Rest on the Flight to Egypt

In the space of five days, I lost my driver's license and my wallet. The driver's license disappeared during Hans's birthday party in Central Park. I had to leave it as a security deposit in exchange for twenty fishing poles so all the kids at the party could catch lakeweed and rusty cans. Later, in the rush to serve chips, juice, and sandwiches to a swarm of hungry eight-year-olds, my license vanished. It resurfaced from a pile of papers in the dining room. How did it get there? By then, the wallet was gone. Did I drop it? Did someone whisk it from the car when I stopped to get the *New York Times*? (For years, the *Times* had teased me with home-delivery invitations but then mailed back every check I sent because delivery was not available in this South Bronx zip code. It wasn't on the local newsstands, either. I could get it in Chicago, in Las Vegas, in L.A., even in Buenos Aires—but not in the South Bronx. The last time an article about our church appeared, I had to drive into Manhattan to get a copy).

So I found myself at the Bronx division of the Department of Motor Vehicles on East Tremont Avenue, waiting to get a new registration, since the old one had gone missing with the wallet. I hated the place. It is torture to wait four or five hours for a transaction that might take less than five minutes. But there was one consolation. This was not the Criminal Court, and reading was permitted. On that day I was happy to be there. I was permitted to read—read without guilt, read without "more important" things to do. Of course, there were more important things to do, but since I couldn't do them, I could read. What a wonderful place to be!—the Bronx division of the Department of Motor Vehicles—my own personal reading room.

I went prepared with a book suggested by a friend who knew of my struggles to find an organizing principle for my own writing. She thought this author's solution might be instructive. I was not happy reading for long. Instead, I found myself feeling jealous that this author had found the organizational magic that eluded me. I turned to the back cover and consoled myself by noticing that she was not married and did not have children. On the other hand, she worked full-time as a doctor, so there was not too much comfort. I stopped reading and started to think about my organizational issues. Was it a writing problem or a life problem? What about an organizing principle for my life? Why did I keep losing things?

Something is surely wrong when one is actually pleased to end up at the Department of Motor Vehicles because it provides a chance to read. I began to laugh out loud. I couldn't help it. People were looking at me, wondering if I was going crazy, yet not seeming particularly surprised that someone would lose her mind in this place. I had opted not go on a retreat I wanted to attend because I had no time. Had I gone, I might have found the focus needed to create better-balanced days. But I didn't go. I lost my wallet. I had no time, but also no registration, so there I was—on retreat at the Bronx division of the

Department of Motor Vehicles. A good joke. I would have been crazy not to laugh. St. Teresa must have been shaking her head. She'd written plenty about people like me: "Full of a thousand preoccupations as they are, they pray only a few times a month, and as a rule they are thinking all the time of their preoccupations, for they are very much attached to them." But there was still hope: "from time to time, however, they shake their minds free of them and it is a great thing that they should know themselves well enough to realize that they are not going the right way to reach the castle door."

Soon after this unexpected respite, I went to a meeting of the seminary board in Philadelphia. We began with worship and suddenly my face was wet with unexpected tears. Why was I crying? I needed to cry but felt that there was no place to do it, no free moment, no space to loose the sorrows of my heart. What I felt was more than frustrating disorganization and division in my life, writing and community. It was a deeper sense of loss, what William James referred to as *Zerrissenheit*—the state of being torn to pieces. I felt that I had to change something, but what?

> When God made the Man, he made him out of stuff that sung all the time and glittered all over. Then after that some angels got jealous and chopped him into millions of pieces, but still he glittered and hummed. So they beat him down to nothing but sparks but each little spark had a shine and a song. So they covered each one over with mud. And the lonesomeness in the sparks make them hunt for one another, but the mud is deaf and dumb. Like all the other tumbling mud-balls, Janie had tried to show her shine. (Zora Neale Hurston, *Their Eyes Were Watching God*)

It was early November and not nearly time for Advent, which is the season the Church marks in the four weeks before Christmas. Nevertheless when I saw a sale on Advent calendars, I bought one for each of my children and one for myself, just to be ready. I grew up with Advent calendars and have always loved them. The ones I had as a child came from Germany, where Advent is a significant season. They were covered in silvery glitter that came off on my hands every time I opened one of their little windows. The calendars begin on December 1 and on each day through the 25th there is a numbered window to open, with a picture inside and sometimes a Scripture verse behind it.

In recent years, I bought them for Ana and Hans, not for myself, but this was an exception. I'd try anything to help me show my shine. There was no glitter on the one that grabbed my attention. Instead there was a print of Gerard David's 1519 painting, *The Rest on the Flight into Egypt*. It spoke volumes to my chopped-up days and the scattered glitter of my own *Zerrissenheit*. I was feeling the need for a rest on my own flight to Egypt—and to pursue the flight as well.

The flight in the painting depicts Joseph, Mary, and the infant Jesus. King Herod, first-century control freak par excellence, was threatened by news of the child he'd heard referred to as a king. Victims of his murderous paranoia had already included his sixteen-year-old brother-in-law, whom he drowned, his uncle, aunt, mother-in-law, two sons, and three hundred palace officials deemed untrustworthy. Alerted in a dream, the Three Kings refused to play along with Herod's conspiratorial plan to track down the baby. Like them, Joseph is warned in a dream to change direction. He must flee to Egypt, with mother and child. He is told to do it immediately, in the middle of the night—the flight is a matter of life and death.

Herod was set to slaughter the irreplaceable gift entrusted to Joseph's and Mary's care—their child. To be certain of eliminating the Jesus, Herod orchestrated a sacrificial bloodbath for all the young children in his reach. The Church remembers this day on December 28 as the Slaughter of the Holy Innocents. At Transfiguration church, we take the day to remember the youth of the South Bronx and the powers that threaten them.

David's painting is based on the apocryphal Gospel of Pseudo-Matthew, which describes Mary resting beneath a palm tree on the third day of their flight. According to the story, the baby Jesus in her lap made a palm tree branch bend down so that she could reach its fruit. In David's version, Jesus holds a bunch of grapes on Mary's lap. She's about to take some to quench her traveler's thirst with their sweet juice, but the grapes also portend the blood being spilled even as she rests. A smile plays on Mary's lips, but over beyond the distant hills in the background, we know that other mothers wail with grief.

The grapes foreshadow the bitter future of the very child Mary holds against the graceful folds of blue cloth and his final triumph; they prefigure his words to the disciples at the Last Supper: *"I will never drink again of the fruit of the vine until that day when I drink it new with you in my father's kingdom."* (Matthew 26:29)

But where is Joseph's rest? Joseph is shown off in the corner, busily gathering nuts from a second tree. In fact, the nut gathering appears to require considerable exertion. He is beating the tree with a long stick to shake them free. You can almost hear his labored breath and smell his sweat. It seems that Mary's rest depends on Joseph's work. This is part of the painting's tension and appeal for me. The flight to Egypt and safety is urgent, but so is rest on the journey. So is stopping Herod. Next to Mary, on the ground beside a river, sits a basket like the one woven to protect the infant Moses from Pharaoh, another ruler bent on the elimination of certain children in order to protect his powerful enterprise.

I identify with Joseph and his dream. I don't want to lose gifts and dreams that lead to life. I want to make the necessary changes, move in the right direction, flee toward life. I identify with Joseph, and I am disturbed that he is not allowed to rest. I am disturbed by the screams of unseen mothers over the hills. But I also identify with Mary. Even in the work of death-defying change, there is need for rest—perhaps especially in the work of change, internal or external. But there is Joseph beating the tree, as later Jesus will be beaten on another tree, sweating blood, gasping for breath. There is Mary reaching for grapes with one hand and caressing her son's chubby thigh with the other. So many contradictory symbols and images bunched together, and yet with all of them, David has created a scene of perfect balance and beauty. He has envisioned the tension and slaughter, sweetness and grace, work and sweat, fatigue and refreshment all at once, impossibly and irrevocably bound. He has painted a miracle.

The painting tears me apart and pulls me together. At the store, I wondered at my attraction to this Advent calendar, but now I see it is a mirror of my life. I wondered what would be behind the calendar's daily windows.

CHAPTER EIGHT

WINTER CONSTRUCTION REPORTS

Frozen Tears

It was so cold at the church that I could barely function. I couldn't concentrate. My body and mind were numb. With the construction going on, it was impossible to keep the cold air out. Space heaters couldn't do enough. Sometimes the electricity was cut off, too.

We also had more water problems. On Sunday, water was pouring down the wall of the church, as it had been all night during a torrential rain. The floor tiles were coming up, and the carpet was soaked. There were three inches of water in the bathroom. Even with leftover pails from the contractors, we couldn't find enough containers to catch it all. The same thing happened when Teresa was trying to fix up a convent for a group of nuns and sections of the roof gave way in a rain storm. "I said to our Lord—really, I was on the verge of complaining—that He should either stop ordering me to take on these projects, or help me get them done!" Our help came later in the morning, in the form of more water that we poured into the baptismal font and blessed. Two former gang members who had been coming to me for counseling after their baby daughter was born were baptized along with their child. They left gang insignia behind and came to be washed and marked indelibly with the sign of the cross. After church, we looked at a catalog full of paint chips. None of us could really tell the difference between the fifty varieties of white, much less translate the tint of a tiny chip to the walls of a big room.

The next day saw another indelible imprint among us. The new concrete floor was poured. Burnice, Faith—her real name, and our intern at the time—and some other women finished a Bible study and went to see the construction progress. "This space is so big it makes you want to dance!" said Faith, and so we did, spinning ourselves silly under the vaulting ribs of our still-visible ceiling. Later on, Burnice and her children made handprints in the wet concrete. Then, Burnice took her finger and carefully traced the words already written on her heart, "Space for Grace." Of course, these emblems of ownership were covered over when the new floor tiles were set down, but they endure under the surface nonetheless.

It turned out that the reason for the cold was not only outside air coming in. There was no inside heat. An underground pipe had split open at some point, but no one realized it. Who could see it? It was the pipe that carried oil between the tank and the boiler. Now it had to be dug up, repaired—something else for the contractors to do—and paid for. On the other hand, there was more to celebrate. The new closets for our food pantry and clothing were in place. One small room was outfitted with extra sockets for the computers we would buy with a grant received for training youth and adults. Instead of seeing dust, tools, dirt, and mess, we were imagining those computers up and running. Life in a construction zone requires a lot of imagination—and patience, and extra heavy sweaters in the winter.

It was November 30, the anniversary of Etty Hillesum's death. She died in Auschwitz in 1943 when she was twenty-nine. I never knew of her until Sister Ellie, my spiritual director, lent me her journal, *An Interrupted Life*. Hillesum prayed that she might be "the thinking heart of these barracks . . . the thinking heart of a whole concentration camp." Her thoughts defied the violence around her with hope and grace. Like Burnice praying beside her potted plants, Etty found a sanctuary growing in the midst of unnatural evils. Locked in a cell, she recalled the white blossoms of jasmine behind her house: "But somewhere inside me the jasmine continues to blossom undisturbed, just as profusely and delicately as ever it did. And it spreads its scent round the house in which you dwell, O God."

Again, it struck me how hard it is to think in the cold. Hatred, racism, and injustice can be numbing too. That is why it is so important to think about it, to reflect. This is one thing I really value in the style of community organizing we engage in here" in the South Bronx—the value placed on reflection. It is one way to rekindle the fires of human thought that sometimes freeze over from the cold in this city.

Rosa called and asked me to come over. When I went to see her, I found out that for two days, she had had no electricity, no heat, and no hot water. Her two children, who both suffer from asthma, hadn't gone to school, but spent the day under blankets in bed. Late the previous night she got news that her cousin, whom she loved dearly, had died in Guatemala. And that wasn't all. Rosa told me about her godson, Carlitos. He became sick with a fever. His mother, also from Guatemala, is undocumented and had heard news that city hospitals could now turn in immigrants without papers. She feared deportation if she took her son to the hospital. When nothing would lower his fever, which continued to rise, she took him to the emergency room. It was too late. He died within the hour. Simple antibiotics administered in time would have saved his life. Carlitos was four. He didn't die of the fever. He died of the cold.

There wasn't much to say. We locked arms for warmth and rested our heads together, warm tears slipping between our cheeks. The church was without heat again, too. It had been snowing all day, and construction once again interrupted our electricity and phone lines, but unlike Rosa, I could go home and get warm.

Back at the house, I found that Gregorio had brought me a big bunch of roses, yellow tinged with spring pink. I once attended the funeral of a church member's mother at which the priest told of a lovely custom from his native village in Spain. When a young woman is engaged to be married, she is given a cloth bag. The bag becomes a repository for rose petals. Whenever she receives roses on any occasion, throughout her life, the fallen petals are collected and placed in this bag. Upon the woman's death, the petal-filled bag is sewn together and placed as a pillow under her head in the coffin—a pillow of petals. I don't have the bag, but I have collected petals for many years—pink and yellow, red and white, solid, and tinged...unfaded in memory; they flower in the hollows in my heart on days when icy death lurks near.

* * *

Amanda, who helped in the after-school program, delivered her baby, a little girl named Brandy. I was thinking of a present and decided that instead of a baby gift, I would get something for the new mother, something pampering and luxurious like bubble bath, massage oil, or scented soap. It was on my to-do list. Then in came Amanda. I was surprised to see her at church as she'd only gotten home from the hospital the day before. She came into my office, wet, shivering, and in tears. Amanda was using the address of a relative in order to get her welfare check, which was being stolen from the broken mail-boxes in her own building. This relative took the last check for herself and neglected to give Amanda a letter with the date of her next face-to-face appointment. Amanda missed the appointment and came out of the hospital with a new baby, only to discover that she had no benefits, no food stamps, and no money.

Having no phone, Amanda spent all morning at a pay phone in the street trying to straighten out the mess. It was cold and raining. She had to leave the baby alone inside in order to make the calls. Her breasts were aching. When she finally got through to the right person at public assistance, after being switched from extension to extension and then put on hold forever, her change ran out. While she was searching for another quarter, the worker barked, "I don't have time for these games!" and hung up.

I decided that my gift would be practical, not pampering. I told Amanda to go home to her baby, and I picked up the office phone. The redial button helped through forty-five minutes of busy signals. Finally, I could take my turn with extension roulette. Then I was put on hold. Someone forgot to turn off the sound, and I eavesdropped as one woman offered coworkers chocolates from a box her boyfriend gave her while another took lunch orders: chicken wings, ribs, pork fried rice, fries, extra hot sauce. I was glad that Amanda didn't have to listen to this. I found out that she would need to go to the Social Security office, an all-day affair, to get the baby on her budget. First, she needed a letter from her landlord, a birth certificate, and a discharge letter from the hospital, which should have been given to her, but wasn't. More trips. All this within two days of giving birth. I felt like strangling the father, who was off somewhere and showed no interest in any of these problems, but another murder wouldn't help.

I focused the energy of my anger into the phone calls, finally getting through to a supervisor who would make an exception and grant Amanda an appointment if she could get the necessary papers. Amanda wrote a letter which would allow me to pick up her papers from the hospital. It was a pleasant surprise to be met by a helpful clerk, who got me the papers in short order. I left with Brandy's freshly stamped footprints in an envelope as proof of her existence and picked up Amanda for the appointment at the welfare office.

The set-up there requires each person to make a call from downstairs to tell a worker upstairs that they are waiting below. There were long, tense lines at the two working phones. Very long lines. Very high tension. A fight broke out in the line Amanda was in waiting her turn. She was almost pushed to the floor. I could see her shivering again. It wasn't bubble bath tied up with a ribbon, but undoing the red tape seemed more important.

More cold. Burnice received a notice stating that she would have to leave the classes she was attending to prepare herself for the job market and register for the public-assistance "job training program." Under this program, her job preparation would consist of picking up garbage and shoveling snow, in spite of her HIV-positive status. She was to report to the recreation facility in St. Mary's Park, about a half-mile from the church, and get her work assignment for Monday. Merry Christmas. The medicine she was taking to ward off full-blown AIDS was making her nauseous, but she was required to show up, even though she was throwing up.

If Burnice did not present herself in the freezing park to prepare for a job that wasn't waiting for her anyway, then her health-care and rent benefits would be cut off. She was supposed to exchange GED classes for park duty. The only way to continue her education would be to enroll in night school. Who would care for her young children? How would she find energy to shovel snow all day, attend to her children's needs, go to school at night, and keep the virus at bay? Burnice was reduced to tears and begged me to accompany her to St. Mary's Park.

It was a chilling scene. First, we had to wait outside in a line with several hundred men and women, all reporting for workfare assignments. After standing in line for hours, we reached the threshold. At last the door was opened, and it would be our turn next. But no. Instead of the expected interview and form-filling, we faced a large gym with hundreds more waiting people filling the bleachers. We had been in the waiting line to get into the waiting room! "We're processing several thousand a week," the worker I approached told me.

I decided to use my clerical collar to try and bypass the crowd since Burnice was becoming increasingly anxious and ill. The worker agreed that if Burnice returned with a doctor's letter stating that park duty would seriously compromise her health, she could be excused from the snow-shoveling duty and continue her studies. This was great for Burnice, but what of the thousands of others waiting there each week with no advocate and no prospect of a real job when all the snow melted? No one had to convince me or Burnice that the welfare system needed reform, but this was not it. Dante had it right when he described the inner circle of Hell as a place of unremitting cold that even takes away our human capacity to grieve:

> their eyes, which had previously been wet within,
> dripped tears over their features, and the cold
> pressed the tears into the eyes and locked them up.
> Board with board clamp never bound so tight . . .
> weeping itself prevents weeping there.
> (*Inferno Cantos* 32:46–33:94)

Where is the outrage in our churches? Where are the tears?

In the end, Burnice's own welfare reform effort to further her education instead of shoveling snow was a smashing success. She passed her GED test, polished the résumé she had developed over the years by volunteering and working part-time in our social-ministry programs and began a full-time office job, with benefits. In the process, she also briefly became a literary star on Broadway, lighting up Symphony Space, the theater on Manhattan's Upper West Side. Students in adult-literacy classes around the city were invited to participate in a writing program. Thirty of their works were selected to be read by professional actors in a Symphony Space production called, "All Write!"

Burnice titled her winning entry "The Early Morning Cold." This phenome-
nal woman, who's conquered crack, abuse, depression, and intemperate
weather morning, noon, and night, ended her poem:

> My daughter says to me
> "Mom here's the school bus"
> I say "I love you, have a nice day."
> Then, as I walk
> I see the sun on my left.
> It's coming across the sky
> To try and meet the moon
> On this early cold morning.
>
> Now the dark sky is all gone
> A new day has dawned.
> The birds sing their morning song
> And I thank God that I am alive
> On this early cold morning.

Soon and Very Soon

Tweety Bird was everywhere—on balloons, plates, napkins, cups, walls, cake,
piñata, and party bags. Plaster Tweety Birds mounted on Styrofoam greeted
the guests as party favors. Everything was yellow and white.

It was the baptism and first birthday party for Mirta's baby. I took Ana and
Hans, who love Mirta as one of their favorite baby-sitters. Neither of her
brothers was there. When I asked for them, I learned that Hector was in jail
and nobody knew where sixteen-year-old Freddy was. *Va y viene*, they said,
"he comes and goes."

As the children were gathering around the Tweety Bird piñata, eager to
take a turn at slugging him to smithereens, Freddy came in. His colors clashed
with Tweety Bird. He was wearing baggy red pants with a baggy red sweatshirt, and hanging down from his back pocket was a red bandana. Freddy had

joined the Bloods and was showing their colors. I remember him at six years old, sweet and shy and sad. He, Hector and Mirta lived with their elderly grandmother because their own mother was strung out on drugs. The grandmother did her best, but her health was not good, and it was hard to keep up with three teenagers. When their mother died of AIDS, Freddy was fifteen. He sat slouched with his face in his hands, crying uncontrollably through the entire funeral. Many times, his grandmother wanted to bring him to church and baptize him, but the date was always canceled. Then he was initiated into the Bloods.

When Freddy saw me, he smiled and came over to give me a big hug and kiss. There was a deep scar across one cheek. Always small for his age, in my arms he seemed frail, which is probably how he felt and why he was probably armed. Young, dangerous, and endangered.

The next day would be the first Sunday of Advent. We would hear the prophet's vision of swords turned into plowshares. I wondered how this could happen for Freddy. But it was time to leave. The children were struggling to see who could cram the most candy into their party bag. My own kids were in the thick of it, Ana helping the younger ones to glean stray pieces. She convinced Hans to share his Tootsie Rolls with a crying toddler who had been afraid to enter the melee. When we left, we found ourselves walking toward a fight about to erupt between two groups of teenagers. They were not kids I knew, and this wasn't our neighborhood. We hurried to the car.

After the children were in bed, I put up our Advent decorations: the glittery calendars, the Tree of Life tablecloth, the wreath of candles, the lion and lamb, the bowl of stars, each inscribed with a name of someone to pray for. Every day we hang a star from the light fixture over our table and pray for its namesake as it dances in the rising candle heat. Mirta and her family were on one of the stars. For as long as I can remember, Advent has been my favorite time. Before going to bed, I read again the text for next Sunday.

> Every valley shall be exalted,
> and every mountain and hill shall be made low;
> the uneven ground shall become level,
> and the rough places plain. (Isaiah 40:4)

And when will this be? The prophet's words were recorded some 2,500 years ago, and in all those centuries I haven't noticed much movement in the right direction. The gap between the mountains and valleys, the rich and the poor, Longwood Avenue and Fifth Avenue, remains as wide as ever. We turn people away from the food pantry because we've run out of canned stew, canned beans, canned tuna, cereal, and powered milk. But during the busy pre-Christmas season at Dean and Deluca down in SoHo, Gregorio works on his feet twelve hours a day trying to meet the insatiable demand for imported foie gras, truffles, and caviar. Sometimes he wraps up single sales totaling over $1,000. He couldn't join us at the party because he had to work overtime. Judging by the street tension afterward, the lions and the lambs are not too close yet either. The distance between the world as it is and the world as it should be tears at my heart.

At least it was Advent. Probably the reason I love Advent so much is that it is a reflection of how I feel most of the time. I might not feel sorry during Lent, when the liturgical calendar begs repentance. I might not feel victorious, even though it is Easter morning. I might not feel full of the Spirit, even though it is Pentecost and the liturgy spins out fiery gusts of ecstasy. But during Advent, I am always in sync with the season. Advent unfailingly embraces and comprehends my reality. And what is that? I think of the Spanish word, *anhelo*, or longing. Advent is when the church can no longer contain its unbearable, unfulfilled desire and the cry of *anhelo* bursts forth: Maranatha! Come Lord Jesus! O Come, O Come Emmanuel!

Advent means "coming." For Christians, God has already come in Jesus and in ourselves. God is already embedded in our being, as we confess creation in God's image. God is already reaching to our hearts through the hands of those who come into our lives, as we remember at our Advent table beneath the dancing stars. But God is also absent. Come! Come! The Church cries during these four weeks, and to me it is a wailing. My wailing.

After all, you don't long for someone to come when they are already beside you. The absence of a loved one wounds the heart. At times, we have known God's presence, and it is this memory that makes us ache and feel holy absence. You don't long for someone who hasn't already deeply touched your life. I understand this more clearly because I have a friend who is far away across the ocean. My friend's absence wounds my heart and teaches me about Advent. If I'd never known God's presence, then why would I ache with the feeling of absence? How would I know to even care, even bother? But I do.

So how do I remember God? Hans is very matter of fact on the subject. For him, there is no time when he, Hans, did not exist. Hans knows where he was before he was born. When Ana speaks of events that occurred during her first three years of life and pointedly comments, "You weren't here yet, Hans. You weren't born," Hans replies, "Oh, I know. That's when I was with God." He speaks with absolute confidence and a trace of one-upmanship—"Well, maybe you were with Mommy and Daddy, but I was with God!"

When Hans was a baby, someone gave us a tape with world-music lullabies. One of the songs had some favorite music of mine from the Andean region of Peru, Bolivia, and Northern Argentina, with reed flutes, soft drums, and small guitar-like charangos. For me, it is the sound of *anhelo*. Whenever I played this particular lullaby, Hans would cry, so of course I stopped playing it for him. I thought it strange that such a tender song would make a baby cry, the same baby whose colicky screams were soothed by holding him over a running washing machine at 3 a.m.

I experimented. Perhaps he was crying about something else, but my experiments only showed that Hans was indeed crying about the music. Later on, when he was about eighteen months old and able to talk a little, I played it again. His eyes filled with tears and he said: "Music sad. No music sad." Now he loves that music. Maybe as an infant Hans was remembering being with God. Maybe the music reminded him, arousing his tearful *anhelo*.

Somehow, I too believe we all passed through the heart of God on our way to where we are. And memory stirs desire to be touched again. Presence remembered provokes the wound of absence. The luminous moments when we are acutely aware of God's presence make the *anhelo* so much worse, because we are reawakened to what we are sometimes missing.

And what we are missing is not only known as "God." "God" is another word requiring definition. The missing of God reverberates in the missing of a loved one and in the absence of justice and truth, goodness and grace—all those things whose absence wounds the human heart. But how do we know to long for a fulfillment we've never known? When were we touched by perfect love, truth, justice, and kindness? When were we caressed with utter comprehension? When did we first hear the music whose echo now breaks our hearts?

It must have been, as Hans says, when we were with God. And so the only way to come close to it is to live as closely as possible to God now—to try and be at one with the heartbeat of life, to love and to be true, just, kind, and good—to try and nudge the mountains and valleys into an embrace that heals the breach. If God—the source of life, the strength of life, the breath of life—hadn't touched the deepest places of my life, those places would not stir with such desire now.

There is awful irony in the Christmas celebration of the Word made Flesh because what are we left with? Words! Sometimes I want to brush them away in annoyance. The Holy Scriptures, words that come from the heart of God, arrive on this shore like letters from across the ocean. They bring a loved one near, but not near enough! Why celebrate the Incarnation and then go back to unsatisfying words?

For centuries, the theologians have promised us that the Holy Word is indeed the holy presence. Yes, but—or as Hans would say, "Yeah, right!"—something is missing. Yes, we believe in the real presence of Christ in the sacraments. But something is missing, or why would the church, which clasps the Scriptures to its breast day and night through all these years, poring over the words for clues and comfort, cry O Wisdom Come! O Adonai Come! O Root of Jesse Come! O Key of David Come! O Rising Sun of Justice Come! O Desire of Nations Come! O Come, O Come Emmanuel! O Come! These ancient prayers are cries for understanding, strength, liberation, justice, clarity, truth, community, and the perfect fullness of the presence of God. These "O antiphons" moan for the closure of every distance, until God is all in all.

These moans are why I feel so blessed to work here. Of course, God is everywhere, but Jesus was clear about his unique presence among the poor, the hungry and thirsty, the naked and sick, the stranger and the prisoner. Perhaps that's why I feel so close to life in this place, so blessedly alive. It is life in the face of death here, where the distances are most acute, between lions and lambs, Tiffany's and Illusions 99¢—all the divisions like class, race, and gender that rend the tissue of our humanity—and here, where the valleys cry to rise up and meet the hills. Here love comes to level out uneven ground and make rough places plain, and pleads for our collaboration. When will the work be finished? The wait is nearly unbearable, but here I can bear it because here is where *anhelo*'s song has seized my soul.

"Soon and very soon!" we sing each Sunday. "Soon and very soon! No more crying, no more dying, no more hunger, no more fighting!" We sing at the top of our lungs. We clap. We throw our bodies into the beat as we prepare to throw ourselves into the work ahead. Outside, a siren's high-pitched wail goes racing toward the next crisis. "Soon" can't come soon enough.

Songlines

Still no heat in the church. The cold gave new meaning to a "smokin'" sermon—clouds billowed out from my mouth. It was that cold! By the second service, my fingers were so icy that I felt badly about blessing babies and small children brought forward during Communion. I should have kept my coat on, like everyone else, but didn't think about it until it was too late.

I told the congregation about St. Teresa, who wrote of the cold winter in her unheated convent. When it became unbearable, she had the sisters grab their castanets and led them in dancing around and singing to get warm. We tried to warm up by jumping and clapping and singing more than ever, which helped.

> Our captors asked us for songs
> and our tormentors asked us for mirth, saying,
> "Sing us one of the songs of Zion!". . .
> How could we sing the Lord's song in a foreign land?
> (Psalm 137:3–4)

With Honduran music on the tape player, Delia spent all day cleaning and preparing for our Bible study that evening at her and her husband's apartment. I remember when I first met Delia and her three children. The youngest, Ferdinand, was born with Down's syndrome, and Honduras offered no educational opportunities or help for a poor family with such a child. Her husband Alberto, also from Honduras, was already somewhere in the U.S. at the time. Delia took Ferdinand and her two daughters and began the long pilgrimage here. She remembers river crossings and cold desert nights trying to keep warm, with only the clothes on their backs. She remembers riding in the *coyote's** truck, hiding with her children under piles of bug-infested vegetables, desperately trying to hush Ferdinand's cries of fear and hunger. She remembers the day she had to hand over all the money she'd saved for their new life, as well as her watch, as a payoff to the driver who threatened otherwise to rape her oldest daughter, Aurora, aged ten. And Delia remembers the songs of Zion.

One summer Sunday, Delia and the children appeared at the church door. I would like to think that their coming was the result of a successful evangelism strategy, but Delia remembers better: "The Holy Spirit pointed out this church to us." When the time came for the offering, Delia approached me: "We don't have any money yet, but we can sing." So Delia, Aurora, Ferdinand, and Nelly stood before the congregation and sang, as ancient immigrants once sang on a distant Babylonian shore. They sang a song of Zion in a new land.

For more than a year, they slept on someone else's floor. Alberto was finally found, and he and Delia were married in the church. Aurora and Nelly were bridesmaids, and Ferdinand carried the rings. Now they were hosting a group in their own apartment—an extended family of immigrants from Honduras, Guatemala, Puerto Rico, the Dominican Republic, Panama and, in my case, New Jersey. Carsten was visiting from Germany and Anna-Kari, our intern, came from Minnesota. In the midst of our Bible study on Sarah and Abraham's immigrant journey, the subject of immigration law came up. Horror stories were shared about friends already being rounded up in factories and put on planes, of young people unable to continue their education, and of hospital care denied. The undocumented immigrants in the group were feeling increasingly threatened.

I thought of a meeting I had recently attended concerning a case of clergy sexual misconduct and of all the talk about not crossing boundaries, of "building hedges" around relationships and about the havoc and hurt caused by people who don't know where the borders are. No argument there, but raising too

---

* A *coyote* is a person who smuggles immigrants without the requisite legal documents across the border.

many boundaries is just as damaging. The conversation about immigration policy continued in the van ride home and ended with Rosa telling about a distant relative in Guatemala who owns a thirteen-room house. The salient feature of thirteen rooms was greeted with appropriate exclamation.

Once, when Rosa visited this mansion, she brought a friend to stay the night and was asked: How did she think there was room? The van burst into side-splitting, window-rattling laughter. How did she think there was room? For people who live ten to a room, who have friends who can't even get a room but rent beds for eight-hour shifts, what a fantastic joke! Thirteen rooms—and no room. The undecipherable riddle of wealth.

I had just finished reading Salman Rushdie's *The Moor's Last Sigh*. Copious betrayals, losses and deaths are not caused by those who trespass boundaries, but by those who raise them—painting and plotting lines of separation, ultimately dividing nations, cities, cultures, religions, properties, businesses, homes, staircases, families, and the heart itself—riven and desecrated by all these demarcations. Toward the end, Rushdie writes of "that most profound of our needs . . . our need for flowing together, for putting an end to frontiers, for dropping the boundaries of the self."

Dropping the boundaries of the self! Here is a phrase to give the willies to those who would patrol our emotional borders. Our churches, seminaries, and candidacy committees make sure that we attend workshops and clinically supervised counseling practicums that are intended to prepare leaders to carry themselves with integrity, borders intact. We rightly worry about individual clergy misconduct and those who misuse their position to abuse others. It is a tragic problem that can destroy lives, but why don't we see the absence of another passion as an equally grave threat to our integrity and life? More passion in the right places might correct some of the very misconduct that concerns us. We virtually ignore the issue of all those borders that should be battered, breached, bent, and burned because they leave billions of people in misery. At best, we tinker, fret, and pass motions at the edges.

The Bible study led us back and forth between ancient Mesopotamia and the Bronx. We shared Holy Communion, and we sang. It is always the singing that bridges our distances and stirs weary feet onward through this Babylon. We sang as we gathered, we sang as we prayed, we sang as we studied, we sang as we ate—between bites of tortillas and mouthfuls of cake. *How could we sing the Lord's song in a foreign land?* (Psalm 137:4) How can we not? We follow the wise counsel of St. Augustine: "You should sing as wayfarers do—sing, but continue the journey. Do not be lazy, but sing to make your journey more enjoyable. Sing, but keep going." We're singing our way forward, singing our way home—not the homes lost or found, but the home that's still to come.

In *The Songlines*, Bruce Chatwin writes about the aboriginal people of Australia who believe that the world was sung into existence by those who wandered through a blank expanse singing out the names of everything they saw. These first songs were sung in a primeval "Dreamtime." The paths of the journeys or the footprints of their songs were called "Songlines" or "Dreaming-tracks," which to this day are understood as the true map of the land. The songlines are also lifelines back to where one belonged before the imposition by Europeans of other boundaries tore up the land. As Enid Lacey, a bookstore owner Chatwin met, said, "The song and the land are one." The songs were also lifelines between distant tribes who heard each other's songs and followed the trail of notes to a newfound communion.

The Psalms were all originally songs. Spoken or sung, they, too, are songlines and dream-tracks. The singing in Delia and Victor's apartment, all the singing we do with each other here, brings us together and maps out new borders of a region where the INS has no claim.

At no time am I more aware of worlds sung into existence than at Christmas which bore our members back to their roots. It was a rocky road back. The older Puerto Rican members of our congregation grew up singing German hymns translated into Spanish. They sang these hymns for so many years, that they became an adopted part of their heart language. Sometimes it's given me liturgical vertigo. I remember one day when a group of German theological students from Bavaria visited the church in the morning. A few days earlier, we had another group from Hesse. Such groups come to New York to see how our churches cope with urban issues such as immigration and multicultural urban communities that are impacting the German church as well. They are interested in the relationship between worship and social engagement. They are interested in antidotes to the arthritic hymns and liturgical lethargy that seem to infect much of the German church, making worship particularly unappealing for young people—such as themselves.

I mentioned that to be Lutheran is not to sing music written by Martin Luther and his colleagues in sixteenth-century Germany. Singing sixteenth-century German hymns at the end of the twentieth century in the South Bronx might even be highly anti-Lutheran, if we take his Reformation principle to heart—worship and music in the language of the people.

We spent several hours talking, went for a neighborhood walk, and ate a big lunch of rice and chicken, rice and beans, fried plantains and salad. When the Germans left, I went to visit Alma, who was back from the nursing home and doing better. She wanted me to sing with her. And what did Alma wish to sing? Born and raised in Puerto Rico, Alma invariably wishes to sing old German hymns. The same hymns the visiting Germans were struggling to be rid of. So there we sat, in the Bronx, singing from an anti-Lutheran Lutheran *Gesangbuch en español*. With each hymn, Alma became more animated. Color sprang to her cheeks. Arthritis was forgotten. No lethargy there. As I said, I'm dizzy just thinking about it.

I also found this musical assimilation highly frustrating. It did not serve our efforts to reach out in hospitality to new people who would not have shared this history and would not identify with this music. And I definitely didn't think that we should perpetuate a system of cultural imperialism in the church. I am reminded of Bartolomé de las Casas' chronicle of the Spanish "evangelists" who enslaved indigenous peoples in the Americas, forcing women into exhausting work with a poor diet that caused the milk of nursing mothers to dry up and their children to die. Too often, North American and European missionaries have done the same thing, holding people in bondage to an alien culture and causing the mother's milk of their own spiritual heritage, language, and music to dry up so that their children are not adequately nourished.

But something changed during my first December at Transfiguration. In the weeks before Christmas, we were having a Bible study in the home of an elderly member, Luzmila. Afterward, the people began singing hymns. Someone recalled childhood Christmas traditions and the folk music that surrounded the festivities. The hymnals with their Spanish-German hymns were put down, and they began to sing *aguinados,* Puerto Rican Christmas songs, from memory.

Luzmila got up and went to an old chest in the corner. She lifted the lid and pushed through layers of old bedspreads, shawls, and tablecloths until, from the very bottom, she lifted out an oblong object wrapped in tissue paper. Slowly she unwrapped it—a *guiro!* (A Puerto Rican rhythm instrument.) At that point, Goyo noticed a set of dusty maracas tied together and hanging on the wall as decoration. He took them down, untied them, and carried them into the kitchen to wash them off.

What had been dug up from beneath the layers, dusted, and washed off was their own precious island heritage. What singing, laughter, and dancing followed! And what a joyous Christmas Eve we celebrated as the transition from living room to sanctuary was finally made. It is true that people can become accustomed to, even fond of, nonindigenous music and style. It is hard to extricate the faith from the cultural packaging people first encounter. Over time, it gets associated with their own life experience, but there is a vibrant and powerful difference when songs are sung in a native tongue, with native instruments and melodies. To accept less than this in worship shows disdain for the energetic diversity that is an intended part of creation.

Every Christmas here since my first when the *guiro* was unwrapped and the maracas were washed off, the Hispanic members and friends of Transfiguration have followed their songlines back to tropical *navidades.* The songlines are lifelines home. Since the original members here were all Puerto Rican, their tradition has been the dominant one, but now many others have been woven in, just as the distant aboriginal tribes followed new trails of notes toward one another.

The memories of a Caribbean Christmas conjured up by the *guiro* and maracas were of the *parranda,* Puerto Rican-style Christmas caroling. The carols, or *aguinados,* are always accompanied by the *guiro,* maracas, guitar, and/or *cuatro* (a kind of guitar). In Puerto Rico, the *parranda* would go from house to house in a series of *asaltos.* The *asaltos* are what they sound like, "assaults." The members of the household being assaulted are supposedly taken by surprise and "forced" to let in their singing guests to offer them traditional food and drink.

Many of the songs include verses to prod those who might have forgotten their hosting responsibilities. One of my favorites goes:

Open the door, open the door,
I'm in the street . . .

Once the singers get inside they continue . . .
over there I see something covered up . . .
I wonder if it might be a roast pig?

Another song is even more direct: "If you don't have anything for us, send someone out to get it!"

These songs are less spiritual than the Mexican *posadas* songs, which stick to the journey of Mary and Joseph into Bethlehem. The *posadas* (Spanish for "inn") groups knock on doors, imitating Mary and Joseph's search for lodging. After initial denials, they are invited in where food and drink abound, but the holiday victuals are not mentioned so overtly in the music. On the other hand, soul and stomach get equal time in Mary's own Christmas canticle recorded in St. Luke's gospel: "my soul magnifies the Lord," sang Mary. "He has filled the hungry with good things."

Both the *parrandas* and *posadas* traditions, which in varying forms seem to exist throughout most of Latin America, emerged where Christmas comes in the summer or where it feels like summer all year round. In addition, the homes to be "assaulted" or sought out for *posada* are usually low-rise buildings, with doors within easy reach. December in the decidedly untropical Bronx is another matter altogether.

We have had to adapt and improvise. A few times we tried to travel from home to home with our *parranda*. This meant that we were out walking in a freezing rain (which never failed to fall, as did the temperature, on the days we planned our *asaltos*) or that we had to find enough cars to try and transport our group from place to place. And forget about the surprise element. Most people live in high-rise apartment buildings with locks on the outside metal doors so that no one can even hear any knocking unless we called ahead to announce ourselves, we'd never get in.

Our revised tradition is to get people to volunteer to be assaulted in the weeks before Christmas. Every week, we visit a different home. The hosts, far from being surprised, spend hours if not days preparing the special *parranda* foods. The rest of the group arrives with *guiros*, maracas, and guitar, and we spend the evening singing, praying, talking, laughing, and eating. The *aguinaldos* are not all or even mainly about food, and we do celebrate the Christmas story in joyous music and readings, but the foods and the songs, like the songs and the land, are inseparable. And what is the food anyway, if not a taste of home? The wonderful thing is that the songs and tastes have created a new community feast in a new land. Coconut bread from Guatemala is on the table with tamales from Honduras, rice from the Dominican Republic, and *empanadas* (meat turnovers) from Argentina.

But for me, after almost twenty years of gustatory immersion in the Puerto Rican navidades, I can no more imagine Christmas without opening steaming *pasteles* (mashed plantain or yucca, stuffed with meat and vegetables) from their banana-leaf wrappings, to eat along with *pernil* (roast pork), rice, *yuca al escabeche* (yucca in garlic sauce), *tembleque* (coconut flan), and *arroz con dulce* (rice pudding), than I can imagine Christmas Eve at home without fish (a custom from Northern Germany), and Christmas morning without German *stollen* (sweet bread studded with raisins, nuts and candied fruits), and Christmas afternoon without a big turkey dinner with all the trimmings.

Christmas is hard for Gregorio, because there are virtually no others around us who share his memories of music and food from Argentina. As is true for so many, the missing of distant family and flavors is always more intense during the holidays. Since Christmas was a more significant day in my family than in his, we follow more of my traditions at Christmas and segue to Argentina for New Year's, which is more important for Gregorio. Then our kitchen fills with delicious smells from the stove as Gregorio rolls out dough for his *empanadas* while tangos and sambas fill the air. While he cooks, he eats the extra *pasteles* given to us as gifts. I make the Argentine flan and *dulce de leche* (milk jam) while listening to Mercedes Sosa, an Argentine folksinger.

Whatever the shepherds were eating that night out in the fields keeping watch over their flocks when the angels appeared with *aguinaldos* straight from the heart of heaven, I'm sure it never tasted ordinary again. All these songlines have led us home and brought us together around the table from all over the world. When John of Patmos envisioned the new Jerusalem from his island exile he wrote in Revelation of a holy city where "the gates are never shut by day—and there will be no night. . . . People will bring into it the glory and honor of the nations." (Revelation 21:25) No locks, no gates, no borders, and the blueprint of the city is outlined in song.

O Holy Night

Camila was trembling when she came to help decorate the church for Christmas. First thing that morning, when she took the garbage to the alleyway outside her basement apartment, she heard what she thought was a cat inside a navy-blue sports bag lying there—except that it didn't quite sound like a cat. It was a newborn baby girl, wet with afterbirth and quivering with cold. Fortunately, Camila's duties as the building's super had her up early with the garbage, because otherwise the baby would have died if she'd remained unfound much longer.

Before coming to church, Camila checked the hospital and learned that the unnamed baby was doing fine. In spite of this good news, Camila's hands were shaking as she wrapped gold foil around the plastic pots that the poinsettias came in and placed them around the altar. Carmen, with her son Stevenson underfoot, was in the kitchen polishing the brass candelabras. Cynthia, a young woman in recovery from crack addiction, came by with her Advent coin folder all filled with $10 worth of quarters. She wanted to make sure that the money would make it to the offering and not tempt her from the path she was following.

I brought Stevenson from the kitchen so he could help arrange the nativity set in front of the altar. We carefully unwrapped the lambs and camels, kings and shepherds, and Mary, Joseph, and baby Jesus with plaster arms forever reaching out. Everything was set up except for the baby. He wouldn't arrive until Christmas Eve, when Stevenson would carry him in, first in the procession, as we stood in the candlelight singing our opening hymn, "Oh Come All Ye Faithful," "*Venid, Fieles Todos.*" The children vie for the honor of carrying in the baby Jesus and I try to choose a child who has gone through a recent loss. A month and a half after losing his mother and brother in the crash of Flight 587, Angelo did it. I hope it helps them to know that this baby has come for them.

I gave Stevenson the tiny figure and remembered when he himself was small enough to fit into my hand, lying in his scratchy manger of tubes and wires while the neonatal intensive care unit worked its miracle. Stevenson clutched the figure tightly in his fist and I showed him how to hold the baby cradled in his open palm. "So they can see his arms?" he asked. Yes, so they can see his arms.

When Hans was about four years old, he used to ask me about heaven when I put him to bed. I told Hans everything I knew about heaven, which didn't take too long. "Will we have a body there?" he wanted to know. "Yes," I said, "a new body." "But will we have arms?" Hans continued. "I don't know," I answered, "We don't know those kinds of details." "But will I have arms?" Young children can be quite persistent. Night after night, Hans raised his urgent question, "Will we have arms?" "Will we have arms?" until I wanted to scream: "Hans, if I've told you once, I've told you a hundred times, I don't know if we will have arms, and I don't care!" Instead, it finally occurred to me to ask the obvious question. "Hans, why do you want arms in heaven?" He looked at me like I was from another planet. "So that Opa and I can hug." Opa is my father, for whom Hans is named. Christmas is about a God with arms.

The Three Kings came to church to try on their robes. Melchoir is picked on because he's overweight and shy. His brother was recently killed in a street fight. Gaspar has never met his dad, and his mother is addicted to crack. Balthazar, a.k.a. Melvin, didn't know it, but would soon be arrested. His father called while I was working on my sermon for Christmas Eve. From what I could gather, he'd been with some boys he didn't usually hang out with, one of whom had stolen a piece of fruit from a green grocer's sidewalk stand. The owner came out with a baseball bat and mayhem ensued. One of the boys had a knife and stabbed him, puncturing a lung. Melvin was around the corner, but was arrested while most of the others got away. I trust Melvin. No doubt he shouldn't have been with this group, but I knew he didn't carry a knife, and I knew he didn't steal.

His lawyer called and urged me to go to the arraignment as a sign of community support. Our intern, Carol, who valued Melvin as a mentor with her confirmation class and as a help with Sunday school, wanted to be there too. So did our youth director. Melvin is a dedicated tutor in our afterschool program and sings in the choir. I told the lawyer that his client was in church virtually every day. The lawyer looked skeptical but read off Melvin's list of church activities to the judge, pointed out that there were no prior arrests and had us all stand to show support. The prosecutor stated that Melvin "had no community ties," and requested a bail of $10,000. No community ties! I wanted to jump up and scream in protest, but had to sit there in silence. The judge lowered the bail to $5,000, a princely sum for a pauper family.

I talked with Melvin's family about raising the money. His father is disabled and his mother suffers from depression. The father told me that he didn't know a single friend who was employed. Like him, they were all on disability. Before long, Melvin was taken to Riker's Island. The next day was Christmas Eve. I went to a bail bondsman. But even after paying the bondsman, the courts would be closed until after Christmas. Our third king would spend Christmas Eve behind bars, but he didn't know it yet.

He was with Melchoir and Gaspar trying on their velvet robes, braided gold belts, and royal headpieces. Then they headed for the bathroom to check themselves out in a mirror. Instead of a Christmas play, our children put on a bilingual drama of the Three Kings on the Sunday closest to January 6, Epiphany. The custom comes to Transfiguration from Puerto Rico, where the celebration of *Los Tres Reyes* rivals, or perhaps surpasses, Christmas. In many Latin American countries, the major cultural holiday (with corresponding commercialization) is January 6th rather than December 25. The department stores of Buenos Aires advertise the visit of the Three Kings rather than Santa Claus. Traditionally, the Three Kings celebration is a time for street processions, songs, worship with dramas and more processions, giving gifts, and partying with friends and family.

At the church, our celebration has evolved to include the children's dramatic presentation of the Christmas story, culminating in the arrival of the Three Kings. The drama is another way for the children to enter into the story. We sing traditional songs in Spanish and English, and after worship, there's a big fiesta which used to include several piñatas—one for the smaller children and one for the older group. Having a hundred keyed-up kids stand in a circle, ready to charge at the shower of candy while they took turns wearing a blindfold and wielding a big stick, turned out not to be such a wonderful idea. Repeated admonitions not to step over the line that kept them a safe distance from the swinging stick were lost in the mounting din. The year that an eighty-year-old woman narrowly missed being conked on the head and a child was lucky to escape with a bloody nose, rather than a broken one, was enough for me. We have since devised another entertainment that satisfies the lust for fun and sweets but leaves out the blood and potential lawsuits.

Melchoir, Gaspar, and Balthazar came back from the bathroom pleased with their regal appearance, but their pleasure wouldn't last long. In Balthazar's case, it would be especially short-lived as beautiful robes gave way to cuffs and prison attire. The circumstances of the boys lives have severed any potential pride in royal bloodlines. Yet most of our past and present kings have been to the Simba Circle camp in the summer in Iowa. We hope these brief days of royalty and their ongoing experiences at the church will set the stage for them to feel more like real, gift-bearing kings. We want them to be able to do what the original Three Kings did—outsmart Herod. As it turned out, on the day after Christmas, Melvin was released on his own recognizance, a wiser, more sober king.

There is an annual Simba reunion each winter in Milwaukee, which our boys had never attended because of the great distance. Gaylord Thomas, whose vision and persistent efforts brought the camp into being and keeps it going, has a passion for the Simbas' welfare that extends far beyond the summer. After Trevor's mother was murdered, Gaylord arranged for him and Melvin to fly out for the reunion. It was their first time on a plane and at a hotel. When our intern, Martin, and I picked them up at the airport on their return and took them out to eat, we heard all about the trip. One phrase stood out, "They treated us like kings!"

During a school break a few months later, they met Gaylord again and flew to Santa Cruz to assist with the initiation of a Simba-like group based on Native American traditions. When Trevor's picture appeared with some of the local youth on the front page of the Santa Cruz Sentinel, he felt proud, and when they got a well-deserved ovation back in the Bronx for their leadership on the other side of the country, that felt good, too. Then I got a call from Gaylord. As part of the program in Santa Cruz, the boys had participated in a sweat-lodge ceremony, part of which included connecting with ancestors. Seventeen-year-old Trevor had prayed for his mother and then he said, "There's someone else I want to pray for . . . I want to pray for forgiveness for the man who killed her. He needs help." The elders were astounded. Sometimes the transfiguration we work for seems a long way off, and sometimes, suddenly, it just blazes up in our midst.

Every year, our Three Kings play ends as Melchoir, Gaspar, and Balthazar place their gifts before the infant Jesus (sometimes a real baby and sometimes a doll). They enter with the gifts as the congregation sings "We Three Kings":

O star of wonder, star of night, star with royal beauty bright;
Westward leading, still proceeding, guide us to thy perfect light.

Trevor used to be one of the kings. In the sweat lodge, he proved himself to be a guiding star.

The boys took off their costumes and left as Deneen came in to practice her solo for Christmas Eve. A depressing number of young girls were in bad sexual relationships. A pregnant thirteen-year-old girl came in to talk with me. She'd been having sex since she was ten. Another girl, seventeen and active in our youth program, was seven months pregnant. She didn't show at all, and no one knew, not even her mother, whom I convinced her we had to tell. A man, twenty-nine, came in wanting to marry a seventeen-year-old he'd been living with for the past three years. I told him that it was illegal, and he said that he knew it. He had already been arrested and put in jail for it, but the girl's mother bailed him out. She didn't want her daughter at home, and this seemed like a good arrangement to her. I told him that I wanted to meet the girl, but he refused. I guess I was supposed to marry them sight unseen. He'd have to find someone else, though I hoped he didn't.

In all this sex, there seems to be little genuine pleasure. When I talk with the girls, they say they don't enjoy it much of the time. We have youth groups, Bible studies, classes, speakers, mentors; we listen and listen and talk and talk. For some of the girls, it makes a significant difference, but not for all, not for enough. The hunger for love, acceptance, and touch is overwhelming. The tragic thing is that all this sex gives so little of what they crave and leads to consequences none of them want.

Sometimes the motivation is anger. One fourteen-year-old described her sexual exploits: "I just hit and run, hit and run." Her stepfather began molesting her when she was little, and this is how she's getting back. She uses her sexuality as a weapon, in a macho way. She purposely seeks out older men and says she hopes they get arrested. When I mentioned the dangers inherent in her behavior, she opened her mouth and showed me the razor blade hidden inside. She had mastered a trick to flick the blade out and back in with her tongue. Now she's worried that she might be infected with HIV. She acts tough, and then she cries because the other kids call her a slut.

One thing is clear to me with respect to adults and to young people. Giving solid, detailed information about HIV/AIDS, other sexually transmitted diseases, and pregnancy prevention is necessary. We do it, but it is not enough, since information without the will or self-respect to use it is virtually useless. Some of the very men and women in the community who work as HIV/AIDS-prevention outreach workers, who have attended trainings and who give workshops, have themselves been infected with the virus—after they began this work. Lack of information is obviously not the only problem. If this is true for adults, how much more is it true for the teenagers?

Deneen came to practice a solo for Christmas Eve. We went over to the organ, and I gave her the music. She stood there looking at the words.

"Can we talk first?"

"Of course."

Deneen ended up telling me about how she was having sex with her boyfriend and was worried about getting pregnant or getting AIDS. It struck me that she wanted to get pregnant because she consciously and repeatedly had intercourse with no birth control and then remarked that her boyfriend was willing to use a condom. "Yes," she admitted, "my mother told me that if I got pregnant, she'd kick me out." Why did she want her mom to kick her out? Her stepfather began having sex with her when she was six and only stopped when she was ten and after she told an aunt. Now he leaves her alone sexually but makes her life hell in other ways. "My mother treats him like a king who can do no wrong and makes me feel like garbage." Deneen had decided that the answer would be to have a baby who would love her.

She sounded ambivalent about sex with the boyfriend, and when I asked her what was good and not good about it, she said that the jewelry he gave her was good. She didn't know what wasn't good. She showed me two large gold rings and her necklace. I asked what else made her feel good besides the boyfriend, and she told me that it was singing and acting, things she only does in church. Perhaps it would help to find more singing and acting things she can be involved in.

Do I "condone" these relationships? Should the church mark these youth people with scarlet letters? Demand that they sign pledges of abstinence or kick them out? I think these are stupid questions. Obviously these relationships are not good. This kind of sex not only threatens the emotional, mental, and spiritual well-being of those involved, it jeopardizes the "lovers'" very lives. But realistically all we can do is persist in loving, listening, praying, teaching, and lifting up alternatives. At least, I think that Deneen is beginning to see that having a baby won't solve her problems. Maybe she just says it to please me. Maybe she believes it. She promised to ask her aunt to take her to the clinic for birth-control pills tomorrow. Then she practiced her solo for Christmas Eve: "O Holy Night." She sings like an angel.

My favorite Christmas hymn will not be sung. No one knows it here, so I sing it to myself. I sang it to the children as a lullaby. That's what I do with some of my old favorites that don't work here because of the cultural context. I use them for lullabies.

Lo, how a Rose e'er blooming from tender stem hath sprung!
Of Jesse's lineage coming, as folk of old have sung.
It came a floweret bright, amid the cold of winter,
When half spent was the night.

Hope flowers in the cold like the tropical poinsettias placed around the sanctuary. Melvin's family came in and embraced me with tears. Our voices filled the candlelit church as Stevenson walked toward the manger holding the baby whose arms do indeed reach toward us, seeking connection in the cold, bright air.

CHAPTER NINE

SPRING CONSTRUCTION
REPORTS

Spring Cleaning with St. Jangama

I decided to try and have the house clean and organized by Easter. One of our interns told me of a Jewish friend who explained keeping kosher as participating in the act of creation. According to the friend, order in the kitchen keeps chaos at bay. In the Genesis account, God wrests creation from watery chaos or *tehom*, a close relation to the ancient sea monster, Tiamat. So I'm battling Tiamat in our closets and under our furniture. Tiamat wreaks havoc in my date book, too. I'm in an ever-losing battle trying to wrest time to clean, pray, write, be with the children, be with Gregorio, be a pastor, pay bills, shop, cook, enter stuff into the computer to be more organized, etc. Then, when I try to remember everything I am supposed to be doing, I forget. Sometimes we find ourselves in ridiculous positions. Shall we make love or vacuum? The dust balls multiply.

But my cleaning issues were nothing like Burnice's. For three days, water had been showering onto her kitchen from a burst pipe above the broken ceiling tiles. The stove was covered in plastic garbage bags. In the bathroom, you had to hold up an umbrella in order to use the toilet. The landlord was "working on it." Tiamat smirked, and her cousins, the monsters Homelessness and Despair, poked their heads into the bedroom where Burnice wept.

The rich
will make temples for Siva.

What shall I,
a poor man, do?

My legs are pillars,
the body the shrine,
the head a cupola,
of gold.

Listen, O lord of the meeting rivers,
things standing shall fall,
but the moving ever shall stay.
  Basavanna (twelfth-century Indian poet
and devotee of the Hindu deity Siva)

In the language of Hindu devotional poetry *sthavara* (the standing) shall fall and *jangama* (the moving) ever shall stay. St. Jangama? She is the patron saint of the inner city—at least, she should be! Jangama doesn't exist in the canon of saints, but *jangama* is definitely a driving force in our midst.

"Things standing shall fall ..." At times, the ongoing instability of the inner city threatens to overwhelm the lives and structures of our neighborhood and our work as a church. AIDS, asthma, shootings, inadequate housing, addiction, and unemployment persist, in spite of all the positive changes. One life is transformed and then, another falls apart. Beautiful new homes go up, apartments are renovated but so many new homeless families are crowding into the Bronx Emergency Assistance Unit office that many have ended up sleeping right there on the floor. A woman finally gains the strength to move away from an abusive husband, but she must then leave her leadership roles in this church and community too. Her children are baptized, enthusiastic participants in many church activities and then they disappear. A teen leader and mentor to younger children is arrested for being in the wrong place at the wrong time in the wrong skin. Another is randomly gunned down. People in recovery enter the workforce for the first time, but the only jobs they find require work on weekends, nights, around the clock in some cases—cleaning homes, washing dishes, tending the homebound. Time for family, community, and church evaporates.

As a pastor, I keep wanting to build something stable, solid, and lasting and often seem to be failing. Things progress and then seem to fall back. I've always liked the phrase "burning patience" quoted by Pablo Neruda when he received the Nobel prize for literature:

> I wish to say to the people of good will, to the workers, to the poets, that the whole future has been expressed in this line by Rimbaud: only with a burning patience can we conquer the splendid city which will give light, justice and dignity to all.

But sometimes my patience wears thin. What does it mean to be patient when young people you love kill or are killed? What does it mean to be patient when we find ourselves mourning more and more young adults dying of AIDS and seeing their children become orphans? What does it mean to be patient when politicians, businesses, and even fellow Christians write off an entire community? And there is plenty of impatience with my private failures too —feeling constantly torn between family and church responsibilities, never enough time to do anything right, feeling that everything is so fragile and might collapse at any moment like Burnice's ceiling—and it will be my fault as the pastor who should oversee it all—and knowing that such thoughts give far too much importance to myself.... Lack of perspective, lack of breathing space. "Things standing shall fall ..." Does that mean me?

Sometimes when I'm short of patience, I focus on the little things, which I find myself doing more and more. Today, this teenager is going to college, the first in her family to graduate from high school—"I can't decide whether I want to be a teacher or a psychiatrist or a pediatrician!" Today, this woman is speaking up for justice—"I sat at the table of history today, Pastor, instead of just reading about it!" Today, this man is experiencing forgiveness. Today, this child feels cherished in the house of God.

Then I worry that this is a way to avoid incompetence and helplessness in bigger matters. I question whether I am contracting my vision, lowering my expectations—exactly what we pastors are warned that we must never do. It seems that every time I open a church magazine, I am instructed to raise my expectations, higher and higher. But over the years I have lowered my expectations, and it has made me feel freer and happier. I am more accepting of my limitations and more aware of the grace of God working when I cannot.

I am often reminded of a brief conversation with a chaplain on the burn unit of the New York Presbyterian Hospital where most of the September 11th burn victims were, including Felipe. No matter what time of day or night I visited the unit, this chaplain was there. I wondered how she managed day after day facing so much pain and suffering, lives torn apart like shredded, charred skin. One day when I saw her in the hallway, I asked her how she was holding up. She looked at me like I was crazy and gave voice to my worst fears: "I'm not holding up," she said. Then there was a pause, as she took a deep breath. "I'm not holding up," she repeated. "I'm being held up."

For we who are held by such grace, the questions seem not to be, "What good do we do and what difference does it really make?" but "How can we not do good?" I take comfort from St. Teresa who concludes her *Interior Castle*, (which surely must have discouraged a few novices who found their progress unutterably slow): "In a word, my sisters, I will end by saying that we must not build towers without foundations, and that the Lord does not look so much at the magnitude of anything we do as at the love with which we do it."

I also take comfort from St. Jangama who reminds me that instability is the only thing that lasts in this earthly city. It's ironic that many clergy choose to avoid the inner city in favor of a more secure environment for themselves and for their families. Then some of these same ministers complain that their churches are set in their ways, stuck, rigid, unmoving—which is to say, stable! A fully-satisfied church where nothing moves or changes is a dead church. In the end, stasis may be more deadly than instability. And stasis is definitely no problem here! In fact, there is tremendous vitality amidst the instability. In my experience here, we live *en la lucha* (in the struggle) and life is scrapping and sparring all over the place, unwilling to sit still or go down and give up the ghost. The moving ever shall stay because it bears within a dynamic, creative, and indefatigable power—the power of *la lucha* against monstrous forces that threaten to devour us, but have not and will not because we struggle on. Jesus himself wandered the streets and shores with no place to lay his head, described as pitching his tent among us, not constructing monuments. His followers should probably expect more of the same. Of course, in my own instability, I vacillate between frustration with the precarious nature of things here and awe at Jangama's resilience. In the end, she wrests me from fatigue and rekindles the restless, burning patience that fuels our struggle.

Luther's response to this issue is also a favorite of mine: "If I knew that the world were going to end tomorrow, I would plant an apple tree today." I drew an apple tree on both our children's birth announcements. Our plans to build are like Luther's planting, an investment in the future that is out of our hands. We do what we can to build the splendid city and let go of the rest. And I write, like Hans with his K'Nex compulsion. I try to use blocks of language to shore up what is swept away and stem the losses in our efforts to create "the splendid city"—a stable congregation in a solid building in a community with an infrastructure that supports life.

Only God knows the ultimate blueprint and timetable. In the meantime, I vow to keep up the parallel efforts of making order with the mess on my desk, or rather messes—the writing project at home and the building project at church. A friend told me that our word "poetry" comes from the Greek, *poiein*, and means "to pile up, to build, to create."

Words strain,
Crack and sometimes break, under the burden,
Under the tension, slip, slide, perish,
Decay with imprecision, will not stay in place,
Will not stay still.

So said T. S. Eliot, and it often feels that way, but St. Jangama sees it differently: "Things standing shall fall, but the moving ever shall stay." I certainly hope so.

Outside the church, a few men were burning garbage that had accumulated—heaps of dry weeds, sticks, and rotten tree limbs, empty cartons that once held donated food and clothing long since given away, and assorted debris that eluded the regular garbage collection. With the construction, we had a lot of that. This was a good Lenten activity, Lent being the church's traditional time for renewal and repentance—literally turning around, getting reordered, reorganized—spring cleaning from the inside out. I wished it were so easy to dispose of the accumulated deadwood in my own life, the empty desires and anxieties that I kept reopening and checking, unable to accept the evidence that they contained nothing worthwhile. I wished I could place myself wholly in the cleansing fire and let all the junk turn to ash, emerging with only the pure, the good, and the true.

Spring cleaning inside the church was out of the question. Construction dust was everywhere. We couldn't keep everything continually covered because then we'd need to vacate the church altogether. In any case, covering up didn't do much good. Like tiny mice, the motes of dust squeezed through every crevice. In my office, I found the dust had sneaked between the papers of every file I opened in every closed drawer. The whole place felt unsettled. The construction crew was always needing something else moved from here to there. They promised that we were nearing the end, about two months more, but "soon" and "very soon" were beginning to feel interminable. Some days I just longed for the familiar dust and customary chaos of our preconstruction life.

> Sometimes Death, puffing at the doore
> Blows all the dust about the floore:
> But while he thinkes to spoile the roome, he sweeps.
> Blest be the Architect, whose art
> Could build so strong in a weake heart.
> (George Herbert, "The Church")

We picked out floor tiles. They needed to be practical, able to hide spills and dirt, but strong and beautiful, too. These were special floors. Our Space for Grace. Our holy ground. Solomon overlaid his stone temple floors with gold. These floors would bear the weight of living stones, cots for the homeless, cases of food, chairs, and tables for Sunday school, church dinners, ESL classes, youth gatherings, and the after-school program. Our floors would also be overlaid with purest gold to defy "Death, puffing at the doore."

The Fall of Grit

Tanya died during dinner, eating sandwiches with her six children. They thought she was choking, but it was heart failure. She was only thirty-nine years old. I had worried about this for some time, given her heart condition and obesity, but it was still a shock. On Sunday, she was in church, something that had been hard for her to manage for the past month. She and her children filled their own pew.

Tanya liked to talk. I once went with her on a three-hour drive to a meeting, and she talked nonstop for the three hours there and the three hours back. She had the same approach to prayer. Each week, when the congregation was invited to pray, Tanya jumped in before anyone else and began with the same words: "I thank you Lord for this day. I thank you Lord for such a beautiful day!" Ana commented, "Mommy, she said it even when it was cold and raining." Tanya always gave the word "beautiful" a lyrical delivery, turning it into a song by itself, and then she'd be off, on another marathon of prayer.

Eating brought on Tanya's death, but it was also her life. Sunday after Sunday, Tanya came to eat what she called "my breakfast with Jesus," an expression she learned from Burnice. She'd raise her hand and rock with pleasure as the bread and wine were brought to the altar and the congregation sang:

We're gonna sit at the Welcome Table.
We're gonna sit at the Welcome Table one of these day, Hallelujah!
No more hunger 'round that table . . . all God's children 'round that
    Table.

For a few years, Tanya came to the table walking on her own. Then she came leaning on a cane, then supported by her teenage sons. When that was too difficult, she would remain in her seat, and someone would carry Communion to her. Then the weeks when she couldn't make it down the front steps of her apartment building became more frequent, so I brought Communion to her home. "Breakfast in bed," she joked and went on to pray her prayer. I imagine her sitting at the Welcome Table now: "I thank you Lord for this day. I thank you Lord for such a beautiful day!" Her mother and sister came from North Carolina to take the children back with them.

A month later we lost Nina. It was a sad time of saying goodbye at her funeral. We not only lost another young mother, but we lost her recently baptized children, too—Kaprice, Crystal, Jovanna, John, Tanesha, and Derrick. The last two were taken in by a new foster family, and Nina's own four went with their grandmother to another state. Nina was thirty-one. Between her and Tanya's death, half of our children's choir was gone.

Tanya was not the only young woman walking around here with a cane. Nina had had one, too. It is terrible how many women in their thirties and forties are walking around with canes. It's a sign of poverty producing sickness. Most of the women are weakened by multiple health problems such as high blood pressure, heart disease, asthma, diabetes, and cancer. And it seems clear that in many cases, drug abuse does permanent damage to the body's immune system, apart from HIV. So many women in recovery, who have not abused drugs for several years and who are not HIV-positive, seem to have a much higher incidence of serious health problems. I don't know of any study that links drug abuse with cancer, but I am convinced that there is a connection which is then aggravated by the ongoing stress of trying to pay your bills, raise your children, watch your back, and care for others with no one there to care for you. On the other hand, some of these women have never abused drugs and are free of HIV. Poverty is a sickening virus unto itself.

When I see these beautiful young women bent over canes, my heart clenches like a fist. In some years, the majority of the funerals I performed were for women younger than myself, mostly mothers. The week Tanya died, there was grim news from the Hunt's Point garbage-disposal front: the dismembered body of a "heavy-set Hispanic woman in her 40's" was found in several blue plastic bags at one of the recycling plants. "Police ask anyone with information to call (1-800-577-TIPS)." Does anyone want tips about all the other women being torn apart in this place?

Rita was in the hospital with AIDS and told me when I visited that it was her anniversary. I assumed it was some recovery milestone until she told me that it was exactly six years ago when she got back positive results on her HIV test. At the time, she was in prison on drug charges but had been drug-free for four years. Until this hospitalization, she'd lived at the Carver Hotel on Prospect Avenue. It's one of the worst single-room-occupancy places I've ever entered: crawling with roaches, rodents, and drugs. It reeks. I don't have asthma but find it hard to breathe there. Many of the residents do have asthma and/or tuberculosis as well as various respiratory problems. The sound of coughing behind closed doors is constant.

Rita didn't have many visitors and talked nonstop. She felt guilty that her husband contracted the disease from her, but he knew she was infected and still refused to use a condom. When she got home following her last hospitalization, he threw her on the floor and grabbed her by the throat. Only when she lost consciousness and began shaking did he let her go, later saying that he was scared she was going to die. He called during my visit and told her he was coming with money to pay for another day's worth of phone and TV service. Rita hung up the phone with a pleased smile, taking this gesture as a sign of affection.

She was restless with a bad headache and worried that her medication was not coming on schedule. She'd gotten a diagnosis of toxoplasmosis and wondered if I knew anything about it. It was the same parasitic infection I'd had as a teenager. This cheered her up. After all, I had it, and look at me. I didn't mention that my immune system had been in comparatively good shape. She told me that the past week was her forty-second birthday. Mine was a month away. We held hands and prayed. She didn't want to let go, so we just stayed that way for a while, holding hands, holding on to each other, holding on to life.

Before I left, Rita told me that she longed for a blue rosary like one her grandmother had bequeathed to her. It had been stolen while she slept at a shelter. This was a simple wish, but rosaries were not in big supply at our Lutheran church. I went to the gift shop of a local Roman Catholic church and stocked up on plastic and glass-bead rosaries—pink, white, and blue. Rita was thrilled with the blue one I gave her. She held it up to the glare of the hospital's fluorescent light. "It's like a string of sapphires!" she exclaimed. The next time I saw her, she was almost unconscious with morphine, but that didn't keep her from mouthing the words to Psalm 23 as we prayed together. I couldn't do much else other than help her overworked nurse turn her to change her diaper.

When I got home, I found that my mother had set the table. Gregorio was recovering from the flu, but he went out anyway and came home with bird of paradise flowers for me. It was my birthday. Ana had a strep throat and chicken pox and I was starting to feel sick as well. My mother came to care for us and cooked a dinner that we all managed to enjoy, as the birds of paradise spread their wings over the table. There was a long period in my life when I could not pray verse fourteen of what I've come to regard as a birthday Psalm, number 139: *I praise you for I am fearfully and wonderfully made!* It was as though a big stone blocked my soul whenever I'd hit that line. Sometime over these years, without my really noticing it, gentle angels have rolled that stone away. We were eating cherry pie, my birthday favorite, when the phone rang.

Rita's funeral took place two days later. At least there were no young children left behind. During the visit when I gave her the rosary, she'd told me about a day from her own childhood when she and Lucy, both abandoned by their mothers, lived together in a home run by nuns. The home had a barn where horses were kept and one of the horses was blind. Rita felt that it was being mistreated. Her idea was to skip class and sneak into the barn and set the poor, blind horse free.

Lucy didn't need much convincing to skip class. Before long, the two girls were in the barn, and soon horse and girls were free in the fields instead of being stuck in their respective stalls. Unfortunately, their flash of freedom did not last long. A nun spotted them from a window, and soon the liberated horse was sent to the stable, and the girls were sent to their rooms.

As Rita told the story, it was obvious that she savored those brief moments of liberation even if they had resulted in a punishment. As she lay dying, the memory brought laughter and smiles to her face. She also told me that she wanted to have her ashes scattered over the waters in view of another free-spirited woman, the Statue of Liberty. I think it's illegal, but once the ashes hit the water, what could be done about it?

Rita's death pulled the heavy darkness back over Lucy's eyes. Nevertheless, at the end of the funeral, Lucy stood and requested us to sing "Thank you, Lord." Soon afterward, she kept her promise to Rita and scattered her ashes off the Staten Island Ferry. She had wanted to do this alone and later told me that nobody noticed as she poured the dust of her friend into the waters. Somebody noticed, I said.

When Camila's sister, Mirthelina, died in a bus crash that killed forty people in Santo Domingo, she could not attend the funeral because of her status as an "undocumented alien." Camila served on our church council, for which the only requisite document is a baptismal certificate. She requested that we have a memorial service here.

Mirthelina's family in New York was full of questions, including the ones that came over the phone lines from Santo Domingo: Do the dead come back and take over other bodies? Can the dead speak to us? Can we hear their voices? Do they meet us in our dreams? Why is the furniture moving around in the night? It is her restless spirit? If you die before your time, then will the spirit stay around until the real date you were supposed to die? If there is unfinished business and the person is angry, will they come back in your dreams? In your living room? Why do they keep appearing to us but we can't touch them? (Mirthelina was not the only dead relative to make appearances.)

As the pastor, I am supposed to know the answers to these questions. I don't. I can only share what I believe:

I believe in . . . the communion of saints
the forgiveness of sins
the resurrection of the body
and the life everlasting.

I tried to explain our creed to Camila and her family. I believe that our connection with those who have died continues, waking and dreaming. This is part of the communion of saints. I don't believe that the limitations of this life continue after death, which means that unspent anger and unfinished business are things of the past for those who die. This is part of how I would interpret the forgiveness of sins. Unfinished business is for us, not for the dead. I still don't know if, in the afterlife, we'll have the arms to hug with that Hans wants but I'm positive that there will be no hit lists in heaven.

I had no comments to share on furniture moving in the night but was glad that it wasn't moving while I was sitting on it, drinking the strong coffee they gave me as we contemplated these ultimate mysteries. Is it possible that the highly charged energy of grief moves things around? Why not? It certainly turns us upside down inside our skin. Why not on the other side, too? Reality is not limited to my tiny corner of it.

The world of church/state relations can also be surreal. I experienced it when the residence that was Michelle's home for the past few years held her memorial service. A number of Michelle's friends at the house came regularly to the church largely because of Michelle's enthusiasm and caring. The social worker planning the service told me over the phone that she wished she could send all the women at the house to the church because it has had such a positive influence on those who had come, all of whom are living with some form of mental illness or are in recovery from substance abuse. On the other hand, her supervisor would be at the service, and she couldn't show bias toward any religious group. She regularly turned away Jehovah's Witnesses who came to the door, so she couldn't favor my church. Understood. But Michelle was not a Jehovah's Witness. In any case, she suggested it would be great if I could please say something without being "too religious." Michelle's friends from the house would expect her pastor to say something. In addition, I was asked to help think of some ritual, some ceremony that would be meaningful but not "too religious," perhaps a tree planting? And could I please give a blessing (a nonreligious blessing, of course)?

The social worker wanted ritual, symbol, remembrance, celebration, and thanksgiving. She even wanted blessing, but it dared not be "too religious." Of course, all these things are the very stuff of religion. She wanted to mark and celebrate a life as special, a life set apart and remembered with gratitude in the face of death; "set apart," this is one definition of holy. We would be engaged in a holy act, but it must not be religious. Actually, I didn't care if we called it religious as long as it was holy. I'd rather be holy than religious any day. I even agreed that a tree planting was something Michelle would have liked. The other residents of the house liked it too. The small grass plot outside the building had no trees, and being private property, to plant one wouldn't require the blessing of the Parks Department.

I went to the service prepared to be holy but not too religious. On the other hand, I realized that what the social worker meant was essentially that I was expected to refrain from naming certain names. Definitely, I should not mention Jesus, and it would be better not to mention G-o-d either. Would I be thrown out if I did? In a way, this was like pouring Rita's ashes into the sea: once the words were out, who could bottle them back up?

We gathered in the sitting room. Some of the residents were already challenging the plan for the day by taking sandwiches from the kitchen, which were not supposed to be eaten until after the "memorial gathering" (not service), was over. I overheard staff discussing this infraction. They decided to let it go. The residents were viewed as nervous and stressed. Nothing should be said to upset them further. Small pieces of paper and pencils were distributed to each person in the room. We were instructed to write a memory of Michelle on the paper, which we would then read to the group. Most people spent the time fidgeting, folding, unfolding, and refolding the paper. Everyone had something to say that could not begin to fit on the little slips. The printed program we received remembered Michelle for "her energy, her enthusiasm, her love of dancing and of music and of red, her joyous laughter, her many kindness to the residents, her quiet passion for reading and her loud passion for life."

The first person to speak was the visiting supervisor. She talked of Michelle's life-giving spirit, her joy, her love for her church, and even her faith in G-o-d. The residents, whom I supposed to be the ones we were protecting from name-calling, continued to ignore the plan. When it was time for their "words of remembrance," many spoke of how Michelle led them to the church and to a faith which would help them now. Gwen said that she could still hear Michelle's voice telling her to get up out of bed and get to church, despite the depression that held her down. After all, Gwen continued, Michelle kept up her spirits in the midst of sickness and pain and Michelle even got up from the dead to speak to her now, so she should get up from her own bed! This sounded suspiciously like resurrection talk.

When it was over, we trooped outside, bearing our folded up slips of paper as instructed. It was time for the tree planting. Across the street, people were lining up for their afternoon cup of methadone. We formed a circle around the tree. The pieces of paper were to be placed next to the roots, planting our memories and thanksgivings there. It was also a planting a prayers. Several of Michelle's friends voiced moving prayers as they planted their folded papers at the roots. The prayers, like the sneaked sandwiches, were allowed so as not to further upset these fragile souls. It was only the supposedly healthy pastor who needed to watch her language and avoid the appearance of being too religious—no prayers from the clergy, please! Only from from the mentally ill, who don't know any better.

I'd brought my rain stick for the blessing. It is acceptable to have religious symbols from the rain forests of Guatemala, since these are not associated with any recognizable faith affiliation. I lifted the stick high in the air and invited the gathered group to close their eyes and listen to the sound of rain, gently at first, coming down with life-giving water like the wash of Michelle's own baptism into the passion, death, and resurrection of her Lord. I tipped the stick straighter and the sound got stronger, the sound of "loud passion." The Irish poet Seamus Heaney caught the sound:

> Upend the rain stick and what happens next
> Is a music that you never would have known
> To listen for. In a cactus stalk
>
> Downpour, sluice-rush, spillage and backwash
> Come flowing through. . . .

He might have been describing Michelle lying in the hospital as deep rivers of song streamed toward me through her stick-dry throat:

Who cares if the music that transpires
Is the fall of grit or dry seeds through a cactus?
You are like a rich man entering heaven
Through the ear of a raindrop.
     "The Rain Stick" in *The Spirit Level*

We were drenched in blessing, and I felt satisfied. Life was celebrated with thanksgiving. Life stretched out roots and branches in the face of death. Prayers were said. Blessing was shared. It was time to eat the remaining sandwiches. "Shouldn't we say grace?" one of the mentally challenged residents asked. By then, the social worker was worn down. "Pastor, would you bless the food?" Of course . . . in the name of Jesus. Amen.

Dust to Dust

Remember that you are dust and to dust you shall return. The words we say over and over on Ash Wednesday, as the ashes are distributed, have often struck me as unnecessary. Each day brings fresh reminders of our dustiness. We already know that we are dust. Even before September 11th reminded the nation, we knew it here. And yet Ash Wednesday is hugely popular in the Bronx, along with Palm Sunday. In each case, people come for something tangible—ashes pressed on your skin, palm branches you can hold in your hand. People who otherwise never come to church arrive pleading, "Can I please have some ashes?" "Are there any palms left?" Of course, the bread and wine in our weekly celebrations of Holy Communion are just as palpable, if not more so, as we take them into our bodies. But non-church attenders tend to view the sacrament as off-limits, whereas ashes and palms are for the masses.

There's another link between these days. We make the ashes by burning leftover dried palms from Palm Sunday the previous year, adding a little oil so they stick better as we mark them on foreheads in the shape of a cross. You can also buy them from church catalogs that advertise: "Fresh cut palm ashes . . . please order early . . . we supply the finest grade of palm ash available anywhere . . . washed and ready to use ashes for Ash Wednesday . . . prices available on request . . ." Washed ashes? Graded ashes? Priced ashes?

On the Sunday after the September 11th attack, some of our Sunday school children walked down the block to take their handmade cards to our local fire station, which lost three men when the Towers collapsed. Once there, the children saw photographs of the fallen heroes over their lockers and in one locker, a pair of boots caked in ash, boots recovered from the rubble.

"Were those his real boots?" six-year-old Derrick asked. Yes they were.

"Was he wearing them in there?" Yes he was.

"Can I touch them?"

The fireman hesitated. The boots and every particle of dust they bore were precious. You could tell he didn't want that dust dislodged. "Let's just look," I said, as another fireman appeared with a plate of homemade chocolate chip cookies for the children. It was dust that had something holy about it, dust that bore a message of saving love, dust from Calvary, priceless.

That is why we mark each forehead with ash in the sign of a cross, not just a reminder of death, but a reminder that dusty as we are, we are all priceless —lifted from dust, headed for dust and bound for glory. The Nobel Prize– winning poet Nelly Sachs writes of the transformation of dust in her poem "Butterfly." She wrote in German as a Jew exiled in Sweden, as genocide swept her people up in smoke:

> What lovely aftermath
> is painted in your dust.
> You who were led through the flaming core of earth
> through its stony shell . . .
> What lovely aftermath
> is painted in your dust.
> What royal sign
> in the secret of the air.

We had two scheduled services for Ash Wednesday, one in English and one in Spanish, until the year we had an unscheduled one. Carmelo, who owned the corner store by the church, wanted me to bring him some ashes since he couldn't leave the store. I figured that taking ashes to the storebound fit into the same category as taking Communion to the homebound. When I came down the street with the bowl of ashes, I passed the group of men and women who hang out in front of the store in order to have easy access to the beer sold inside. We always exchange greetings. I invariably invite them to church, and invariably they don't come. But on this particular day when they saw me coming with the ashes, as if on cue, they all knelt down on the sidewalk, obedient to some internal rubric. They begged me for ashes, and then some of them got up and went to find their friends. In the end, there was a congregation of about twenty-five kneeling by the bodega.

This was the beginning of a new relationship. Soon afterward, the corner congregation came looking for me when one of their them was the victim of a hit-and-run accident. José was thrown from his wheelchair by a speeding car and killed. He was a passionate Puerto Rican independista, who became more impassioned with every beer. Whenever he saw me, usually several times a week, he would launch into a political tirade that I could never fully understand but which clearly championed the independence of Puerto Rico with something about Cuba and Castro thrown in. Our encounters would end with me trying to avoid his beery kisses by substituting a handshake. Invariably, he would end up kissing my hands until I managed to pull them away. His own hands looked like they hadn't had contact with soap or water in years, and I always returned to the church to wash, which disturbed me, as though I were trying to rinse away our meeting itself.

Nobody knew of any family José might have had beyond his corner comrades. They dug into their beer money to make a collection for the funeral and went to the funeral home begging for help. The owners were willing to do it but obviously would do only the bare minimum. I was soon to find out how bare that minimum would be. One member of the group had been delegated to ask me if I would officiate at the service. When I arrived, José's body was draped in a large Puerto Rican flag that his friends had borrowed. Something was leaking from the back of his head onto the pillow on which it rested, and the stain was spreading.

No one showed up at the service other than José's bodega buddies and the funeral director's wife, there to make sure that nothing untoward occurred. I thought a round of beers would have been appropriate but didn't offer to buy one. I'd brought my guitar and began singing songs with a liberation theme in honor of his politics. I then moved on to more religious music in honor of his soul. Actually, I don't entirely separate these things, nor did he, something we had in common. After the music, we moved into some shared memories, Bible readings, preaching, and prayers. When I got to the commendation, I reached out to touch José for one last time. I realized it was the first time that I had initiated such contact and felt a wave of sadness.

On Ash Wednesday the following year, we decided to be intentional about taking the service to the street. We offered regular worship in the sanctuary, but in the afternoon we went outside. More than a hundred people came asking to be blessed and marked with the ashes. They asked for prayers for strength in recovery from addiction, prayers related to health and relationship struggles. We weren't more than twenty feet from the front doors of the church, and yet I knew that very few of those people would ever have walked through the church doors to request the same prayers and blessing. Why not? They are people who feel ashamed to enter the church. They are not homebound or storebound, but shamebound and afraid of crossing the border, afraid of being met with judgment and rejection. They didn't realize how identical their condition was to that of the members who would later gather to worship inside the doors, many also HIV-positive, in various stages of addiction recovery, abused, homeless, poor—like all of us, for as Luther put it, we are all beggars. But there was no way for those outside to know this if those inside were not willing to come out and worship on the street, becoming by their very bodily presence a door into the welcoming body of Christ.

Willing people like Angie. The first time I visited, Angie was in her bathrobe lying on a couch, downed by depression over her childhood when her father would come into her room at night and violate her, depression over wasted years getting high to numb the pain and doing anything to get by, depression over her HIV status. Angie sent her son, Tiriq, to our summer program a few years ago, just to get him out of the house so she could be uninterrupted on the couch.

On the summer program application form, Angie had noted her interest in baptism for Tiriq, the reason for my visit. We prepared for the baptism and read of the God who. . . . *out of the great love with which he loved us even when we were dead . . . made us alive together with Christ and raised us up with him.* (Ephesians 2:4ff.). Bit by bit Angie rose up, coming to worship, to Bible study, to volunteer at our shelter where homeless people can eat good food and sleep in warm beds each Wednesday night. She enrolled, along with adults from around our synod, in a two-year Christian leadership class called Diakonia. Angie, a highly intelligent woman, absorbed it all with growing excitement.

Everyone in the class had to give a presentation on Lutheran theology, telling why they were Lutheran. One night, the students assigned to present were absent, and the pastor teaching the class asked if anyone would be willing to step in. No one was, because they didn't have their written papers at hand since it wasn't their turn. Evidently they needed their notes to remind them of why they were Lutheran. Except for Angie. Her paper wasn't prepared, but she was. "It is living, no rather dying, suffering and facing damnation, not thinking, reading and speculating that makes a theologian." said Luther. Angie had that covered.

Angie got a glass of water and set it in front of her. Then she slowly opened a Mary Kay jewelry case and took out a pink pouch which was filled with multicolored pills. She took out about ten pills and swallowed them, one by one, in silence. The class was riveted by this unusual theological presentation. When the last pill was swallowed, Angie stood up. "That's my HIV medication," she said. "I'm Lutheran because the church welcomed me as I am, an HIV-positive, recovering addict, and a child of God filled with grace. Taking care of my health is part of my stewardship. Now, by the grace of God I want to live. I want to live for my son. I want to live for the people still out there on the streets as I was. I want to live because Jesus Christ lives in me and through me. It's not just my body anymore. I'm part of his body, a temple of the Holy Spirit." Then this budding Lutheran theologian sat down. But she doesn't sit down much.

Angie rose up to become a pillar and president of our church. Often at night, she went out and ministered to the street people she called her night flock, offering words of hope, praying, sharing Scripture. She accompanied some of them to church, knowing that they'd be afraid to enter on their own. She was their door into the sanctuary. And now, Angie has stepped through the doors of the Lutheran Theological Seminary in Philadelphia where she is studying to be a pastor. What lovely aftermath is painted in her dust!

Plumbing Problems

Plumb 1. A weight suspended from the end of a line to determine water depth or establish a true vertical. 2. To straighten or make perpendicular. Usually used with up. 3. To examine closely; probe into.

Plumb line 1. A line from which a weight is suspended to determine verticality or depth. 2. A line regarded as directed exactly toward the earth's center of gravity.

The house is still not clean, but with only two weeks to go, it looks like Easter will come anyway. We had a meeting of women working around the church and spent most of the time reflecting on Jesus in the garden of Gethsemane on the Mount of Olives, where he prayed before his arrest. To get there, John reminds the reader that Jesus and the three disciples with him had to cross the Kidron Valley, literally "the winter-flowing valley," because water rushed through its stream bed only during winter rains. The Kidron Valley was a dump of sorts. When zealous reformers went through the area to wipe out idol worship, they grabbed the wooden and stone idols, smashed them, burnt them and threw the remains in the wadi (valley), which doubled as a graveyard. (2 Kings 23:6,12) The altars left as rubble had first been raised to idols such as the child-eating Molech. (2 Kings 23:10) So Jesus and his disciples were passing through a geography where life wrestled with death. We call it the Bronx. Jesus took them across the dry bed of a river where Molech had been drowned even as Moses had led their ancestors to freedom through the dry bed of the Red Sea. But what kind of promised land lay ahead of them? The edge of another dump outside Jerusalem that was used by the Romans for crucifixions.

The Mount of Olives where Jesus took his disciples had its own historical resonance. It was a grove of tears long before Jesus, Peter, James, and John set foot there.

The king (David) crossed the Wadi Kidron and . . . went up the ascent of the Mount of Olives, weeping as he went, with his head covered and walking barefoot. (2 Samuel 15:23,30)

King David went to pray at a time when he faced betrayal and attack. The Mount of Olives had a garden of olive trees named Gethsemane.

The women at church had to cross through their own valleys strewn with the wreckage of idols to arrive at their Gethsemane. And what did they find there? More struggles with illness, housing worries, unreliable men, and needy children like Darrin. He weighed only one pound at birth and has always been small for his age. I visited him in the neonatal intensive care unit where he lay barely visible among the machines and tubes. The doctor took me aside to say that infections were marauding through his tiny body and that I should "prepare the mother for the worst." When I baptized him with drops of sterile water, Burnice looked up and said with a mother's fierce love, "Now that he's baptized, I know he'll be just fine."

Darrin's survival did seem miraculous, but he's not exactly fine, either. What is the future for children whose fragile systems are flooded with toxic cocktails before their hearts have begun to beat? Before their lungs have taken a first breath? From the evidence, some appear to emerge to be fine indeed while others, many others, are not. Trying to find the right resources, the right classroom setting in a system that doesn't even serve kids with normal challenges is exhausting and discouraging—and virtually impossible, if like Burnice you are trying to hold down a job to pay the rent and feed your family at the same time.

Postnatal traumas have lingering effects, too. Burnice was worried sick about her sixteen-year-old son, Eddie, who was out on the street dealing. She came in to talk about possibly having him arrested, which surprised me. But Burnice was desperate, and nothing had worked to dissuade him. She was also afraid for her other children if he got into a dispute and someone came looking for revenge, a very reasonable concern and one with a long timeline. Another young man I knew was locked up and then allowed briefly out, escorted by armed guards, to attend his mother's funeral. A car filled with young men kept driving by the funeral home looking for him, so he had to be hustled out the back door. During my sermon, the carload, armed with automatic weapons, came in to "pay their respects." Almost simultaneously, the police arrived and made the arrests. It was over a conflict that had taken place five years earlier.

Eddie was a loving kid, but there were too many years when no one was there to nurture him. I'd recently visited him in the hospital after his hand got injured in a fight. He had ignored it until gangrene set in. While not glad about the gangrene, once antibiotics put him out of danger on that score, I was pleased to see him off the street and hoped that now we could talk. Eddie was sitting still in a dark room, not even listening to music on his Walkman. The blinds were pulled shut, and the light was off. For a while, we just sat in the darkness. I didn't know what to say, but slowly words came, and Eddie was able to speak a little from a place where the light had not been extinguished. He still dreamed of becoming a computer technician. It was not an impossible dream. He had the intelligence, and there were training programs that offered GED and computer classes.

When Eddie got out of the hospital, Burnice made an appointment to sign him up. The night before, he had a high fever. She went to the corner store to buy aspirin. When she came home, her husband was gone. The money they'd been saving in the dresser drawer was also gone. Before his fever left, Eddie was back on the street. Burnice said she hoped an arrest would make him reconsider his direction.

It was getting late in the olive grove, and Jesus asked his disciples to stay awake and watch in prayer as he himself went aside to pray. Three times, Jesus asked, and three times the disciples lay down and fell asleep. They failed. We fail. I fail. Solidarity, attentiveness, and persistence in prayer fall by the wayside. Over and over and over again. *"This very night, before the cock crows, you will deny me three times"* (Matthew. 26:34), Jesus told Peter against his protests.

Stardeshia came in with a question about her upcoming baptism. She told me about "a friend" who had an ulcer and needed medicine. When she went to the doctor, he told her that he had just the medicine she needed but would not prescribe it for her. Why not? She was a regular user of marijuana. "As long as you smoke pot, there's no point in my prescribing this medicine, because the chemical reaction of the medicine with the pot makes the medicine ineffective—so prescribing it would be a waste." The question Stardeshia then asked me was whether or not her inconsistent behavior and her doubts would cancel out the power of her baptism as marijuana cancels out the power of the medicine. What a great question! Theology hits the street. Nothing we do cancels out God, but some things can definitely dull our ability to live alert to that amazing grace. And then the cock crows.

When Stardeshia left, Sonia arrived to discuss her children's Easter baptisms. She's been alone raising three children since her husband died a few years back and is rarely in church because of a cleaning job she has over the weekends. The children, however, have not missed a single Sunday since they began attending after coming to the summer program. I asked her about her husband's death and sat quietly waiting for words to come, after her immediate tears. He died of "the virus" contracted through sleeping with prostitutes. "I've never slept with any man but him. I've never used drugs. I had no idea. I trusted him." And now she too has the virus. All of her family lives in Guatemala. She dares not tell them because her mother has a weak heart and "it would kill her." Only her brother is here, a brother who has not spoken to her in the year since finding out. "Why?" There is no answer that can fill that pit.

Peter, James, and John were the same three disciples that Jesus took up with him to the Mount of the Transfiguration, but the Mount of Olives is another story:

> And having gone forward a little, he fell on his face praying and saying, "My Father, if it is possible, let this cup pass from me. Nevertheless, not as I will but as you will." ... And being in agony, he was praying more earnestly. And his sweat became as if drops of blood falling down to the earth. (Matthew 26:39, Luke 22:44)

Transfiguration on the mountaintop was one thing, but this the disciples can't bear to watch. This does not look like the promised land to them. They fail to see the miracle of God's own bloody sweat searing itself irrevocably into the dust. *He found them sleeping; for their eyes were very burdened, and they did not know what they should answer him.* (Mark 14:40)

Did Jesus really sweat blood? Some say that what is meant is that Jesus' sweat was so copious it flowed like blood. Others cite medical texts describing hematidrosis, a stress-induced condition that causes "intense dilation of subcutaneous capillaries that burst into the sweat glands," causing bloody sweat. But this is not a question that weighs on the minds of the disciples I know. What matters to them is that Jesus knows what agony is all about. What matters is that Jesus knows them.

Our women's meeting came to an end. We shut our eyes and stood together in wide-awake silence, our hands gripped tight like olive branches twined together. It was ten o'clock in the morning, but we stood there under Gethsemane's moonlit sky. The betrayer was at hand. We strained to stay awake and watch for one another.

While all this was going on, Lenny was busy. He carried boxes of cleaning supplies down to the basement. He changed light bulbs, fixed a broken table and chair, and folded enough bulletins to last us through Pentecost. He brightened after each completed task. Lack of job opportunities just kills people. Work, after all, is even part of life in the biblical paradise. Lenny also asked to be baptized during the Easter season.

The next morning when I came to church, he was thirty feet in the air, on top of a ladder set precariously upon two pews, screwing in light bulbs. "Pastor, I used to be scared of heights! I fell off a ladder as a child," he announced, "but I'll do anything for my church!" Another mountaintop experience for Lenny. The place of leftovers was becoming a place of belonging and purpose, but such changes are scary and don't always last. Before the week was over, Lenny disappeared. No one had seen him. Off the ladder again.

It was a cold spring day and the food pantry was in action, but there was no heat. I went down to the basement to check the boiler and discovered a flood. Tiamat had been busy. More chaos. According to the Building Department this was a construction site, but some days I wondered. Water was pouring in from broken pipes on the ceiling. Pieces of pipe lay all over. Someone had taken a crowbar, broken down two doors, and ripped the place apart. The purpose was to take and sell the copper pipes. Also missing were several hundred dollars' worth of supplies we'd just ordered: cases of toilet paper, plates, cups, soap, mousetraps, etc. A fire extinguisher had been torn from the wall. Several bicycles waiting to be given away were missing along with all of our standing fans and some folding chairs. But the most expensive loss would be the boiler and plumbing repairs. And now we'd have no heat, no water, and no bathrooms for Palm Sunday, a day second only to Easter in church attendance, and sometimes surpassing it. "If this is how you treat your friends," St. Teresa chided God after falling off her mule into the mud one day, "no wonder you have so few."

It was too late to cancel the after-school program, but an organization next door said that the children could use their bathroom. They also gave us blankets for the children in case they became too cold. We let them watch a movie in the sanctuary where it was a little warmer. People working around the church felt deflated, believing they knew who was behind the break-in. The very one who helped carry down the boxes of supplies a few days before and had now gone missing.

The bright side, when I called about renting a portable toilet for Sunday—a business listed under "Mr. John"—I was put on hold and treated to a brass rendition of Handel's "Water Music" and a proud voice informing me that, "Mr. John handled the Papal Mass." I supposed that Mr. John could easily handle Palm Sunday at Transfiguration.

When the after-school program was over, I took Jasmine, a teenage tutor, to get her clothes. She was moving into a youth shelter called Sheltering Arms. Jasmine, born when her mother was sixteen, had grown up living with her grandmother, who had recently died. Jasmine then moved back in with her mother and other siblings, near the church. She was the family scapegoat. Nothing she did was ever right. Her mother would go out and buy dinner at the Chinese takeout place and eat with the other kids in front of Jasmine without offering her any. "You're too fat," she'd be told.

Besides tutoring, Jasmine sang in the choir and attended confirmation class. She tried talking with her mother about the problems at home but was told, "If you don't like it, you don't have to live here." But where could she live? Sheltering Arms seemed to be the best alternative. She asked me if I could drive her there so that she didn't have to carry plastic garbage bags of clothing on the bus. As Jasmine gathered her things together, her mother ignored her and talked with her brothers about going out to buy them some new sneakers. There were six other children in the home and another due the following month.

In addition to myself, some of the women at church tried visiting and talking with Jasmine's mother, all to no avail. In confirmation class, Jasmine wondered why God allows children to starve. I wondered about her unspoken questions. I wondered at her courage. I wondered how I was going to teach the fourth commandment: Honor your father and mother.

Waiting for Jasmine, I watched a man on the TV ranting about how he didn't even attend college but now he's a multimillionaire because of his fool-proof real-estate investing system. He was a busboy, and now he lives in a $1.5 million house. The younger children were engrossed in this show, sitting on the floor picking at the layers of flaking linoleum. We were all treated to a tour of the $1.5 million house.

Jasmine had excellent grades and planned to be a heart surgeon. She wrote poetry. Poetry, music, books, and church—these were what seemed to keep Jasmine together. Her things were now all in the bags except for her newest possession, the Walkman she got at church for Christmas. It was missing, but no one in the apartment could say where it was. No one would help her to look for it. Finally, Jasmine gave up. As we walked out the door, her mother picked up her purse to go buy the shoes. Jasmine ventured a tentative, but clearly audible, good-bye. There was no reply.

Eddie was still on the street selling. We spoke when I went out to buy ice cream at the corner store. His stepfather had kicked him out of the house, and Burnice was having second thoughts about going to the police. She held these men she loved tight in prayer, but her arms ached with emptiness. Now she worried that Eddie would be killed on the street. We lived on the same block and heard the same gunshots. Why was this happening now, now that she had turned her own life around? Why? The question was digging a deep hole in her heart. For Eddie things were turning in another direction. He had recently learned that his mother was HIV-positive. Maybe that was one of his reasons for pulling away so hard, as though saying: "You weren't there for me then and now that you are, you're going to die anyway, so to hell with it." I too felt helpless with no idea what kind of counsel to give and no idea on reaching Eddie. Burnice begged me to try and talk with him again, but by that point, he was almost always high.

Burnice held my hand so hard it hurt. We don't want to see resurrection after death. We want to see it now. It was Holy Thursday, but we read the words of Psalm 22, the Psalm for Good Friday:

My God my God, why have you forsaken me?
Why are you so far from helping me, from the words of my groaning?
I cry by day, but you do not answer;
and by night, but find no rest.

On Holy Thursday, like most churches, we celebrate Holy Communion and reflect on Jesus' final meal with his disciples. There are differences in understanding exactly what Jesus meant when he took bread and wine at his Last Supper with the disciples, offered a thanksgiving prayer (Eucharist) and said: "*This is my body given for you. This is my blood shed for you.*" Nevertheless, these biblically recorded words are repeated in Christian churches of all denominations when Holy Communion is celebrated. At least that's what I thought until I visited a megachurch in Las Vegas that featured a sanitized Eucharistic prayer with no mention of blood. The pastor explained that "seekers," people unfamiliar with church traditions or people who've found the church irrelevant in the past and are searching for spiritual meaning in their lives, would be turned off by the mention of blood. I looked around at the gleaming floors and plush carpeting. No doubt, blood would be an unseemly intrusion.

The pastor continued to explain how we needed to take people's culture and context seriously. On that note, he was preaching to the choir, but where we differed radically was on what that means. Is bloodless Communion really so culturally relevant? What culture would that be? People in Las Vegas don't bleed? I know that most of the architecture is fake, but it seems an insult to imply that the people are, too.

Ignoring pain has serious consequences. If our sanctuaries remain bloodless enclaves of sweetness and light, we risk far more than offending spiritual seekers. Cutting, a form of self-mutilation most commonly practiced among teenage girls, is on the rise. Girls who cut often explain it as a way of externalizing pain that they don't feel able to express otherwise. These girls sometimes describe the cutting of their bodies as a way to feel real, seeing their own red blood. Watching the blood is an important part of the behavior. It is often done by girls who have kept their pain long submerged.

I think that bad theology—and I put bloodless Communion in that category—can carry with it an edge of pathology, however well-intentioned it may be. Communion is not about wearing a smile on the outside when you're dying inside, like the decals plastered on broken buildings. It's about finding life in a power that has proven to be stronger than any wounding force.

There are others who find offense in the blood and body language for very different reasons than those voiced by the pastor in Las Vegas. Elisabeth Schussler Fiorenza speaks for many feminists when she asks: "How can we point to the Eucharistic bread and say 'This is my body' as long as women's bodies are battered, raped, sterilized, mutilated, prostituted and used to male ends?" Some feel that lifting up the cross implies the elevation of victimization and abuse. Tragically, it is all too true that many women have suffered, and even died, as victims of domestic violence under the rubric of "bearing their cross." But that is a twisted use of the cross.

When we sing about "power in the blood" here in the Bronx, we're not glorifying suffering and advocating victimhood. We're taking life seriously. Blood is not just death. From the womb, life and blood are inseparable. My babies came out shining with my blood. Burnice's were born bright with hers. I'm sure it is also true in Las Vegas. I bleed every month. My heart bleeds with pain when blood is spilled. This doesn't make me a victim. It makes me a woman. It makes me human. Jesus' blood made him human. Without it, he's no better than a molded action figure. Our faith is that he died in the fight for life—and that he didn't die in vain. He didn't die as a passive victim. He died because of his powerful passion for us, resisting all dehumanizing powers. His blood doesn't call us to lie down and rest in peace, but to rise in strength.

This is what drew me back to Christianity, knowing a God who could bleed to death and yet live. We who bleed in the Bronx want to live, too. We want "power in the blood." Middle-class megachurches have many good and necessary things to teach the rest of the church about mission. I admire their passionate, creative efforts to relate the faith to contemporary contexts. I applaud their removal of many sacred cows overdue to be toppled into the *wadi*.

We try to do the same. I simply don't know a context on the face of the earth where bloodless Communion is relevant to human life. It is precisely that cup that Jesus agonized over on the Mount of Olives. The anemic Eucharistic prayer of a bloodless church dishonors Gethsemane where Jesus struggled and Golgotha where Jesus died. It dishonors those who have died in the fight for justice and truth. And it fails to take our own wounds seriously, whatever zip code we live in.

Before she died, before I realized she would die, my childhood friend Tracy and I made small cuts in our arms and rubbed our bleeding flesh together, mixing our blood, sealing our sisterhood. In Holy Communion, we also mix blood. Jesus rubs his flesh against our own in solidarity. It is not his death, but life that fills our mouth and enters our hearts with power.

And so on Holy Thursday, we remember Jesus' Last Supper, considered by many to have been a Passover meal. We read the biblical Exodus story and share other stories of resistance and liberation—from slavery in this country more than a century ago, to Mexican teenagers brought here recently and held captive in apartments to perform forced sex for money that is handed over to their cruel taskmasters. Gladys told of horrors in the Dominican Republic during the brutal dictatorship of Rafael Trujillo, under which Dominicans suffered for thirty-one years (1930-1961), and of her family's escape to New York. And we prayed for our own Exodus from the unspoken bondage among us, from the thieves who come in the night, looting, cutting pipelines, and flooding the basement of our souls with grief.

We washed each others' hands. We broke bread and lifted the cup: *This is my body given for you. This is my blood shed for you.* We stood in a circle round as the Earth, holding hands, flesh against flesh, dust to dust, bound in one blood with a cross at the center—our plumb line.

When it was time for our outdoor Good Friday procession, it began to snow, sleet, rain, and hail. We decided to move the procession inside. With so many people already half-sick with colds and sore throats, including me, it seemed to be the right decision. Others were relieved because they remembered a few years back when a group of young people was reenacting the story of each station of the cross. When we came to the tenth station, Jesus Is Stripped, we were under the Prospect Avenue train station. Drug dealers on the corner crossed themselves and stopped selling while we prayed. So far, so good.

Our eyes were closed, or at least bowed down. Fortunately, the dealers were not so devout. They saw a car approaching and yelled at us to get down, but it was too late. The car was there, with guns sticking out of every window. We were between the guns and their intended targets. Everyone froze, and ages passed. Finally, instead of shooting straight out, the gunmen shot up in the air as a warning and drove by. We rushed down the block to find a safer spot for Station eleven—Jesus Is Nailed to the Cross.

There was still no heat since the break-in, and the church was really cold. Imagine visits to Mr. John in the icy rain! The plumber assured us that all would be repaired by Sunday.

And Still We Rise

You may write me down in history
With your bitter, twisted lies,
You may trod me in the very dirt
But still, like dust, I'll rise.
(from "Still I Rise," Maya Angelou)

I heard the birds near midnight. I was lying in bed about to go to sleep, when I heard birds singing. I've grown used to unexpected birds in the Bronx. I hadn't known there would be roosters crowing at 5 A.M. or seagulls circling the street on garbage days, but birdsong at midnight? Insomniac nightingales escaped from the Bronx Zoo? Maybe I was mistaken. I lay there and listened. Soon, it came again. I got up and went to the window, but having already taken out my contact lenses, I couldn't see a thing. "What are you doing? Come back to bed." said Gregorio. "Listen to the birds," I answered and went to the bathroom to put the contact lenses back in. It took a while, but I finally located the birds. Their song was serious stuff. The riffs were in code. These "nightingales" were lookouts for drug dealers. Their inventive songlines up and down the street were a matter of freedom or arrest. Their vigil was a question of life or death.

Our Easter vigil begins in the dark, too, with a fire on the sidewalk and a song on our lips. We kindle a fire, light our candles and walk into the church to wait for Easter. While we wait, we tell stories: the creation in Genesis, Sarah and Abraham, Noah's ark and the rainbow, the averted sacrifice of the child Isaac, the Exodus, Jonah and the whale, and Daniel, Shadrach, Meshach, and Abednego in the fiery furnace. I've told versions of all of them here.

In our vigil, most of the stories are acted out, often by children and teenagers—because these stories that illumine our night of vigil are their birthright. Over the years, the big boxes that brought beds for our overnight homeless program have been transformed into boats, fiery furnaces, puppet theaters and, my favorite, the wide mouth of a whale from which Jonah shot out, sliding on his stomach across the floor as someone made an appropriate burping sound into the microphone: *Then the Lord spoke to the fish, and it spewed Jonah out upon the dry land.* (Jonah 2:3)

We began with "In the beginning," and that story belonged to Angie, who danced the days of creation to an African drumbeat. She brought James Weldon Johnson's poetry to life—flinging stars, surging with waters, stomping out valleys, splitting the air with the wings of birds. And when she came to the final lines:

This Great God,
Like a mammy bending over her baby,
Kneeled down in the dust
Toiling over a lump of clay
Til he shaped it in his own image;

Then into it he blew the breath of life
And man became a living soul.
Amen. Amen.

Angie bent down over the motionless form of her own son, Tiriq, and raised him up to complete the dance in her arms. "It's not just my body anymore. I'm part of his body," she'd said. She lit up the sanctuary, a pillar of fire in our darkness. Angie the pillar.

The stone that the builders rejected has become the chief cornerstone.

This is the day that the Lord has made;
let us rejoice and be glad in it. (Psalm 118:22, 24)

This Psalm we read on Easter Sunday never seemed more apt than it did as our building program neared completion. Among the lilies we had ladders and other signs of work still pending. After almost ten years of construction struggles, we knew plenty about rejection: rejected plans, rejected permits, rejected loans, rejected people. On Easter morning, when the women went to the gravesite, they found the stone blocking the mouth of the tomb rolled away. Perhaps the women remembered Jesus' words to those who maintained a system of injustice inside the religious infrastructure: If you destroy this temple, in three days, I will raise it up. They thought he was speaking of the Jerusalem Temple, under construction for an unenviable forty-six years! Forty-six years and, if it were destroyed, Jesus could raise it up in three? They laughed. But Jesus wasn't interested in their grandiose building that rose up while others were ground down. He was referring to another temple they tried to break into dust, his body. Angie's body. Burnice's body. Lucy's body. Tiriq's body. Eddie's body. Felipe's body. Venus' body. Trevor's body. Rosalina's body. Forty-six years? Angie was forty-seven.

One by one, the obstacles were rolled away like stones. The date for dedicating our new space was only four weeks away. The end was in sight, but a lot could happen in four weeks, for better or for worse! Our addition is constructed so that one wall of the sanctuary can be opened onto the new space for overflow seating. We needed it on Easter. People streamed in, and we became the waves that sank the chariots and horses that pursued us—the guns and bullets, the needles and vials, the test results, and dispossess slips, the hungry nights and weary days. We came out of Egypt and danced on the shore, gathered at the water's edge, as Angie assisted with the baptisms—wiping dripping faces and handing out candles.

That year we had a dozen. One of them was three-year-old Yesenia. Her mother, Maritza, was baptized, too. As the water ran down Maritza's cheeks, mixing with her tears, Yesenia began to dance in a little circle in the aisle of the church, crying out, "Yeah Mommy! Yeah Mommy!" Yesenia, who'd spent most of her life in a drug-rehab program that allowed mothers to stay with their young children, had something to dance about. We all did. The pothole had become a pool, teeming with life. We were standing at the center of so much that is wounded and wrong, in a well of catastrophe that is, at the same time, a center from which springs amazing grace. I wrote that in the preface to this book. I see it in the font.

For waters shall break forth in the wilderness, and streams in the desert. (Isaiah 35:6) Three months after September 11, we celebrated thirty-five baptisms, more than we've ever had at one time. One of them was Rosalina, Felipe's daughter. He had just been released from the hospital and had to wear a special kind of body suit covering his burns and skin grafts, but Felipe was able briefly to be present to see his daughter baptized, this daughter whose alphabet song had reached through his pain and pulled him back from the brink.

"And here in dust and dirt, O here / The lilies of His love appear." wrote Henry Vaughan. Like lilies in the dust, Rosalina and the others who were baptized stood among us, a reason for rejoicing even through our tears. Although it is not usually our custom, in addition to giving out candles, we gave all the baptized a rose that day because they had truly flowered in the desert of our grief. Our national presiding bishop, Bishop Mark Hanson, was present and performed the baptisms. He had visited Ground Zero the day before. He later commented that the pit of Ground Zero and the font of Transfiguration would be joined forever in his mind, death giving way to life.

Easter is actually not a day but a season, Eastertide that lasts fifty days until Pentecost. The dedication of our new space was set to take place in the middle of Eastertide, and there was a flurry of preparation carrying us toward the big day—and several surprises that washed ashore. Alan called from Albany. The last time I'd seen Alan, he was cursing at me from the wheelchair the EMS crew tied him into so they could carry him away. He had been a leader in our men's group and stayed in the church for several months after losing his apartment. The arrangement was intended to be a security measure for the church during construction as well as a way to help Alan while he looked for a job and apartment. Instead we became the unwitting enablers of his progressive alcoholism. The situation hit bottom on the day I arrived to hear sounds like a wounded animal might make coming from the bathroom, along with loud banging. Alan had locked himself in there, and besides loudly moaning, he was tearing the fixtures from the walls and floor. I called 911.

Understandably, Alan's backsliding had a negative impact on the men who heretofore had looked up to him as a role model in the midst of their own substance-abuse struggles. The men's group fell apart. Alan, on the other hand, slowly began to get his life together. He entered a long-term treatment program in Albany, graduated from it and decided to settle there. He called to share news of his progress and told of spending all of his free time practicing and performing with a singing group made up of men in recovery. He offered to come down from Albany with the group for a fund-raising concert. The men call themselves "Resurrection!" They now have made several CDs.

News of Alan's resurrection gave hope to Burnice. She never did call the police, but they contacted her after Eddie was arrested. A merciful judge gave him a choice between prison and an eighteen-month drug-rehabilitation program for youth. This was an incredible break for Eddie, and he was smart enough to know it. He was also pleased that the program offered both GED and computer classes.

Ben was a member of the diminished men's group. He had been in and out of church because of mental-health struggles related to time in Vietnam. At that point, Ben was in. On Sunday he sang each song with arms outstretched. He spent all of Monday and Tuesday up near the ceiling, giving the sanctuary a fresh coat of paint to get it ready for the dedication. The sanctuary was not part of the actual construction project, but it was being renovated by the congregation. The woodwork had been washed and restained by a youth group from Pennsylvania. Ben and some friends of his laid down a new floor, and a new carpet for it was donated by Minerva. There was no question but that it would be red.

In the Lutheran Church, we change the color of the paraments (cloths) that hang from our sanctuary furniture (the altar, the pulpit) for different liturgical seasons. Red is the color for celebrations of the Holy Spirit, like Pentecost. Once, when I was in the sanctuary with a group of women, and it was time to change colors, the women staged a protest. We needed to switch from red to white, I explained. Pentecost was over, and Trinity Sunday was coming, and then it would be green for the many months of what we sometimes call "ordinary time." My explanations of the liturgical calendar with different seasons and colors satisfied nobody. They loved the way red brightened the space and presented a powerful defense. "Won't we be celebrating in the power of the Holy Spirit next Sunday, too?" Our rubrics gave way to the higher wisdom of these adamant women, and it stayed rebel red for Trinity Sunday. Most Lutherans are not given to being thrown to the floor in spiritual ecstasy and more's the pity; I wish it would happen to me. But at least our Pentecostal red rug was laid down the center aisle in testimony to the Spirit that runs through us.

As the construction crew began removing their ladders, Lucy was watering the lilies, and Ben was high up by the ceiling waving the paintbrush around to gospel music on his tape player. In *The Sanctified Church*, Zora Neale Hurston recaptures a sermon preached in 1929 that pictures people taken up "thru the open bosom of a unclouded sky" and receiving "in their hands de hosanna fan." Ben was up there waving his paintbrush while the music played. Ben waved his hosanna fan in the sanctified church.

We were well into the decorating stage now, the part I love. At home I figure that if the flowers are beautiful and the art is interesting, your eyes will be drawn there and away from the mess everywhere else. Photographs of door paintings made by youngsters in years past were blown up and framed, creating splashes of color on the freshly painted white walls. The door pictures function as icons, windows connecting our limited vision with something larger. A group of mothers and children worked on making intricate tissue-paper flowers to decorate tablecloths, a Central American custom. And there was more sobering art, too. Two large picture frames were filled with photographs of the neighborhood memorials to slain youth. Local mural art and dead youth are so inseparable that when different scenes were being painted on our doors, someone who stopped to watch commented, "It's great to see a painting out here that's not about someone dead."

So why did we hang up the memorial photos in our Space for Grace? Not only as a reminder of the fifth commandment, You shall not kill, which hangs with them, but because the stakes in that space are high. As we hung the photographs, I thought of my father. It was from him I came into this Lutheran heritage. He grew up in Lübeck, Germany, and was confirmed in that city's beautiful St. Mary's Church. During the Second World War, the two great bells that rang from one of the cathedral's high gothic towers crashed to the floor during a bombing raid that left much of the church in ruins. My mother recalls that during her honeymoon visit there with my father, they worshipped in an open-air sanctuary. The restoration work had not yet reached the roof. All rubble has long since been cleared away, and the arched, gothic roof is now on, but the bells have been left just as they fell, untouched and broken on the cracked stone floor, roped-off in the back of the church. When my mother took us there on a visit, Hans kept returning to that spot while we admired the many other artistic treasures housed in the cathedral. He was drawn to and captivated by the sight of the huge, broken bells. Their message was as loud and clear as when they rang on high. We hung the memorial photographs in hopes that they, too, would call us toward a better future.

It was natural for me to remember my father. My mother and I were both present at his death from colon cancer. We each held one hand as his breaths came spaced further and further apart until there was only space. I always think of him at important moments, and other times too, but I was surprised and deeply moved when the church decided to mount a plaque in his honor over the door of our new wing. I wondered that they chose to honor this man they never knew, who had died two years before my ordination, this man who with my mother always gave me space for grace to be myself. I realized that over the years, they and I had come to know more than we ever would have imagined about one another.

The dedication was now one week away, the last vestiges of construction debris had been hauled off, and Alberto was up all night polishing and buffing the new floors. He said that *la cumbia y el cafe* kept him going—dance music and coffee. Some people would say that it was just a clean, shiny, waxed floor, admittedly a rarity in our busy church. But for us it was something even more special, a portent, a sea of glass:

> I saw another portent in heaven, great and amazing . . . and I saw what appeared to be a sea of glass mixed with fire. And those who had conquered the beast . . . standing beside the sea of glass with the harps of

God in their hands. And they sing the song of Moses ... "Great and amazing are your deeds Lord God Almighty!" (Revelation 15:1–3)

They stood there the next Sunday with tambourines instead of harps in their hands. The sea of glass was transfigured with a sea of faces, as waves of people flowed through the doors, people streaming in by foot from the neighborhood and by busloads and car caravans from other churches, people filling every inch of Space for Grace, a standing-room only crowd jammed together in joy and borne up on this rising Eastertide.

There was Nikia living with a foster family after being raped by her stepfather; Nelly and Aurora who rode across the border huddled in fear under a pile of vegetables; Dashawn, six feet and sixteen years who ordered girl Happy Meals on the way to Simba Camp so that his little sisters could have the toys; his friend, Trevor, Melvin, and Robert. The sisters were there, too—Danielle, Shakira, and Desiree, who saw their mother die in the stairwell. There was Gracie wondering when the virus would turn to full-blown AIDS and take her mother; and Eric and Tracy who had already lost theirs. There was Nelson who knows he's a child of God; and his big sister, Venus, and the whole flock of siblings she shepherds each week. They all stood there in front of the church singing their hearts out.

And it dawned on me. It was happening before our very eyes; the ruins were breaking forth together into singing. It was as the prophet had said: *Break forth together into singing, you ruins of Jerusalem.* But these children are no one's ruins. Despite the many-headed beast that seeks to terrify and destroy, they stood before our sea of faces as conquerors beside the sea of glass, singing their song of victory: "Great and amazing are your deeds, Lord God Almighty!" The church rose to its feet. *All creation stands on tiptoe,* says Paul, *to see the children of God coming into their own.*

Space for Grace

"Sherman, I'm sure that's the turnoff to Manhattan."
"You're right sweetheart, but there's no way I can get over there now."

"Where does this go?"

"The Bronx." ...

A vague smoky abysmal uneasiness was seeping into Sherman's skull. The Bronx ...

Well ... how bad could it be? ...

His sense of direction was slipping away ... all at once there was no more ramp, no more clean cordoned expressway. He was at ground level. It was as if he had fallen into a junkyard ...

"Where are we Sherman?" ...

"We're in the Bronx." ...

What a lot of people all of a sudden ... Half of them seem to be out in the street... He could feel his heart beating with a nervous twang ... Three youths stood beneath a streetlight; three dark faces. They stared at the Mercedes ... Maria wasn't saying a word. The concerns of her luxurious life were now tightly focused. Human existence had but one purpose: to get out of the Bronx.

(Tom Wolfe, *Bonfire of the Vanities*)

"How good that we are here!" That was the farthest thing from the lips of the discouraged members I first met at Transfiguration. Peter would have been sympathetic. When he went along with James and John up to the mountaintop where Jesus was transfigured—his face shining like the sun, his clothes become swaths of flame—Peter is blown away by the vision. After all, he'd spent most of his life on rough boats with rougher fisherman, eyeballing dead fish. Then he is transported to a scene of magnificence not even achieved at the glittery parties attended by Wolfe's Sherman and Maria where guests came transfigured by surgery and sheathed in as much dazzlement as money could buy. *"Lord, how good it is for us to be here! Let us make three dwellings, one for you, one for Moses and one for Elijah."* Peter doesn't want to leave the party. He's ready to invest in some lofty real estate.

But living up high in the rarefied air isn't the point of transfiguration. It was never intended as breathing space for a precious few, never meant as a private experience of spirituality removed from the public square. It was a vision to carry us down, a glimpse of unimagined possibility at ground level. When Peter proposes construction, he doesn't get the permit: "*A cloud came and over-*

shadowed them . . . then a voice came from the cloud that said, 'This is my Son, my Chosen; listen to him!'" And Jesus led them down. Way down.

When they came down from the mountain . . . a man from the crowd shouted . . . "I beg you to look at my son. He is my only child. Suddenly a spirit seizes him, and all at once he shrieks. It convulses him until he foams at the mouth; it mauls him and will scarcely leave him." (Luke 9:37–39)

When Peter and the others came down the mountain, they found a father and a child gasping for life. But Jesus rebuked the unclean spirit, healed the boy, and gave him back to his father. And they found transfiguration.

And so it is. When the disciples of this Bronx church unlocked the doors of their private shelter and stepped out into the neighborhood, they did meet the distress of a community convulsed and mauled by poverty, corruption, and crime. But they also discovered transfiguration as a congregation in connection with others. "Transfiguration" behind closed sanctuary doors existed in name only. The glorious reality was outside in the most unexpected places. Like Peter, we wanted to build, but the construction of Space for Grace was hardly a mountaintop experience! It was, and is, a costly investment on the ground level, worth every tear, every prayer, every cent. It is an investment to honor all that has been invested in us.

Listen again to the father: "I beg you to look at my son. He is my only child." His words echo those of another: *"This is my only Son, my Chosen, listen to him."* The voice on the mountain and the voice in the valley are one and the same.

"How good that we are here!" Although some groups still voice fear and dismay at the scene before them when they step out of the subway at Prospect Avenue, most visitors notice a positive change. Even ten years ago, the picture painted by the prophet Ezekiel of a valley of dry bones was an apt description for the many vacant lots littered with garbage and the burnt, skeletal remains plastered with eerie decals depicting scenes of artificial life.

Today, the corner lot is not a place of overgrown weeds and abandoned cars used to hold and sell guns. Countless homes are restored and inhabited.

Real curtains hang in real windows. The field of rotting buildings down the block is now a green park where children play baseball and men play soccer. The outlook on my block is repeated on many blocks around the South Bronx. Numerous groups have invested time, money, and passion in this renewal. The *New York Times* delivers—most days.

This is the new Bronx, the Bronx that several years ago got an award as one of the top ten All American Cities by the National Civic League. The criteria for the award was based on advances in problem-solving, diversity, education, and building. I am proud that we have been part of the rebuilding with Nehemiah Homes, the Bronx Leadership Academy, our Space for Grace. But awards like this are premature. An award for education? In the field of education, Ezekiel's image of dead bones disconnected from life, from hope, and from a future is more apt than ever. It's been easier to rebuild the outer structures of our city than to demolish the internal framework in order to construct a wholly new civic life.

These days, it's quieter at night. We are more likely to be kept awake by boom boxes than bullets. But it's too soon to breathe easily with Molech still on the loose and this is still part of Asthma Alley. There is more work to do.

Every valley shall be lifted up and every mountain and hill be made low, the uneven ground shall become level and the rough places plain. Then the glory of the Lord shall be revealed and all people, all people shall see it together. (Isaiah 39:4–5)

We await the final transfiguration, breathing space for everyone.

How good it is to be here. What happened to Transfiguration, happened to me as well. I arrived when I was not yet thirty. After almost twenty years, I am not the same person I was when I first came. How could I be? Who I am has been shaped and formed by the people of the South Bronx in ways I cannot fully recognize or understand. Some changes are easy to name. Any coffee other than the strong Spanish brew I learned to enjoy here is generally not worth drinking. Sometimes, my mind reaches to recall the right word—in English! I have learned from my sisters and brothers how to keep on when it seems impossible. Their refrains have reframed my view of life: "God will make a way out of no way" and *"Se hace camino al andar"* (you make the way by walking).

I have learned the joy of worshiping with body, as well as mind and soul. This is not just an addition, it is a new dimension, being put together in a new way. I have experienced healing, and find myself more at home with my own identity. Some of this is what one might expect to happen between the ages of twenty-nine and forty-eight, but it's been way beyond expectation for me.

I think the most powerful thing that has happened to me here is that as Transfiguration has seared my soul, I have been irrevocably "threatened by resurrection." The phrase comes from the poet, Julia Esquivel, writing of life and struggle in her native Guatemala. Her verses are steeped in the blood of her people. She writes of the blood that has flooded her land, her body, her soul. And she writes of life.

I began with the Bronx mother who raced to get a basin of water to scrub her murdered son's blood off the street and held off the traffic until she was finished. I needed to stand vigil too, to grieve, and remember. But grief is not the end. The people I mourn and celebrate and love will not allow me to live as though they have not lived. They will not let us return to business as usual. They will not let us give up—"They have threatened us with Resurrection." Esquivel ends her poem with an invitation, as I too would like to end:

Accompany us on this vigil
and you will know what it is to dream!
Then you will know how marvelous it is
to live threatened with Resurrection!

How marvelous it is. How good that we are here. How marvelous, indeed.

EPILOGUE

As I write this epilogue it is midwinter of 2003. In May, I will have been here for nineteen years and in May I will celebrate my final Sunday as Transfiguration's pastor. I will be moving across the river, into Manhattan, to serve at Trinity Lutheran Church on W. 100th Street and Amsterdam Avenue. After their call committee wrote to tell me that they decided I was not the right pastor for them, they continued to reevaluate their future direction. A year after the rejection letter, I received another phone call from Bishop Bouman. Trinity had reconsidered and wanted to know if I would as well.

Throughout the year, the church had been in my prayers. I prayed that the Spirit would guide the right pastor to them, knowing that it was not myself. Once again, I find that I did not know what I thought I knew. Trinity voted to call me as their next pastor and after much internal struggle, prayer, and conversation, I accepted. As I write, real *malabarriga* has seized my gut because now is the time when I am indeed called to get out of my boat.

What will happen to Transfiguration? The short answer is, I don't know—but a fuller response is required. Over the years, seventeen seminary students have spent their internship year in training with us. Perhaps one will return, with love for what has been and passion for what is still to come. If not, I trust that Bishop Bouman will make certain that another pastor is found. Most importantly, there are lay leaders deeply committed to the life of this church and this neighborhood. And they have friends in many places.

When I announced my leaving, one council member, Gladys, gave voice to what some others were feeling, "Why fill up one hole by making another?"

She is the same wonderful woman who leaves a fresh rose for me to find on my desk every Sunday morning. Recently, she gave me a rose encased in a snow globe of glass to grace my new desk. Maybe the "hole" at Transfiguration will become another space for grace. There's precedent for that!

What will happen at Trinity? The rebuilding of Manhattan post-September 11 has focused on the configuration of structures and spaces downtown, but the architecture of human relationships in our city is even more important for real urban renewal. Will the classes only exist in an architectural face-off, projects vs. condos, while the people who live in them have no genuine relationships? What about the welcome that immigrants find in a city ever more security-conscious and wary of those who cross our borders? Is there room at Trinity for Our Lady of Guadalupe, a sign of welcome to any Mexican immigrant? Trinity is a "Reconciling in Christ" congregation, meaning that it explicitly welcomes gay and lesbian persons. While it is easy to say that the church "welcomes everyone," those who have felt repeatedly rejected will hardly believe it without more specific signs of hospitality. The housing projects near Trinity are named after Frederick Douglass. I imagine Douglass hand in hand with Our Lady of Guadalupe, a rainbow Pride flag flying over their heads—a mural of Space for Grace in Manhattan. Trinity, surrounded as it is by such a range of diversity, is in a great location to create new configurations of urban community.

Trinity has also been through some tough times and at this point, the financial situation there is not much better than it is at Transfiguration. Will there even be time to secure its future? The whole venture is both scary and exciting, but that's how life is when we live threatened by resurrection. What will happen at Trinity? I don't know. But isn't that true every day, wherever we are?

I share a prayer from our Lutheran worship book that I have been using frequently during this time of transition:

Lord God, you have called your servants
to ventures of which we cannot see the ending,
by paths as yet untrodden, through perils unknown.

Give us faith to go out with good courage,
not knowing where we go,
but only that you hand is leading us
and your love supporting us.

Se hace camino al andar . . . I hope these stories of transfiguration will help
along the way as we travel towards the splendid city.

NOTES

PREFACE

XVIII TERESA OF AVILA: Citations from Teresa of Avila, unless otherwise noted, are from *The Interior Castle* (New York: Image Books, Doubleday, 1989).

ONE Church Doors

5ff "PLANNED SHRINKAGE AND THE CROSS BRONX EXPRESSWAY": The policy of "planned shrinkage," the construction of the Cross Bronx Expressway, and the roles of Robert Moses and Roger Starr are discussed in detail in a number of books, including: Jill Jonnes, *We're Still Here* (New York: Atlantic Monthly Press, 1986). Robert A. Caro, *The Power Broker* (New York: Vintage Books, Random House, 1975). Jim Rooney, *Organizing the South Bronx*, Chapter 2, "Why Did the South Bronx Collapse?" (New York: State University of New York Press, 1995).

8ff "THE BRONX HAS BECOME THE CITY'S TOILET": Editorial, *El Diario*, 3 May 1996. See also "Breathing Lessons," Editorial, *The Village Voice*, 29 April 1997, p. 27. These articles are among many that discuss asthma in the South Bronx and the environmental causes.

10 Statistics are from the Community District Profiles issued by the Community Service Society. Further data can be found in a 1999 report by Emily Rosenbaum, Associate Professor of Sociology at Fordam University. Her study is entitled "A Demographic and Socioeconomic Portrait of Mott Haven/Hunts Point, Morrisania/East Tremont, and Highbridge/South Concourse."

14 "LIKE JONAH HIMSELF, I FIND MYSELF TRAVELING": Thomas Merton, *The Sign of Jonas* (Garden City, New York: Image Books, Doubleday, 1956), p. 21.

14 "HOW OFTEN LUNG AND LIVER MUST HAVE PAINED HIM!": Martin Luther, *Luther's Works*, vol. 19 (St. Louis: Concordia Publishing House, 1957), p. 68.

TWO Neighborhood Doors

38 "PRAYER IS A BATTLE": Ushi Nomura, *Desert Wisdom* (Garden City, New York: Doubleday, 1982), p. 103. A more complete version of these stories is available in *The Desert Fathers*, Vintage Spiritual Classics series (New York: Vintage Press, Random House, 1998).

39 "WORLD-MOTHERING AIR": Gerard Manley Hopkins, from "The Blessed Virgin compared to the Air we Breathe" in *The Poems of Gerard Manley Hopkins* (London: Oxford University Press, 1975), p. 93.

61 This and other Hasidic tales have been collected by Martin Buber, *Tales of the Hasidim* (New York: Schoken Books, 1975).

73 "BEYOND JUSTICE: FRIENDSHIP IN THE CITY": Martha Ellen Stortz, "World and World," *Luther Seminary* (fall 1994): 409–418.

73 "THE AREA WAS 'UNREPAIRABLE ... BEYOND REBUILDING' ": Robert Moses quoted in the *New York Times*, 13 January 1973.

74 WINDOW DECALS: Jill Jonnes, *We're Still Here*, ibid., p. 385.

74 MAYOR EDWARD KOCH ON DECALS: *New York Times*, 12 November 1983.

75 INDUSTRIAL AREAS FOUNDATION: To read more about the IAF and church-based community organizing in New York, see the book by Michael Gecan, *Going Public* (Boston: Beacon Press, 2002).

THREE Parsonage Doors

80 "SINCE GOD IS SPIRIT": Uta Ranke-Heinemann, *Eunuchs for the Kingdom of Heaven* (New York: Doubleday, 1990), p. 117.

80 EUGENIA, ST. HILDEGUND AND POPE JOAN: A discussion of these women's place in history is found at the conclusion of the novel *Pope Joan* by Donna Woolfolk Cross (New York: Ballantine Books, 1996).

FOUR Soul Doors—Breathing Space

97 "SILENCE MY SOUL": Rabindranath Tagore, "Stray Birds," *A Tagore Reader*, edited by Amiya Chakravarty (Boston: Beacon Press, 1966), p. 328.

97 "I ASKED THE TREE": from sixth century B.C.E., translated by Rabindranath Tagore.

102 "IN A WAY—NOBODY SEES A FLOWER": Georgia O'Keeffe, *One Hundred Flowers*, edited by Nicholas Callaway (New York: Wings Books, 1987), p. 2.

103 "FOR IT IS ONLY FRAMED IN SPACE THAT BEAUTY BLOOMS": Anne Morrow Lindbergh, *Gift from the Sea* (New York: Vintage Books, Random House, 1991), p. 114.

103   "I HAVE TO BE PART OF COMMUNITY": cited by Cathleen Medwick in *Teresa of Avila: The Progress of a Soul* (New York: Doubleday, 1999), p. 104.

104   "DEBAJO DEL MANZANO, BENEATH THE APPLE TREE": from *The Collected Works of St. John of the Cross*, Kieran Kavanaugh, O.C.D., and Otilio Rodriguez, O.C.D., trans. (Washington, D.C.: ICS Publications, 1973), pp. 413, 415. The same book includes a biographical sketch of John of the Cross that includes the story of his imprisonment.

107   "LAS MANOS DEL HOMBRE NO TIENEN MÁS SENTIDO": Federico García Lorca, "Gacela of the Flight" in *The Selected Poems of Federico García Lorca* (New York: New Directions, 1961), p. 166.

FIVE   Gathering Resources

115   "THE SHADOWS CAST BY THE HERMITAGES": cited by Cathleen Medwick, *Teresa of Avila: The Progress of a Soul* (New York: Doubleday, 1999), p. 98.

117   "GIANTS KEEP COMING": Samuel D. Proctor and William D. Watley, *Sermons from the Black Pulpit* (Valley Forge, Penn.: Judson Press, 1984).

SIX   Summer Construction Reports

128   *Makes Me Wanna Holler,* Nathan McCall (New York: Random House, 1994).

133   NEHEMIAH HOMES: To read in greater detail about the South Bronx Churches' organizing work that made this construction possible see the chapter by Lee Stuart, "Come, Let Us Rebuild the Walls of Jerusalem" in *Signs of Hope in the City*, edited by Robert Carle and Louis Di Carlo (Valley Forge, Penn.: Judson Press, 1998), pp. 129ff.

134   "THE STREET IS FOR CELEBRATION": Thomas Merton in *Love and Living* (New York, Bantam Books, 1979), pp. 41ff.

136   "THE SCHOOL CONSTRUCTION AUTHORITY IS SCRAMBLING": "Board of Ed Demands Accounting of 100M," *Daily News*, 26 October 1998, p. 12.

136   "THE FOUR YOUNG MOTHERS PRAYING": See the chapter by Lee Stuart, "Redefining the Public Sphere: South Bronx Churches and Education Reform" in *Signs of Hope in the City*, ibid., pp. 140ff. This chapter also includes an account of the development of the Bronx Leadership Academy.

139   "I THOUGHT OF ABBA JOSEPH": see Ushi Nomura, *Desert Wisdom*, ibid., p. 90.

141ff   NYC DEPARTMENT OF JUVENILE JUSTICE: The report referred to is the "Facility Development Project, A Guest Overview," produced under Mayor R. Giuliani and Commissioner Tino Hernandez: 1998. See also, "Youth in Detention: Some Facts and Figures" prepared by the same.

144   "DEAD-ZONE SCHOOLS": see *Futures Denied: Concentrated Failure in the New York*

City Public School System, a report of Parents Organized to Win Education Reform, produced by the Industrial Areas Foundation-Metro N.Y. and the Public Education Association, March 1997.

145 "LIVIN' HIGH OFF KIDS": *Daily News,* 3 November 1994, p. 5.

145 ALFRED D. LERNER: Lerner's comments can be read in "Court Reverses Finance Ruling on City Schools," *New York Times,* 26 June 2002, sec. A, p. 1.

147 "THOUGH THE COURT FEELS THAT THE REINSTATEMENT": from "Crew-Cut Board Wins One," *Daily News,* May 1998, p. 12.

152 "STONE WITHIN STONE": Pablo Neruda, *The Heights of Macchu Picchu* (New York: Farrar, Straus & Giroux, 1974), pp. 57, 59.

157 "I AM COGNIZANT OF THE INTERRELATEDNESS OF ALL COMMUNITIES": Martin Luther King, "Letter from Birmingham City Jail" in *A Testament of Hope* (San Francisco: HarperCollins, 1991), p. 290.

163 "AS LONG AS WE ARE ON EARTH": Thomas Merton, *New Seeds of Contemplation* (New York: New Directions, 1972), p. 72.

164–65 "SINGING SOMETHING": For more, see *A Singing Something: Womanist Reflections on Anna Julia Cooper* by Karen Baker-Fletcher (New York: Crossroad, 1994).

168–69 "IT STARTED THAT WAY: LAUGHING CHILDREN, DANCING MEN": Toni Morrison, *Beloved* (New York: Alfred A. Knopf, 1987), p. 88.

SEVEN Fall Construction Reports

171–72 "THIRTY SPOKES SHARE THE WHEEL'S HUB": Lao Tsu, *Tao Te Ching* (New York: Vintage Books, Random House, 1972), p. 11.

186 "THERE IS SOMETHING ABOUT POVERTY": Zora Neale Hurston, *Their Eyes Were Watching God* (New York: Harper & Row, 1990), p. 193.

191 *Children in Danger; Coping with the Consequences of Community Violence,* James Garbarino, Nancy Dubrow, Kathleen Kostelny, and Carole Pardo (San Francisco: Jossey-Bass Publishers, 1992).

195 "THERE IS A BASIN": Zora Neale Hurston, *Their Eyes Were Watching God,* ibid., p. 23.

200 "FULL OF A THOUSAND PREOCCUPATIONS": *The Interior Castle,* ibid., p. 32.

200 "ZERRISSENHEIT": William James in Anne Morrow Lindbergh, *Gift from the Sea,* ibid., p. 56.

200 "WHEN GOD MADE THE MAN": Zora Neale Hurston, *Their Eyes Were Watching God,* ibid., p. 86.

EIGHT   Winter Construction Reports

204   "THE THINKING HEART OF THESE BARRACKS": Etty Hillesum, *An Interrupted Life* (New York: Henry Holt and Company, 1996), p. 225.

204   "BUT SOMEWHERE INSIDE ME THE JASMINE CONTINUES TO BLOSSOM": Etty Hillesum, ibid., p. 179.

208   "THEIR EYES, WHICH HAD PREVIOUSLY BEEN WET WITHIN": Dante, *Inferno*, Cantos 32:46–33:94.

217   "YOU SHOULD SING AS WAYFARERS DO": *Augustine excerpt* from *A Sourcebook about Liturgy* (Archdiocese of Chicago: Liturgy Training Publications, 1994), p. 35.

217   *The Songlines*, Bruce Chatwin (New York: Penguin Books, 1987).

NINE   Spring Construction Reports

231-32   "THE RICH/MAKE TEMPLES FOR SIVA": in *Speaking of Siva*, A. K. Ramanujan, trans. (Baltimore: Penguin Books, 1973), p. 88 and see discussion in the introduction.

233   "BURNING PATIENCE": Pablo Neruda, Nobel Lecture, *Toward the Splendid City* (New York: Farrar, Straus & Giroux, 1974), p. 35.

235   "WORDS STRAIN": T. S. Eliot, "Burnt Norton," in *Four Quartets* (London: Faber and Faber, 1970), p. 19.

236   "SOMETIMES DEATH, PUFFING AT THE DOORE": George Herbert, "The Church-floore," *Major Poets of the Earlier Seventeenth Century*, edited by Barbara Lewalski and Andrew Sabol (New York: Odyssey, 1973), p. 247.

244-45   "UPEND THE RAIN STICK AND WHAT HAPPENS NEXT": Seamus Heaney, "The Rain Stick" in *The Spirit Level* (New York: Farrar Straus Giroux, 1996), p. 3.

246   "WHAT LOVELY AFTERMATH": Nelly Sachs, "Butterfly" in *O the Chimneys* (New York: Farrar, Straus and Giroux, 1969), p. 91.

249   "IT IS LIVING, NO RATHER DYING, SUFFERING": Martin Luther's *sämmtliche Schriften*, 22 vols. (St. Louis: Concordia Publishing House, 1957) 4:455.

258   "HOW CAN WE POINT TO THE EUCHARISTIC BREAD": Elizabeth Schussler Fiorenza, *In Memory of Her* (New York: Crossroad, 1983), p. 350.

260   "YOU MAY WRITE ME DOWN IN HISTORY": from "Still I Rise" in *The Complete Collected Poems of Maya Angelou*, (New York: Random House, 1994), p. 163.

261   "THIS GREAT GOD": James Weldon Johnson, "The Creation" in *God's Trombones* (New York: Penguin Books, 1990), p. 20.

263 "AND HERE IN DUST AND DIRT, O HERE/THE LILIES OF HIS LOVE APPEAR":
These oft-quoted lines are sometimes attributed to George Herbert, but they are actually the final lines of "The Revival" by Henry Vaughan.

265 *The Sanctified Church*, Zora Neale Hurston (Berkeley, Calif.: Turtle Island Foundation, 1981), p. 102.

267-68 "SHERMAN, I'M SURE THAT'S THE TURNOFF": Tom Wolfe, *The Bonfire of the Vanities* (New York: Bantam Books, 1988), pp. 8off.

271 "THEY HAVE THREATENED US WITH RESURRECTION": Julia Esquivel, *Threatened with Resurrection* (Elgin, Ill.: Brethren Press, 1994), pp. 59ff.

271 "SE HACE CAMINO AL ANDAR": This phrase has become so commonly used that the author is often forgotten. The original is by Antonio Machado (1875–1939) and reads in its complete form: *Caminante, no hay camino, se hace camino al andar* . . . (Traveler, there is no path, you make the way by walking it.).

ACKNOWLEDGMENTS

I need to begin by thanking Dwight Boud, my high school English teacher, whose timely and painstaking attention to my early efforts made all the difference. I thank those who read my manuscript in its many, oh so many variations. Every page is marked by their wise suggestions and life-giving encouragement—Gordon Lathrop, Jann Boyd, Edward Dufresne, Lee Stuart, Michael McQuarrie, Ellie Shea, John Grange, Susan Schulman, Stephen Bouman, Lynda Bogel, Kim Zalent, Bernd Kappes, Jon Pahl, Karen Brau, and Terry Boggs.

The last five of Transfiguration's interns belong on this list as well—Andrea Walker, Paul Block, Anita Mohr, Martin Malzahn, and Carol Book. They showed up for work, not knowing that book editing and author support were part of the deal, and they have been and remain dear companions sharing the sorrows and joys of ministry and publishing. Special thanks and *un abrazo* to Christina del Piero for being a voice of unfailing hope throughout.

It would have been impossible to complete this book without the sabbatical breathing space and grant assistance I received from the Louisville Institute. I am deeply grateful to Jim Lewis, David Wood, and Bill Brosend for their ongoing support. Special thanks are due to David Wood, who called me out of the blue when my manuscript was in limbo and put me on the path to my agent, John Thornton. And thanks to Richard Lischer for graciously making the contact on my behalf.

John has been far more than an agent. He has shepherded this manuscript and this author with goodness, kindness, adroitness, and grace. My cup runneth over. I am equally blessed with a wonderful editor at Beacon, Gayatri Patnaik, and her assistant, Kerri, who have exceeded every expectation I ever had about what an editor might do or be. I am grateful to all the folks at Beacon for their vision, commitment, and hard work.

Of course, there would be no book without this ministry that has been borne of a great cloud of witnesses and coconspirators. I thank the mentors who set me on this path and whose witness keeps me going: Franklin Fry, Harvey Peters, William Stafford, John Egan, Tom Kochenderfer, John Cochran, Mary Forell, Tom Sinnott, and Paul Hagedorn. I thank my mentors in community organizing, especially Jim Drake and Lee Stuart. Deep thanks are also owed to all of the bishops and their staffs, without whom Transfiguration would not have survived nor thrived: James Graefe, William Lazareth, James Sudbrock, and Stephen Bouman.

I am grateful to my pastoral colleagues in the Bronx for their dedication, humor, and faithfulness and to the numerous people and churches who have contributed generously to the ministry of Transfiguration. While there are so many persons whose caring has supported this work, I am particularly grateful to Dr. Edward Davies, Dr. Melissa Sedlis, and Virginia Connor for all that they have done for my family over so many years.

To the true authors of this book—the people of Transfiguration and the South Bronx—any word of thanks is inadequate. I can only try to live each day in a way that honors you. Likewise, words are insufficient to thank my mother, Barbara, indefatigable in generosity and succor of every sort. And to Gregorio, Ana, and Hans—I thank each one of you for being exactly who you are and for sharing your lives with me. Your love is my breathing space. I know that after living through this long labor, you will never look at a book in the same way again.

Solo Deo Gracias!

CREDITS